The Romance Of Modern Invention

Williams, Archibald

The Romance of Modern Invention

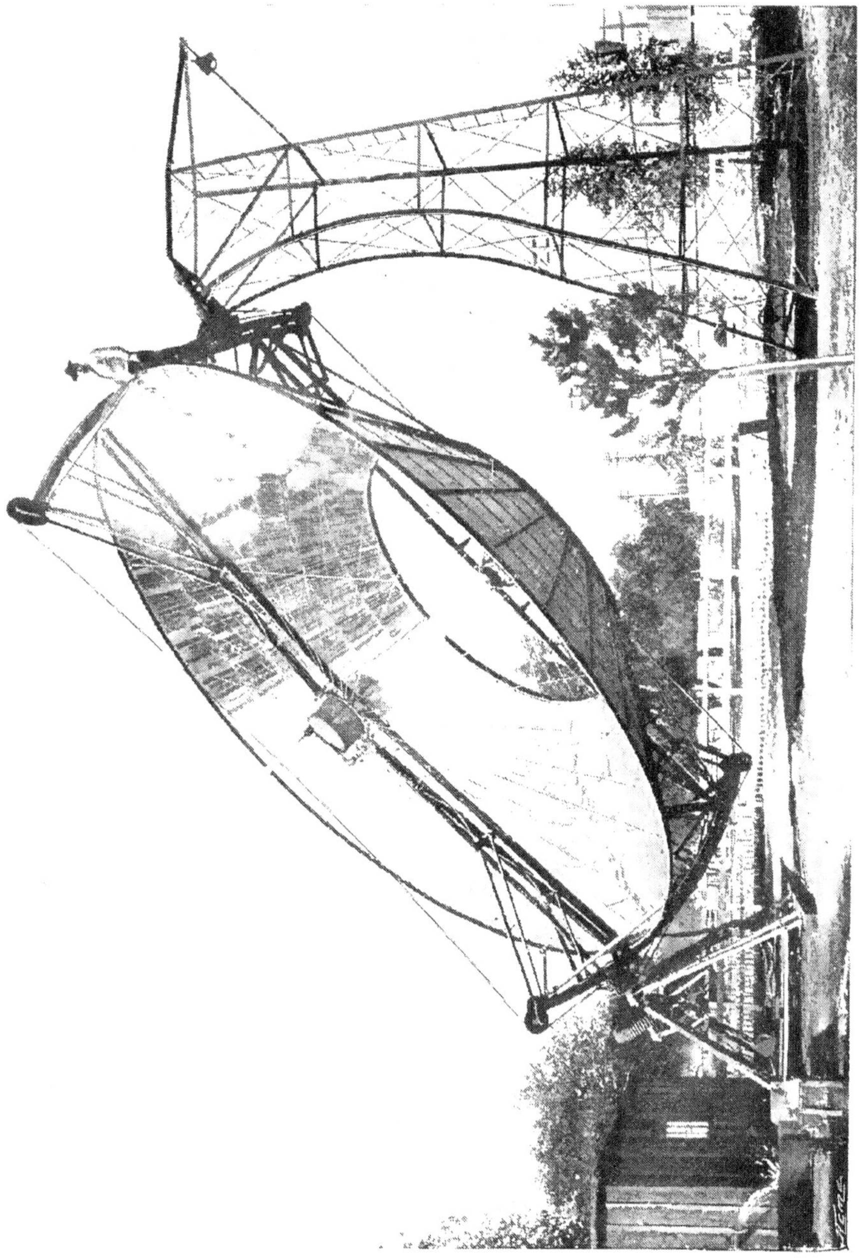

THE ROMANCE OF MODERN INVENTION

CONTAINING INTERESTING DESCRIPTIONS IN NON-TECHNICAL LANGUAGE OF WIRELESS TELEGRAPHY, LIQUID AIR, MODERN ARTILLERY, SUBMARINES, DIRIGIBLE TORPEDOES, SOLAR MOTORS, AIRSHIPS, &c. &c.

BY

ARCHIBALD WILLIAMS, B.A., F.R.G.S.

AUTHOR OF "THE ROMANCE OF MODERN MECHANISM"
"THE ROMANCE OF MODERN ENGINEERING"
&c. &c.

WITH TWENTY-FIVE ILLUSTRATIONS

PHILADELPHIA
J. B. LIPPINCOTT COMPANY
LONDON: SEELEY & CO. LIMITED
1910

Preface

THE object of this book is to set before young people in a bright and interesting way, and without the use of technical language, accounts of some of the latest phases of modern invention; and also to introduce them to recent discoveries of which the full development is yet to be witnessed.

The author gratefully acknowledges the help given him as regards both literary matter and illustrations by:—Mr. Cuthbert Hall (the Marconi Wireless Telegraphy Co.); Mr. William Sugg; Mr. Hans Knudsen; Mr. F. C. B. Cole; Mr. E. J. Ryves; Mr. Anton Pollak; the Telautograph Co.; the Parsons Steam Turbine Co.; the Monotype Co.; the Biograph Co.; the Locomobile Co.; the Speedwell Motor Co.

September 1902.

Contents

List of Illustrations

List of Illustrations

The Romance of Modern Invention

WIRELESS TELEGRAPHY

ONE day in 1845 a man named Tawell, dressed as a Quaker, stepped into a train at Slough Station on the Great Western Railway, and travelled to London. When he arrived in London the innocent-looking Quaker was arrested, much to his amazement and dismay, on the charge of having committed a foul murder in the neighbourhood of Slough. The news of the murder and a description of the murderer had been telegraphed from that place to Paddington, where a detective met the train and shadowed the miscreant until a convenient opportunity for arresting him occurred. Tawell was tried, condemned, and hung, and the public for the first time generally realised the power for good dormant in the as yet little developed electric telegraph.

Thirteen years later two vessels met in mid-Atlantic laden with cables which they joined and paid out in opposite directions, till Ireland and Newfoundland were reached. The first electric message passed on

August 7th of that year from the New World to the Old. The telegraph had now become a world-power.

The third epoch-making event in its history is of recent date. On December 12, 1901, Guglielmo Marconi, a young Italian, famous all over the world when but twenty-two years old, suddenly sprang into yet greater fame. At Hospital Point, Newfoundland, he heard by means of a kite, a long wire, a delicate tube full of tiny particles of metal, and a telephone ear-piece, signals transmitted from far-off Cornwall by his colleagues. No wires connected Poldhu, the Cornish station, and Hospital Point. The three short dot signals, which in the Morse code signify the letter S, had been borne from place to place by the limitless, mysterious ether, that strange substance of which we now hear so much, of which wise men declare we know so little.

Marconi's great achievement, which was of immense importance, naturally astonished the world. Of course, there were not wanting those who discredited the report. Others, on the contrary, were seized with panic and showed their readiness to believe that the Atlantic had been spanned aërially, by selling off their shares in cable companies. To use the language of the money-market, there was a temporary "slump" in cable shares. The world again woke up—this time to the fact that experiments of which it had heard faintly had at last culminated in a great triumph, marvellous in itself, and yet probably nothing in comparison with the revolution in the transmission of news that it heralded.

The subject of Wireless Telegraphy is so wide that to treat it fully in the compass of a single chapter is impossible. At the same time it would be equally impossible to pass it over in a book written with the object of presenting to the reader the latest developments of scientific research. Indeed, the attention that it has justly attracted entitle it, not merely to a place, but to a leading place; and for this reason these first pages will be devoted to a short account of the history and theory of Wireless Telegraphy, with some mention of the different systems by which signals have been sent through space.

On casting about for a point at which to begin, the writer is tempted to attack the great topic of the ether, to which experimenters in many branches of science are now devoting more and more attention, hoping to find in it an explanation of and connection between many phenomena which at present are of uncertain origin.

What is Ether? In the first place, its very existence is merely assumed, like that of the atom and the molecule. Nobody can say that he has actually seen or had any experience of it. The assumption that there is such a thing is justified only in so far as that assumption explains and reconciles phenomena of which we have experience, and enables us to form theories which can be scientifically demonstrated correct. What scientists now say is this: that everything which we see and touch, the air, the infinity of space itself, is permeated by a *something*, so subtle that, no matter how continuous a thing may seem, it is but a concourse of atoms separated by this something, the Ether. Reasoning drove them to this conclusion.

It is obvious that an effect cannot come out of nothing. Put a clock under a bell-glass and you hear the ticking. Pump out the air and the ticking becomes inaudible. What is now not in the glass that was there before? The air. Reason, therefore, obliges us to conclude that air is the means whereby the ticking is audible to us. No air, no sound. Next, put a lighted candle on the further side of the exhausted bell-glass. We can see it clearly enough. The absence of air does not affect light. But can we believe that there is an absolute gap between us and the light? No! It is far easier to believe that the bell-glass is as full as the outside atmosphere of the something that communicates the sensation of light from the candle to the eye. Again, suppose we measure a bar of iron very carefully while cold and then heat it. We shall find that it has expanded a little. The iron atoms, we say, have become more energetic than before, repel each other and stand further apart. What then is in the intervening spaces? Not air, which cannot be forced through iron whether hot or cold. No! the ether: which passes easily through crevices so small as to bar the way to the atoms of air.

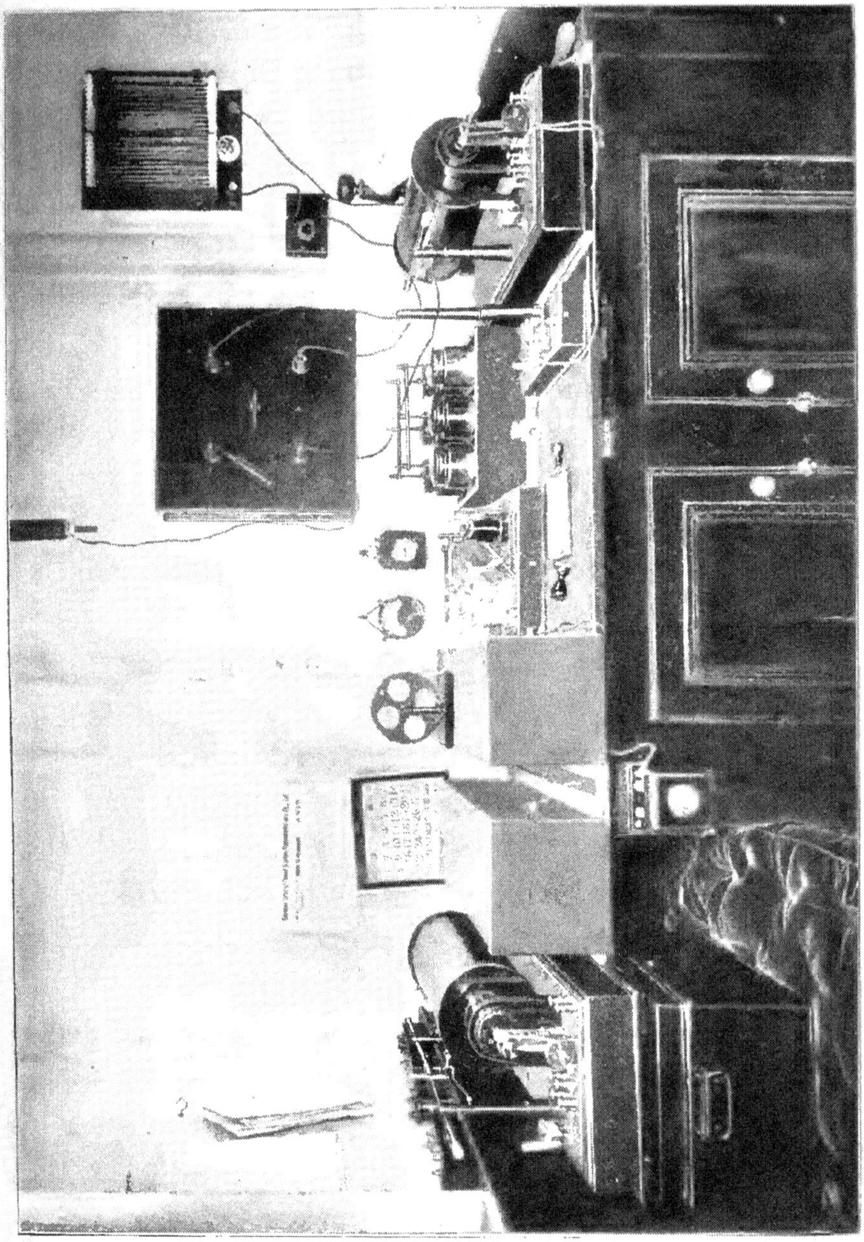

Once more, suppose that to one end of our iron bar we apply the negative "pole" of an electric battery, and to the other end the positive pole. We see that a current passes through the bar, whether hot or cold, which implies that it jumps across all the ether gaps, or rather is conveyed by them from one atom to another.

The conclusion then is that ether is not merely omnipresent, penetrating all things, but the medium whereby heat, light, electricity, perhaps even thought itself, are transmitted from one point to another.

In what manner is the transmission effected? We cannot imagine the ether behaving in a way void of all system.

The answer is, by a wave motion. The ether must be regarded as a very elastic solid. The agitation of a portion of it by what we call heat, light, or electricity, sets in motion adjoining particles, until they are moving from side to side, but not forwards; the resultant movement resembling that of a snake tethered by the tail.

These ether waves vary immensely in length. Their qualities and effects upon our bodies or sensitive instruments depend upon their length. By means of ingenious apparatus the lengths of various waves have been measured. When the waves number 500 billion per second, and are but the 40,000th of an inch long they affect our eyes and are named light—red light. At double the number and half the length, they give us the sensation of violet light.

When the number increases and the waves shorten further, our bodies are "blind" to them; we have no sense to detect their presence. Similarly, a slower vibration than that of red light is imperceptible until we reach the comparatively slow pace of 100 vibrations per second, when we become aware of heat.

Ether waves may be compared to the notes on a piano, of which we are acquainted with some octaves only. The gaps, the unknown octaves, are being discovered slowly but surely. Thus, for example, the famous X-rays have been assigned to the topmost octave; electric waves to the notes between light and heat. Forty years ago Professor Clerk Maxwell suggested that light and electricity were very closely connected, probably differing only in their wave-length. His theory has been justified by subsequent research. The velocity of light (185,000 miles per second) and that of electric currents have been proved identical. Hertz, a professor in the university of Bonn, also showed (1887–1889) that the phenomena of light—reflection, refraction, and concentration of rays—can be repeated with electric currents.

We therefore take the word of scientists that the origin of the phenomena called light and electricity is the same—vibration of ether. It at once occurs to the reader that their behaviour is so different that they might as well be considered of altogether different natures.

For instance, interpose the very thinnest sheet of metal between a candle and the eye, and the light is cut off. But the sheet will very readily convey electricity. On the contrary, glass, a substance that repels electricity, is transparent, *i.e.* gives passage to light. And again, electricity can be conveyed round as many corners as you please, whereas light will travel in straight lines only.

To clear away our doubts we have only to take the lighted candle and again hold up the metal screen. Light does not pass through, but heat does. Substitute for the metal a very thin tank filled with a solution of alum, and then light passes, but heat is cut off. So that heat and electricity *both* penetrate what is impenetrable to light; while light forces a passage securely barred against both electricity and heat. And we must remember that open space conveys all alike from the sun to the earth.

On meeting what we call solid matter, ether waves are influenced, not because ether is wanting in the solid matter, but because the presence of something else than ether affects the intervening ether itself. Consequently glass, to take an instance, so affects ether that a very rapid succession of waves (light) are able to continue their way through its interstices, whereas long electric waves are so hampered that they die out altogether. Metal on the other hand welcomes slow vibrations (*i.e.* long waves), but speedily kills the rapid shakes of light. In other words, *transparency* is not confined to light alone. All bodies are transparent to some variety of rays, and many bodies to several varieties. It may perhaps even be proved that there is no such thing as absolute resistance, and that our inability to detect penetration is due to lack of sufficiently delicate instruments.

The cardinal points to be remembered are these :—

That the ether is a universal medium, conveying all kinds and forms of energy.

That these forms of energy differ only in their rates of vibration.

That the rate of vibration determines what power of penetration the waves shall have through any given substance.

Now, it is generally true that whereas matter of any kind offers resistance to light—that is, is not so perfect a conductor as the ether—many substances, especially metals, are more sensitive than ether to heat and electricity. How quickly a spoon inserted into a hot cup of tea becomes uncomfortably hot, though the hand can be held very close to the liquid without feeling more than a gentle warmth. And we all have noticed that the very least air-gap in an electric circuit effectively breaks a current capable of traversing miles of wire. If the current is so intense that it insists on passing the gap, it leaps across with a report, making a spark that is at once intensely bright and hot. Metal wires are to electricity what speaking tubes are to sound ; they are as it were electrical tubes through the air and ether. But just as a person listening outside a speaking tube might faintly hear the sounds passing through it, so an instrument gifted with an "electric ear" would detect the currents passing through the wire. Wireless telegraphy is possible because mankind has discovered instruments which act as *electric ears or eyes,* catching and recording vibrations that had hitherto remained undetected.

The earliest known form of wireless telegraphy is transmission of messages by light. A man on a hill lights a lamp or a fire. This represents his instrument for agitating the ether into waves, which proceed straight ahead with incredible velocity until they reach the receiver, the eye of a man watching at a point from which the light is visible.

Then came electric telegraphy.

At first a complete circuit (two wires) was used. But in 1838 it was discovered that if instead of two wires only one was used, the other being replaced by an earth connection, not only was the effect equally powerful, but even double of what it was with the metallic circuit.

Thus the first step had been taken towards wireless electrical telegraphy.

The second was, of course, to abolish the other wire.

This was first effected by Professor Morse, who, in 1842, sent signals across the Susquehanna River without metallic connections of any sort. Along each bank of the river was stretched a wire three times as long as the river was broad. In the one wire a battery and transmitter were inserted, in the other a receiving instrument or galvanometer. Each wire terminated at each end in a large copper plate sunk in the water. Morse's conclusions were that provided the wires were long enough and the plates large enough messages could be transmitted for an indefinite distance; the current passing from plate to plate, though a large portion of it would be lost in the water.[1]

About the same date a Scotchman, James Bowman Lindsay of Dundee, a man as rich in intellectual attainments as he was pecuniarily poor, sent signals in a similar manner across the River Tay. In September, 1859, Lindsay read a paper before the British Association at Dundee, in which he maintained that his experiments and calculations assured him that by running wires along the coasts of America and Great Britain, by using a battery having an acting surface of 130 square feet and immersed sheets of 3000 square feet, and a coil weighing 300 lbs., he could send messages from Britain to America. Want of money prevented the poor scholar of Dundee from carrying out his experiments on a large enough scale to obtain public support. He died in 1862, leaving behind him the reputation of a man who in the face of the greatest difficulties made extraordinary electrical discoveries at the cost of unceasing labour; and this in spite of the fact that he had undertaken and partly executed a gigantic dictionary in fifty different languages!

[1] It is here proper to observe that the term *wireless* telegraphy, as applied to electrical systems, is misleading, since it implies the absence of wires; whereas in all systems wires are used. But since it is generally understood that by wireless telegraphy is meant telegraphy without *metal connections*, and because the more improved methods lessen more and more the amount of wire used, the phrase has been allowed to stand.

M. Marconi's Travelling Station for Wireless Telegraphy.

[*To face p.* 16.

Wireless Telegraphy

The transmission of electrical signals through matter, metal, earth, or water, is effected by *conduction*, or the *leading* of the currents in a circuit. When we come to deal with aërial transmission, *i.e.* where one or both wires are replaced by the ether, then two methods are possible, those of *induction* and Hertzian waves.

To take the induction method first. Whenever a current is sent through a wire magnetism is set up in the ether surrounding the wire, which becomes the core of a "magnetic field." The magnetic waves extend for an indefinite distance on all sides, and on meeting a wire *parallel* to the electrified wire *induce* in it a *dynamical* current similar to that which caused them. Wherever electricity is present there is magnetism also, and *vice versâ*. Electricity—produces magnetism—produces electricity. The invention of the Bell telephone enabled telegraphers to take advantage of this law.

In 1885 Sir William Preece, now consulting electrical engineer to the General Post-Office, erected near Newcastle two insulated squares of wire, each side 440 yards long. The squares were horizontal, parallel, and a quarter of a mile apart. On currents being sent through the one, currents were detected in the other by means of a telephone, which remained active even when the squares were separated by 1000 yards. Sir William Preece thus demonstrated that signals could be sent without even an earth connection, *i.e.* entirely through the ether. In 1886 he sent signals between two parallel telegraph wires 4½ miles apart. And in 1892 established a regular communication between Flatholm, an island fort in the Bristol Channel, and Lavernock, a point on the Welsh coast 3⅓ miles distant.

The inductive method might have attained to greater successes had not a formidable rival appeared in the Hertzian waves.

In 1887 Professor Hertz discovered that if the discharge from a Leyden jar were passed through wires containing an air-gap across which the discharge had to pass, sparks would also pass across a gap in an almost complete circle or square of wire held at some distance from the jar. This "electric eye," or detector, could have its gap so regulated by means of a screw that at a certain width its effect would be most pronounced, under which condition the detector, or receiver, was "in tune" with the exciter, or transmitter. Hertz thus established three great facts, that—

(*a*) A discharge of static (*i.e.* collected) electricity across an air-gap produced strong electric waves in the ether on all sides.

(*b*) That these waves could be *caught*.

(*c*) That under certain conditions the catcher worked most effectively.

Out of these three discoveries has sprung the latest phase of wireless telegraphy, as exploited by Signor Marconi. He, in common with Professors Branly of Paris, Popoff of Cronstadt, and Slaby of Charlottenburg, besides many others, have devoted their attention to the production of improved means of sending and receiving the Hertzian waves. Their experiments have shown that two things are required in wireless telegraphy—

(i.) That the waves shall have great penetrating power, so as to pierce any obstacle.

(ii.) That they shall retain their energy, so that a *maximum* of their original force shall reach the receiver.

The first condition is fulfilled best by waves of great length; the second by those which, like light, are of greatest frequency. For best telegraphic results a compromise must be effected between these extremes, neither the thousand-mile long waves of an alternating dynamo nor the light waves of many thousands to an inch being of use. The Hertzian waves are estimated to be 230,000,000 per second; at which rate they would be 1½ yards long. They vary considerably, however, on both sides of this rate and dimension.

Marconi's transmitter consists of three parts—a battery; an induction coil, terminating in a pair of brass balls, one on each side of the air-gap; and a Morse transmitting-key. Upon the key being depressed, a current from the battery passes through the coil and accumulates electricity on the brass balls until its tension causes it to leap from one to the other many millions of times in what is called a spark. The longer the air-gap the greater must be the accumulation before the leap takes place, and the greater the power of the vibrations set up. Marconi found that by connecting a kite or balloon covered with tinfoil by an aluminium wire with one of the balls, the effect of the waves was greatly increased. Sometimes he replaced the kite or balloon by a conductor placed on poles two or three hundred feet high, or by the mast of a ship.

We now turn to the receiver.

In 1879 Professor D. E. Hughes observed that a microphone, in connection with a telephone, produced sounds in the latter even when the microphone was at a distance of several feet from coils through which a current was passing. A microphone, it may be explained, is in its simplest form a loose connection in an electric circuit, which causes the current to flow in fits and starts at very frequent intervals. He discovered that a metal microphone stuck, or cohered, after a wave had influenced it, but that a carbon microphone was self-restoring, *i.e.* regained its former position of loose contact as soon as a wave effect had ceased.

In 1891 Professor Branly of Paris produced a "coherer," which was nothing more than a microphone under another name. Five years later Marconi somewhat altered Branly's contrivance, and took out a patent for a coherer of his own.

It is a tiny glass tube, about two inches long and a tenth of an inch in diameter inside. A wire enters it at each end, the wires terminating in two silver plugs fitting the bore of the tube. A space of $\frac{1}{32}$ inch is left between the plugs, and this space is filled with special filings, a mixture of 96 parts of nickel to 4 of silver, and the merest trace of mercury. The tube is exhausted of almost all its air before being sealed.

This little gap filled with filings is, except when struck by an electric wave, to all practical purposes a non-conductor of electricity. The metal particles touch each other so lightly that they offer great resistance to a current.

But when a Hertzian wave flying through the ether strikes the coherer, the particles suddenly press hard on one another, and make a bridge through which a current can pass. The current works a "relay," or circuit through which a stronger current passes, opening and closing it as often as the coherer is influenced by a wave. The relay actuates a tapper that gently taps the tube after each wave-influence, causing the particles to *de*cohere in readiness for the succeeding wave, and also a Morse instrument for recording words in dots and dashes on a long paper tape.

The coherer may be said to resemble an engine-driver, and the "relay" an engine. The driver is not sufficiently strong to himself move a train, but he has strength enough to turn on steam and make the engine do the work. The coherer is not suitable for use with currents of the intensity required to move a Morse recorder, but it easily switches a powerful current into another circuit.

Want of space forbids a detailed account of Marconi's successes with his improved instruments, but the appended list will serve to show how he gradually increased the distance over which he sent signals through space.

In 1896 he came to England. That year he signalled from a room in the General Post-Office to a station on the roof 100 yards distant. Shortly afterwards he covered 2 miles on Salisbury Plain.

In May, 1897, he sent signals from Lavernock Point to Flatholm, 3⅓ miles. This success occurred at a critical time, for Sir W. Preece had already, as we have seen, bridged the same gap by his induction method, and for three days Marconi failed to accomplish the feat with his apparatus, so that it appeared as though the newer system were the less effective of the two. But by carrying the transmitting instrument on to the beach below the cliff on which it had been standing, and joining it by a wire to the pole already erected on the top of the cliff, Mr. Marconi, thanks to a happy inspiration, did just what was needed; he got a greater length of wire to send off his waves from. Communication was at once established with Flatholm, and on the next day with Brean Down, on the other side of the Bristol Channel, and 8⅔ miles distant. Then we have—

Needles Hotel to Swanage . .	17½	miles.
Salisbury to Bath	34	,,
French Coast to Harwich . .	90	,,
Isle of Wight to The Lizard . .	196	,,
At Sea (1901)	350	,,
Dec. 17, 1901, England to America	2099	,,

Poldhu Towers, the Station put down by the Marconi Wireless Telegraph Company, Limited, for carrying on a system of transatlantic wireless telegraphy between England and America. From the four towers are suspended the ærial wires which are carried into the buildings in the centre. The towers are 215 feet in height, and are made of wood.

[To face p. 22.

A more pronounced, though perhaps less sensational, success than even this last occurred at the end of February, 1902. Mr. Marconi, during a voyage to America on the s.s. *Philadelphia* remained in communication with Poldhu, Cornwall, until the vessel was 1550 miles distant, receiving messages on a Morse recorder for any one acquainted with the code to read. Signals arrived for a further 500 miles, but owing to his instruments not being of sufficient strength, Mr. Marconi could not reply.

When the transatlantic achievement was announced at the end of 1901, there was a tendency in some quarters to decry the whole system. The critics laid their fingers on two weak points.

In the first place, they said, the speed at which the messages could be transmitted was too slow to insure that the system would pay. Mr. Marconi replied that there had been a time when one word per minute was considered a good working rate across the Atlantic cable; whereas he had already sent twenty-two words per minute over very long distances. A further increase of speed was only a matter of time.

The second objection raised centred on the lack of secrecy resulting from signals being let loose into space to strike any instrument within their range; and also on the confusion that must arise when the ether was traversed by many sets of electric waves.

The young Italian inventor had been throughout his experiments aware of these defects and sought means to remedy them. In his earliest attempts we find him using parabolic metal screens to project his waves in any required direction and prevent their going in any other. He also employed strips of metal in conjunction with the coherer, the strips or "wings" being of such a size as to respond most readily to waves of a certain length.

The electric oscillations coming from the aërial wires carried on poles, kites, &c., were of great power, but their energy dispersed very quickly into space in a series of rapidly diminishing vibrations. This fact made them affect to a greater or less degree any receiver they might encounter on their wanderings. If you go into a room where there is a piano and make a loud noise near the instrument a jangle of notes results. But if you take a tuning-fork and after striking it place it near the strings, only one string will respond, *i.e.* that of the same pitch as the fork.

What is required in wireless telegraphy is a system corresponding to the use of the tuning-fork. Unfortunately, it has been discovered that the syntony or tuning of transmitter and receiver reduces the distance over which they are effective. An electric "noise" is more far-reaching than an electric "note."

Mr. Marconi has, however, made considerable advances towards combining the sympathy and secrecy of the tuning system with the power of the "noise" system. By means of delicately adjusted "wings" and coils he has brought it about that a series of waves having small individual strength, but great regularity, shall produce on the receiver a *cumulative* effect, storing, as it were, electricity on the surface of the receiver "wings" until it is of sufficient power to overcome the resistance of the coherer.

That tuned wireless telegraphy is, over moderate distances, at least as secret as that through wires (which can be tapped by induction) is evident from the fact that during the America Cup Yacht Races Mr. Marconi sent daily to the *New York Herald* messages of 4000 total words, and kept them private in spite of all efforts to intercept them. He claims to have as many as 250 "tunes"; and, indeed, there seems to be no limit to their number, so that the would-be "tapper" is in the position of a man trying to open a letter-lock of which he does not know the cipher-word. He *may* discover the right tune, but the chances are greatly against him. We may be certain that the rapid advance in wireless telegraphy will not proceed much further before syntonic messages can be transmitted over hundreds if not thousands of miles.

It is hardly necessary to dwell upon the great prospect that the new telegraphy opens to mankind. The advantages arising out of a ready means of communication, freed from the shackles of expensive connecting wires and cables are, in the main, obvious enough. We have only to imagine all the present network of wires replaced or supplemented by ether-waves, which will be able to act between points (*e.g.* ships and ships, ships and land, moving and fixed objects generally) which cannot be connected by metallic circuits.

Already ocean voyages are being shortened as regards the time during which passengers are out of contact with the doings of the world. The transatlantic journey has now a newsless period of but three days. Navies are being fitted out with instruments that may play as important a part as the big guns themselves in the next naval war. A great maritime nation like our own should be especially thankful that the day is not far distant when our great empire will be connected by invisible electric links that no enemy may discover and cut.

The romantic side of wireless telegraphy has been admirably touched in some words uttered by Professor Ayrton in 1899, after the reading of a paper by Mr. Marconi before the Institution of Electrical Engineers.

"If a person wished to call to a friend" (said the Professor), "he would use a loud electro-magnetic voice, audible only to him who had the electromagnetic ear.

"'Where are you?' he would say.

"The reply would come—'I am at the bottom of a coal mine,' or 'Crossing the Andes,' or 'In the middle of the Pacific.' Or, perhaps, in spite of all the calling, no reply would come, and the person would then know his friend was dead. Let them think of what that meant; of the calling which went on every day

Guglielmo Marconi.

[*To face p.* 26.

from room to room of a house, and then imagine that calling extending from pole to pole; not a noisy babble, but a call audible to him who wanted to hear and absolutely silent to him who did not."

When will Professor Ayrton's forecast come true? Who can say? Science is so full of surprises that the ordinary man wonders with a semi-fear what may be the next development; and wise men like Lord Kelvin humbly confess that in comparison with what has yet to be learnt about the mysterious inner workings of Nature their knowledge is but as ignorance.

HIGH-SPEED TELEGRAPHY.

THE wonderful developments of wireless telegraphy must not make us forget that some very interesting and startling improvements have been made in connection with the ordinary wire-circuit method: notably in the matter of speed.

At certain seasons of the year or under special circumstances which can scarcely be foreseen, a great rush takes place to transmit messages over the wires connecting important towns. Now, the best telegraphists can with difficulty keep up a transmitting speed of even fifty words a minute for so long as half-an-hour. The Morse alphabet contains on the average three signals for each letter, and the average length of a word is six letters. Fifty words would therefore contain between them 900 signals, or fifteen a second. The strain of sending or noting so many for even a brief period is very wearisome to the operator.

Means have been found of replacing the telegraph clerk, so far as the actual signalling is concerned, by mechanical devices.

In 1842 Alexander Bain, a watchmaker of Thurso, produced what is known as a "chemical telegraph." The words to be transmitted were set up in large

The receiving instrument used by Messrs. Pollak & Virag in their high-speed system of telegraphy. This instrument is capable of receiving and photographically recording messages at the astonishing speed of 50,000 words an hour.

[*To face p.* 28.

metal type, all capitals, connected with the positive pole of a battery, the negative pole of which was connected to earth. A metal brush, divided into five points, each terminating a wire, was passed over the metal type. As often as a division of the brush touched metal it completed the electric circuit in the wire to which it was joined, and sent a current to the receiving station, where a similar brush was passing at similar speed over a strip of paper soaked in iodide of potassium. The action of the electricity decomposed the solution, turning it blue or violet. The result was a series of letters divided longitudinally into five belts separated by white spaces representing the intervals between the contact points of the brush.

The Bain Chemical Telegraph was able to transmit the enormous number of 1500 words per minute; that is, at ten times the rate of ordinary conversation! But even when improvements had reduced the line wires from five to one, the system, on account of the method of composing the message to be sent, was not found sufficiently practical to come into general use.

Its place was taken by slower but preferable systems: those of duplex and multiplex telegraphy.

When a message is sent over the wires, the actual time of making the signals is more than is required for the current to pass from place to place. This fact has been utilised by the inventors of methods whereby two or more messages may not only be sent the *same* way along the same wire, but may also be sent in *different* directions. Messages are "duplex" when they travel across one another, "multiplex" when they travel together.

The principle whereby several instruments are able to use the same wire is that of *distributing* among the instruments the time during which they are in contact with the line.

Let us suppose that four transmitters are sending messages simultaneously from London to Edinburgh.

Wires from all four instruments are led into a circular contact-maker, divided into some hundreds of insulated segments connected in rotation with the four transmitters. Thus instrument A will be joined to segments 1, 5, 9, 13; instrument B to segments 2, 6, 10, 14; instrument C with segments 3, 7, 11, 15; and so on.

Along the top of the segments an arm, connected with the telegraph line to Edinburgh, revolves at a uniform rate. For about $\frac{1}{500}$ of a second it unites a segment with an instrument. If there are 150 segments on the "distributor," and the arm revolves three times a second, each instrument will be put into contact with the line rather oftener than 110 times per second. And if the top speed of fifty words a minute is being worked to, each of the fifteen signals occurring in each second will be on the average divided among seven moments of contact.

A similar apparatus at Edinburgh receives the messages. It is evident that for the system to work satisfactorily, or even to escape dire confusion, the revolving arms must run at a level speed in perfect unison with one another. When the London arm is over segment 1, the Edinburgh arm must cover the same number. The greatest difficulty in multiplex telegraphy has been to adjust the timing exactly.

Paul la Cour of Copenhagen invented for driving the arms a device called the Phonic Wheel, as its action was regulated by the vibrations of a tuning-fork. The wheel, made of soft iron, and toothed on its circumference, revolves at a short distance from the pole of a magnet. As often as a current enters the magnet the latter attracts the nearest tooth of the wheel; and if a regular series of currents pass through it the motion of the wheel will be uniform. M. la Cour produced the regularity of current impulses in the motor magnet by means of a tuning-fork, which is unable to vibrate more than a certain number of times a second, and at each vibration closed a circuit sending current into the magnet. To get two tuning-forks of the same note is an easy matter; and consequently a uniformity of rotation at both London and Edinburgh stations may be insured.

So sensitive is this "interrupter" system that as many as sixteen messages can be sent simultaneously, which means that a single wire is conveying from 500 to 800 words a minute. We can easily understand the huge saving that results from such a system; the cost of instruments, interrupter, &c., being but small in proportion to that of a number of separate conductors.

The word-sending capacity of a line may be even further increased by the use of automatic transmitters able to work much faster in signal-making than the human brain and hand. Sir Charles Wheatstone's Automatic Transmitter has long been used in the Post-Office establishments.

The messages to be sent are first of all punched on a long tape with three parallel rows of perforations. The central row is merely for guiding the tape through the transmitting machine. The positions of the holes in the two outside rows relatively to each other determine the character of the signal to be sent. Thus, when three holes (including the central one) are abreast, a Morse "dot" is signified; when the left-hand hole is one place behind the right hand, a "dash" will be telegraphed.

In the case of a long communication the matter is divided among a number of clerks operating punching machines. Half-a-dozen operators could between them punch holes representing 250 to 300 words a minute; and the transmitter is capable of despatching as many in the same time, while it has the additional advantage of being tireless.

The action of the transmitter is based upon the reversal of the direction or nature of current. The punched tape is passed between an oscillating lever, carrying two points, and plates connected with the two poles of the battery. As soon as a hole comes under a pin the pin drops through and makes a contact.

At the receiving end the wire is connected with a coil wound round the pole of a permanent bar-magnet. Such a magnet has what is known as a north pole and a south pole, the one attractive and the other repulsive of steel or soft iron. Any bar of soft iron can be made temporarily into a magnet by twisting round it a few turns of a wire in circuit with the poles of a battery. But which will be the north and which the south pole depends on the *direction* of the current. If, then, a current passes in one direction round the north pole of a permanent magnet it will increase the magnet's attractive power, but will decrease it if sent in the other direction.

The "dot" holes punched in the tape being abreast cause first a positive and then a negative current following at a very short interval; but the "dash" holes not being opposite allow the positive current to occupy the wires for a longer period. Consequently the Morse marker rests for correspondingly unequal periods on the recording "tape," giving out a series of dots and dashes, as the inker is snatched quickly or more leisurely from the paper.

The Wheatstone recorder has been worked up to 400 words a minute, and when two machines are by the multiplex method acting together this rate is of course doubled.

As a speed machine it has, however, been completely put in the shade by a more recent invention of two Hungarian electricians, Anton Pollak and Josef Virag, which combines the perforated strip method of transmission with the telephone and photography. The message is sent off by means of a punched tape, and is recorded by means of a telephonic diaphragm and light marking a sensitised paper.

In 1898 the inventors made trials of their system for the benefit of the United Electrical Company of Buda-Pesth. The Hungarian capital was connected by two double lines of wire with a station 200 miles distant, where the two sets were joined so as to give a single circuit of 400 miles in length. A series of tests in all weathers showed that the Pollak-Virag system could transmit as many as 100,000 words an hour over that distance.

From Hungary the inventors went to the United States, in which country of "records" no less than 155,000 words were despatched and received in the sixty minutes. This average—2580 words per minute, 43 per second—is truly remarkable! Even between New York and Chicago, separated by 950 odd miles, the wires kept up an average of 1000 per minute.

The apparatus that produces these marvellous results is of two types. The one type records messages in the Morse alphabet, the other makes clearly-written longhand characters. The former is the faster of the two, but the legibility of the other more than compensates for the decrease of speed by one-half.

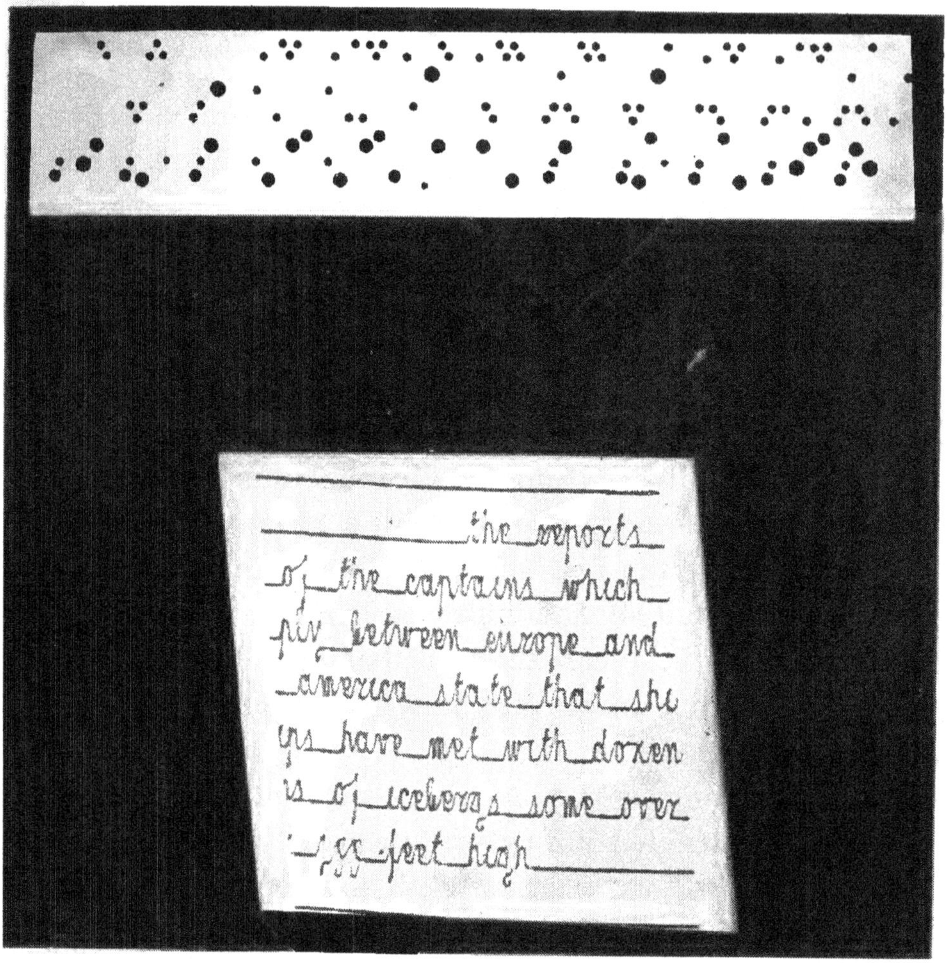

Specimens of the punched tape used for transmitting messages by the Pollak-Virag system, and of a message as it is delivered by the receiving machine.

[*To face p.* 34.

The Morse alphabet method closely resembles the Wheatstone system. The message is prepared for transmission by being punched on a tape. But there is this difference in the position of the holes, that whereas in the Wheatstone method two holes are used for each dot and dash, only one is required in the Pollak-Virag. If to the right of the central guiding line it signifies a "dash," if to the left, a "dot."

The "reversal-of-current" method, already explained, causes at the receiver end an increase or decrease in the power of a permanent magnet to attract or repel a diaphragm, the centre of which is connected by a very fine metal bar with the centre of a tiny mirror hinged at one side on two points. A very slight movement of the diaphragm produces an exaggerated movement of the mirror, which, as it tilts backwards and forwards, reflects the light from an electric lamp on to a lens, which concentrates the rays into a bright spot, and focuses them on to a surface of sensitised paper.

In their earliest apparatus the inventors attached the paper to the circumference of a vertical cylinder, which revolved at an even pace on an axle, furnished at the lower end with a screw thread, so that the portion of paper affected by the light occupied a spiral path from top to bottom of the cylinder.

In a later edition, however, an endless band of sensitised paper is employed, and the lamp is screened from the mirror by a horizontal mantle in which is cut a helical slit making one complete turn of the cylinder in its length. The mantle is rotated in unison with the machinery driving the sensitised band; and as it revolves, the spot at which the light from the filament can pass through the slit to the mirror is constantly shifting from right to left, and the point at which the reflected light from the mirror strikes the sensitised paper from left to right. At the moment when a line is finished, the right extremity of the mantle begins to pass light again, and the bright spot of light recommences its work at the left edge of the band, which has now moved on a space.

The movements of the mirror backwards and forwards produce on the paper a zigzag tracing known as syphon-writing. The record, which is continuous from side to side of the band, is a series of zigzag up-and-down strokes, corresponding to the dots and dashes of the Morse alphabet.

The apparatus for transmitting longhand characters is more complicated than that just described. Two telephones are now used, and the punched tape has in it five rows of perforations.

If we take a copy-book and examine the letters, we shall see that they all occupy one, two, or three bands of space. For instance, *a*, between the lines, occupies one band; *g*, two bands; and *f*, three. In forming letters, the movements of the fingers trace curves and straight lines, the curves being the resultants of combined horizontal and vertical movements.

Messrs. Pollak and Virag, in order to produce

curves, were obliged to add a second telephone, furnished also with a metal bar joined to the mirror, which rests on three points instead of on two. One of these points is fixed, the other two represent the ends of the two diaphragm bars, which move the mirror vertically and horizontally respectively, either separately or simultaneously.

A word about the punched paper before going further. It contains, as we have said, five rows of perforations. The top three of these are concerned only with the up-and-down strokes of the letters, the bottom two with the cross strokes. When a hole of one set is acting in unison with a hole of the other set a composite movement or curve results.

The topmost row of all sends through the wires a negative current of known strength; this produces upward and return strokes in the upper zone of the letters: for instance, the upper part of a *t*. The second row passes *positive* currents of equal strength with the negative, and influences the up-and-down strokes of the centre zone, *e.g.* those of *o*; the third row passes positive currents *twice* as strong as the negative, and is responsible for double-length vertical strokes in the centre and lower zones, *e.g.* the stroke in *p*.

In order that the record shall not be a series of zigzags it is necessary that the return strokes in the vertical elements shall be on the same path as the out strokes; and as the point of light is continuously tending to move from left to right of the paper there must at times be present a counteracting tendency counterbalancing it exactly, so that the path of the light point is purely vertical. At other times not merely must the horizontal movements balance each other, but the right-to-left element must be stronger than the left-to-right, so that strokes such as the left curve of an *e* may be possible. To this end rows 4 and 5 of the perforations pass currents working the second telephone diaphragm, which moves the mirror on a vertical axis so that it reflects the ray horizontally.

It will be noticed that the holes in rows 3, 4, 5 vary in size to permit the passage of currents during periods of different length. In this manner the little junction-hooks of such letters as *r*, *w*, *v*, *b* are effected.

As fast as the sensitised paper strip is covered with the movements of the dancing spot of light it is passed on over rollers through developing and fixing chemical baths; so that the receiving of messages is purely automatic.

The reader can judge for himself the results of this ingenious system as shown in a short section of a message transmitted by Mr. Pollak. The words shown actually occupied two seconds in transmission. They are beautifully clear.

It is said that by the aid of a special "multiplex" device thirty sets of Pollak-Virag apparatus can be used simultaneously on a line! The reader will be able, by the aid of a small calculation, to arrive at some interesting figures as regards their united output.

THE TELEPHONE.

A COMMON enough sight in any large town is a great sheaf of fine wires running across the streets and over the houses. If you traced their career in one direction you would find that they suddenly terminate, or rather combine into cables, and disappear into the recesses of a house, which is the Telephone Exchange. If you tracked them the other way your experience would be varied enough. Some wires would lead you into public institutions, some into offices, some into snug rooms in private houses. At one time your journey would end in the town, at another you would find yourself roaming far into the country, through green fields and leafy lanes until at last you ran the wire to earth in some large mansion standing in a lordly park. Perhaps you might have to travel hundreds of miles, having struck a "trunk" line connecting two important cities; or you might even be called upon to turn fish and plunge beneath the sea for a while, groping your way along a submarine cable.

In addition to the visible overhead wires that traverse a town there are many led underground through special conduits. And many telephone wires never come out of doors at all, their object being to furnish communication between the rooms of the same house. The telephone and its friend, the electric-bell, are now a regular part of the equipment of any large premises. The master of the house goes to his telephone when he wishes to address the cook or the steward, or the head-gardener or the coachman. It saves time and labour.

Should he desire to speak to his town-offices he will, unless connected direct, "ring up" the Exchange, into which, as we have seen, flow all the wires of the subscribers to the telephone system of that district. The ringing-up is usually done by rapidly turning a handle which works an electric magnet and rings a bell in the Exchange. The operator there, generally a girl, demands the number of the person with whom the ringer wants to speak, rings up that number, and connects the wires of the two parties.

In some exchanges, *e.g.* the new Post-Office telephone exchanges, the place of electric-bells is taken by lamps, to the great advantage of the operators, whose ears are thus freed from perpetual jangling. The action of unhooking the telephone receiver at the subscriber's end sends a current into a relay which closes the circuit of an electric lamp opposite the subscriber's number in the exchange. Similarly, when the conversation is completed the action of hanging up the receiver again lights another lamp of a different colour, given the exchange warning that the wires are free again.

In America, the country of automatic appliances, the operator is sometimes entirely dispensed with.

A subscriber is able, by means of a mechanical contrivance, to put himself in communication with any other subscriber unless that subscriber is engaged, in which case a dial records the fact.

The popularity of the telephone may be judged from the fact that in 1901 the National Telephone Company's system transmitted over 807 millions of messages, as compared with 89 millions of telegrams sent over the Post Office wires. In America and Germany, however, the telephone is even more universally employed than in England. In the thinly populated prairies of West America the farm-houses are often connected with a central station many miles off, from which they receive news of the outer world and are able to keep in touch with one another. We are not, perhaps, as a nation sufficiently alive to the advantages of an efficient telephone system; and on this account many districts remain telephoneless because sufficient subscribers cannot be found to guarantee use of a system if established. It has been seriously urged that much of our country depopulation might be counteracted by a universal telephone service, which would enable people to live at a distance from the towns and yet be in close contact with them. At present, for the sake of convenience and ease of "getting at" clients and customers, many business men prefer to have their homes just outside the towns where their business is. A cheap and efficient service open to every one would do away with a great deal of travelling that is necessary under existing circumstances, and by making it less important to live near a town allow people to return to the country.

Even Norway has a good telephone system. The telegraph is little used in the more thinly inhabited districts, but the telephone may be found in most unexpected places, in little villages hidden in the recesses of the fiords. Switzerland, another mountainous country, but very go-ahead in all electrical matters, is noted for the cheapness of its telephone services. At Berne or Geneva a subscriber pays £4 the first year, £2, 12s. the second year, and but £1, 12s. the third. Contrast these charges with those of New York, where £15, 10s. to £49, 10s. is levied annually according to service.

The telephone as a public benefactor is seen at its best at Buda-Pesth, the twin-capital of Hungary. In 1893, one Herr Theodore Buschgasch founded in that city a "newspaper"—if so it may be called—worked entirely on the telephone. The publishing office was a telephone exchange; the wires and instruments took the place of printed matter. The subscribers were to be informed entirely by ear of the news of the day.

The *Telefon Hirmondo* or "Telephonic Newsteller," as the "paper" was named, has more than six thousand subscribers, who enjoy their telephones for the very small payment of eighteen florins, or about a penny a day, for twelve hours a day.

News is collected at the central office in the usual journalistic way by telephone, telegraph, and reporters.

It is printed by lithography on strips of paper six inches wide and two feet long. These strips are handed to "stentors," or men with powerful and trained voices, who read the contents to transmitting instruments in the offices, whence it flies in all directions to the ears of the subscribers.

These last know exactly when to listen and what description of information they will hear, for each has over his receiver a programme which is rigidly adhered to. It must be explained at once that the *Telefon Hirmondo* is more than a mere newspaper, for it adds to its practical use as a first-class journal that of entertainer, lecturer, preacher, actor, political speaker, musician. The *Telefon* offices are connected by wire with the theatres, churches, and public halls, drawing from them by means of special receivers the sounds that are going on there, and transmitting them again over the wires to the thousands of subscribers. The Buda-Pesthian has therefore only to consult his programme to see when he will be in touch with his favourite actor or preacher. The ladies know just when to expect the latest hints about the fashions of the day. Nor are the children forgotten, for a special period is set aside weekly for their entertainment in the shape of lectures or concerts.

The advertising fiend, too, must have his say, though he pays dearly for it. On payment of a florin the stentors will shout the virtues of his wares for a space of twelve seconds. The advertising periods are sandwiched in between items of news, so that the subscriber is bound to hear the advertisements unless he is willing to risk missing some of the news if he hangs up his receiver until the "puff" is finished.

Thanks to the *Telefon Hirmondo* the preacher, actor, or singer is obliged to calculate his popularity less by the condition of the seats in front of him than by the number of telephones in use while he is performing his part. On the other hand, the subscriber is spared a vast amount of walking, waiting, cab-hire, and expense generally. In fact, if the principle is much further developed, we shall begin to doubt whether a Buda-Pesthian will be able to discover reasons for getting out of bed at all if the receiver hanging within reach of his hand is the entrance to so many places of delight. Will he become a very lazy person; and what will be the effect on his entertainers when they find themselves facing benches that are used less every day? Will the sight of a row of telephone trumpets rouse the future Liddon, Patti, Irving, or Gladstone to excel themselves? It seems rather doubtful. Telephones cannot look interested or applaud.

What is inside the simple-looking receiver that hangs on the wall beside a small mahogany case, or rests horizontally on a couple of crooks over the case? In the older type of instrument the transmitter and receiver are separate, the former fixed in front of the case, the latter, of course, movable so that it can be applied to the ear. But improved patterns have transmitter and receiver in a single movable handle, so shaped that the earpiece is by the ear while the mouthpiece curves round opposite the mouth. By pressing a small lever with the fingers the one or the other is brought into action when required. .

The construction of the instrument, of which we are at first a little afraid, and with which we later on learn to become rather angry, is in its general lines simple enough. The first practical telephone, constructed in 1876 by Graham Bell, a Scotchman, consisted of a long wooden or ebonite handle down the centre of which ran a permanent bar-magnet, having at one end a small coil of fine insulated wire wound about it. The ends of the wire coil are led through the handles to two terminals for connection with the line wires At a very short distance from the wire-wound pole of the magnet is firmly fixed by its edges a thin circular iron plate, covered by a funnel-shaped mouthpiece.

The iron plate is, when at rest, concave, its centre being attracted towards the pole of the magnet. When any one speaks into the mouthpiece the sound waves agitate the diaphragm (or plate), causing its centre to move inwards and outwards. The movements of the diaphragm affect the magnetism of the magnet, sometimes strengthening it, sometimes weakening it, and consequently exciting electric currents of varying strength in the wire coil. These currents passing through the line wires to a similar telephone excite the coil in it, and in turn affect the magnetism of the distant magnet, which attracts or releases the diaphragm near its pole, causing undulations of the air exactly resembling those set up by the speaker's words. To render the telephone powerful enough to make conversation possible over long distances it was found advisable to substitute for the one telephone a special transmitter, and to insert in the circuit a battery giving a much stronger current than could possibly be excited by the magnet in the telephone at the speaker's end.

Edison in 1877 invented a special transmitter made of carbon. He discovered that the harder two faces of carbon are pressed together the more readily will they allow current to pass; the reason probably being that the points of contact increase in number and afford more bridges for the current.

Accordingly his transmitter contains a small disc of lampblack (a form of carbon) connected to the diaphragm, and another carbon or platinum disc against which the first is driven with varying force by the vibrations of the voice.

The Edison transmitter is therefore in idea only a modification of the microphone. It acts as a *regulator* of current, in distinction to the Bell telephone, which is only an *exciter* of current. Modern forms of telephones unite the Edison transmitter with the Bell receiver.

The latter is extremely sensitive to electric currents, detecting them even when of the minutest power. We have seen that Marconi used a telephone in his famous transatlantic experiments to distinguish the signals sent from Cornwall. A telephone may be used with an "earth return" instead of a second wire; but as this exposes it to stray currents by induction from other wires carried on the same poles or from the earth itself, it is now usual to use two wires, completing the metallic circuit. Even so a subscriber is liable to overhear conversations on wires neighbouring his own; the writer has lively recollections of first receiving news of the relief of Ladysmith in this manner.

Owing to the self-induction of wires in submarine cables and the consequent difficulty of forcing currents through them, the telephone is at present not used in connection with submarine lines of more than a very moderate length. England has, however, been connected with France by a telephone cable from St. Margaret's Bay to Sangatte, 23 miles; and Scotland with Ireland, Stranraer to Donaghadee, 26 miles. The former cable enables speech between London and Marseilles, a distance of 900 miles; and the latter makes it possible to speak from London to Dublin *viâ* Glasgow. The longest direct line in existence is that between New York and Chicago, the complete circuit of which uses 1900 miles of stout copper wire, raised above the ground on poles 35 feet high.

The efficiency of the telephone on a well laid system is so great that it makes very little difference whether the persons talking with one another are 50 or 500 miles apart. There is no reason why a

Cape-to-Cairo telephone should not put the two extremities of Africa in clear vocal communication. We may even live to see the day when a London business man will be able to talk with his agent in Sydney, Melbourne, or Wellington.

A step towards this last achievement has been taken by M. Germain, a French electrician, who has patented a telephone which can be used with stronger currents than are possible in ordinary telephones; thereby, of course, increasing the range of speech on submarine cables.

The telephone that we generally use has a transmitter which permits but a small portion of the battery power to pass into the wires, owing to the resistance of the carbon diaphragm. The weakness of the current is to a great extent compensated by the exceedingly delicate nature of the receiver.

M. Germain has reversed the conditions with a transmitter that allows a very high percentage of the current to flow into the wires, and a comparatively insensitive receiver. The result is a "loud-speaking telephone"—not a novelty, for Edison invented one as long ago as 1877—which is capable of reproducing speech in a wonderfully powerful fashion.

M. Germain, with the help of special tubular receivers, has actually sent messages through a line having the same resistance as that of the London-Paris line, so audibly that the words could be heard fifteen yards from the receiver in the open air!

Wireless Telephony.

In days when wireless telegraphy is occupying such a great deal of the world's attention, it is not likely to cause much astonishment in the reader to learn that wireless transmission of *speech* over considerable distances is an accomplished fact. We have already mentioned (see "Wireless Telegraphy") that by means of parallel systems of wires Sir William Preece bridged a large air-gap, and induced in the one sounds imparted to the other.

Since then two other methods have been introduced; and as a preface to the mention of the first we may say a few words about Graham Bell's *Photophone.*

In this instrument *light* is made to do the work of a metal connection between speaker and listener. Professor Bell, in arranging the Photophone, used a mouthpiece as in his electric telephone, but instead of a diaphragm working in front of a magnet to set up electric impulses along a wire he employed a mirror of very thin glass, silvered on one side. The effect of sound on this mirror was to cause rapid alterations of its shape from concave to convex, and consequent variations of its reflecting power. A strong beam of light was concentrated on the centre of the mirror through a lens, and reflected by the mirror at an angle through another lens in the direction of the receiving instrument. The receiver consisted of a parabolic reflector to catch the rays and focus them on a selenium cell connected by an electric circuit with an ordinary telephone earpiece.

On delivering a message into the mouthpiece the speaker would, by agitating the mirror, send a succession of light waves of varying intensity towards the distant selenium cell. Selenium has the peculiar property of offering less resistance to electrical currents when light is thrown upon it than when it is in darkness: and the more intense is the light the less is the obstruction it affords. The light-waves from the mirror, therefore, constantly alter its capacity as a conductor, allowing currents to pass through the telephone with varying power.

In this way Professor Bell bridged 800 yards of space; over which he sent, besides articulate words, musical notes, using for the latter purpose a revolving perforated disc to interrupt a constant beam of light a certain number of times per second. As the speed of the disc increased the rate of the light-flashes increased also, and produced in the selenium cell the same number of passages to the electric current, converted into a musical note by the receiver. So that by means of mechanical apparatus a "playful sunbeam" could literally be compelled to play a tune.

From the Photophone we pass to another method of sound transmission by light, with which is connected the name of Mr. Hammond V. Hayes of Boston, Massachusetts. It is embodied in the Radiophone, or the Ray-speaker, for it makes strong rays of light carry the human voice.

Luminous bodies give off heat. As the light increases, so as a general rule does the heat also. At present we are unable to create strong light without having recourse to heat to help us, since we do not know how to cause other vibrations of sufficient rapidity to yield the sensation of light. But we can produce heat directly, and heat will set atoms in motion, and the ether too, giving us light, but taking as reward a great deal of the energy exerted. Now, the electric arc of a searchlight produces a large amount of light *and* heat. The light is felt by the eye at a distance of many miles, but the body is not sensitive enough to be aware of the heat emanating from the same source. Mr. Hayes has, however, found the heat accompanying a searchlight beam quite sufficient to affect a mechanical "nerve" in a far-away telephone receiver.

The transmitting apparatus is a searchlight, through the back of which run four pairs of wires connected with a telephone mouthpiece after passing through a switch and resistance-box or regulator. The receiver is a concave mirror, in the focus of which is a tapering glass bulb, half filled with carbonised filament very sensitive to heat. The tapering end of the bulb projects through the back of the mirror into an ear tube.

If a message is to be transmitted the would-be speaker turns his searchlight in the direction of the person with whom he wishes to converse, and makes the proper signals. On seeing them the other presents his mirror to the beam and listens.

The speaker's voice takes control of the searchlight beam. The louder the sound the more brilliantly glows the electric arc; the stronger becomes the beam, the greater is the amount of heat passed on to the mirror and gathered on the sensitive bulb. The filament inside expands. The tapering point communicates the fact to the earpiece.

This operation being repeated many times a second the earpiece fills with sound, in which all the modulations of the far-distant voice are easily distinguishable.

Two sets of the apparatus above described are necessary for a conversation, the functions of the searchlight and the bulb not being reversible. But inasmuch as all large steamers carry searchlights the necessary installation may be completed at a small expense. Mr. Hayes' invention promises to be a rival to wireless telegraphy over comparatively short distances. It can be relied upon in all weathers, and is a fast method of communication. Like the photophone it illustrates the inter-relationship of the phenomena of Sound, Light, and Heat, and the readiness with which they may be combined to attain an end.

Next we turn from air to earth, and to the consideration of the work of Mr. A. F. Collins of Philadelphia. This electrician merely makes use of the currents flowing in all directions through the earth, and those excited by an electric battery connected with earth. The outfit requisite for sending wireless spoken messages consists of a couple of convenient stands, as many storage batteries, sets of coils, and receiving and transmitting instruments.

The action of the transmitter is to send from the battery a series of currents through the coils, which transmit them, greatly intensified, to the earth by means of a wire connected with a buried wire-screen. The electric disturbances set up in the earth travel in all directions, and strike a similar screen buried beneath the receiving instrument, where the currents affect the delicate diaphragm of the telephone earpiece.

The system is, in fact, upon all fours with Mr. Marconi's, the distinguishing feature being that the ether of the atmosphere is used in the latter case, that of the earth in the former. The intensity coils are common to both; the buried screens are the counterpart of the aërial kites or balloons; the telephone transmitter corresponds to the telegraphic transmitting key; the earpiece to the coherer and relay. No doubt in time Mr. Collins will "tune" his instruments, so obtaining below ground the same sympathetic electric vibrations which Mr. Marconi, Professor Lodge, or others have employed to clothe their aërial messages in secrecy.

THE PHONOGRAPH.

EVEN if Thomas Edison had not done wonders with electric lighting, telephones, electric torpedoes, new processes for separating iron from its ore, telegraphy, animated photography, and other things too numerous to mention, he would still have made for himself an enduring name as the inventor of the Phonograph. He has fitly been called the "Wizard of the West" from his genius for conjuring up out of what would appear to the multitude most unpromising materials startling scientific marvels, among which none is more truly wizard-like than the instrument that is as receptive of sound as the human ear, and of illimitable reproducing power. By virtue of its elfishly human characteristic, articulate speech, it occupies, and always will occupy, a very high position as a mechanical wonder. When listening to a telephone we are aware of the fact that the sounds are immediate reproductions of a living person's voice, speaking at the moment and at a definite distance from us; but the phonographic utterances are those of a voice perhaps stilled for ever, and the difference adds romance to the speaking machine.

The Phonograph was born in 1876. As we may imagine, its appearance created a stir. A contributor to the *Times* wrote in 1877: "Not many weeks have passed since we were startled by the announcement that we could converse audibly with each other, although hundreds of miles apart, by means of so many miles of wire with a little electric magnet at each end.

"Another wonder is now promised us—an invention purely mechanical in its nature, by means of which words spoken by the human voice can be, so to speak, stored up and reproduced at will over and over again hundreds, it may be thousands, of times. What will be thought of a piece of mechanism by means of which a message of any length can be spoken on to a plate of metal—that plate sent by post to any part of the world and the message absolutely respoken in the very voice of the sender, purely by mechanical agency? What, too, shall be said of a mere machine, by means of which the old familiar voice of one who is no longer with us on earth can be heard speaking to us in the very tones and measure to which our ears were once accustomed?"

The first Edison machine was the climax of research in the realm of sound. As long ago as 1856 a Mr. Leo Scott made an instrument which received the formidable name of Phonautograph, on account of its capacity to register mechanically the vibrations set up in the atmosphere by the human voice or by musical instruments. A large metal cone like the mouth of an ear-trumpet had stretched across its smaller end a membrane, to which was attached a very delicate tracing-point working on the surface of a revolving cylinder covered with blackened paper. Any sound entering the trumpet agitated the membrane, which in turn moved the stylus and produced a line on the cylinder corresponding to the vibration. Scott's apparatus could only record. It was, so to speak, the first half of the phonograph. Edison, twenty years later, added the active half. His machine, as briefly described in the *Times*, was simple; so very simple that many scientists must have wondered how they failed to invent it themselves.

A metal cylinder grooved with a continuous square-section thread of many turns to the inch was mounted horizontally on a long axle cut at one end with a screw-thread of the same "pitch" as that on the cylinder. The axle, working in upright supports, and furnished with a heavy fly-wheel to render the rate of revolution fairly uniform, was turned by a handle. Over the grooved cylinder was stretched a thin sheet of tinfoil, and on this rested lightly a steel tracing-point, mounted at the end of a spring and separated from a vibrating diaphragm by a small pad of rubber tubing. A large mouthpiece to concentrate sound on to the diaphragm completed the apparatus.

To make a record with this machine the cylinder was moved along until the tracing-point touched one extremity of the foil. The person speaking into the mouthpiece turned the handle to bring a fresh surface of foil continuously under the point, which, owing to the thread on the axle and the groove on the

A unique group of Phonographs. 1. *The oldest phonograph in existence, now in South Kensington Museum.* 2. *Tinfoil instrument.* 3. *A cheaper form of the same.* 4. *A "spectacle-form" graphophone.* 5. *An exactly similar instrument, half-size scale.* 6. *A doll fitted with phonograph.*

[*To face p.* 56.

cylinder being of the same pitch, was always over the groove, and burnished the foil down into it to a greater or less depth according to the strength of the impulses received from the diaphragm.

The record being finished, the point was lifted off the foil, the cylinder turned back to its original position, and the point allowed to run again over the depressions it had made in the metal sheet. The latter now became the active part, imparting to the air by means of the diaphragm vibrations similar in duration and quality to those that affected it when the record was being made.

It is interesting to notice that the phonograph principle was originally employed by Edison as a telephone "relay." His attention had been drawn to the telephone recently produced by Graham Bell, and to the evil effects of current leakage in long lines. He saw that the amount of current wasted increased out of proportion to the length of the lines—even more than in the proportion of the squares of their lengths—and he hoped that a great saving of current would be effected if a long line were divided into sections and the sound vibrations were passed from one to the other by mechanical means. He used as the connecting link between two sections a strip of moistened paper, which a needle, attached to a receiver, indented with minute depressions, that handed on the message to another telephone. The phonograph proper, as a recording machine, was an after-thought.

Edison's first apparatus, besides being heavy and

clumsy, had in practice faults which made it fall short of the description given in the *Times*. Its tone was harsh. The records, so far from enduring a thousand repetitions, were worn out by a dozen. To these defects must be added a considerable difficulty in adjusting a record made on one machine to the cylinder of another machine.

Edison, being busy with his telephone and electric lamp work, put aside the phonograph for a time. Graham Bell, his brother, Chichester Bell, and Charles Sumner Tainter, developed and improved his crude ideas. They introduced the Graphophone, using easily removable cylinder records. For the tinfoil was substituted a thin coating of a special wax preparation on light paper cylinders. Clockwork-driven motors replaced the hand motion, and the new machines were altogether more handy and effective. As soon as he had time Edison again entered the field. He conceived the solid wax cylinder, and patented a small shaving apparatus by means of which a record could be pared away and a fresh surface be presented for a new record.

The phonograph or graphophone of to-day is a familiar enough sight; but inasmuch as our readers may be less intimately acquainted with its construction and action than with its effects, a few words will now be added about its most striking features.

In the first place, the record remains stationary while the trumpet, diaphragm and stylus pass over it. The reverse was the case with the tinfoil instrument.

The record is cut by means of a tiny sapphire point having a circular concave end very sharp at the edges, to gouge minute depressions into the wax. The point is agitated by a delicate combination of weights and levers connecting it with a diaphragm of French glass $\frac{1}{140}$ inch thick. The reproducing point is a sapphire ball of a diameter equal to that of the gouge. It passes over the depressions, falling into them in turn and communicating its movements to a diaphragm, and so tenderly does it treat the records that a hundred repetitions do not inflict noticeable damage.

It is a curious instance of the manner in which man unconsciously copies nature that the parts of the reproducing attachment of a phonograph contains parts corresponding in function exactly to those bones of the ear known as the Hammer, Anvil, and Stirrup.

To understand the inner working of the phonograph the reader must be acquainted with the theory of sound. All sound is the result of impulses transmitted by a moving body usually reaching the ear through the medium of the air. The quantity of the sound, or loudness, depends on the violence of the impulse; the tone, or note, on the number of impulses in a given time (usually fixed as one second); and the quality, or *timbre,* as musicians say, on the existence of minor vibrations within the main ones.

If we were to examine the surface of a phonograph record (or phonogram) under a powerful magnifying glass we should see a series of scoops cut by the gouge in the wax, some longer and deeper than others, long and short, deep and shallow, alternating and recurring in regular groups. The depth, length, and grouping of the cuts decides the nature of the resultant note when the reproducing sapphire point passes over the record—at a rate of about ten inches a second.

The study of a tracing made on properly prepared paper by a point agitated by a diaphragm would enable us to understand easily the cause of that mysterious variation in *timbre* which betrays at once what kind of instrument has emitted a note of known pitch. For instance, let us take middle C, which is the result of a certain number of atmospheric blows per second on the drum of the ear. The same note may come from a piano, a violin, a banjo, a man's larynx, an organ, or a cornet; but we at once detect its source. It is scarcely imaginable that a piano and a cornet should be mistaken for one another. Now, if the tracing instrument had been at work while the notes were made successively it would have recorded a wavy line, each wave of exactly the same *length* as its fellows, but varying in its *outline* according to the character of the note's origin. We should notice that the waves were themselves wavy in section, being jagged like the teeth of a saw, and that the small secondary waves differed in size.

The minor waves are the harmonics of the main

note. Some musical instruments are richer in these harmonics than others. The fact that these delicate variations are recorded as minute indentations in the wax and reproduced is a striking proof of the phonograph's mechanical perfection.

Furthermore, the phonograph registers not only these composite notes, but also chords or simultaneous combinations of notes, each of which may proceed from a different instrument. In its action it here resembles a man who by constant practice is able to add up the pounds, shillings, and pence columns in his ledger at the same time, one wave system overlapping and blending with another.

The phonograph is not equally sympathetic with all classes of sounds. Banjo duets make good records, but the guitar gives a poor result. Similarly, the cornet is peculiarly effective, but the bass drum disappointing. The deep chest notes of a man come from the trumpet with startling truth, but the top notes on which the soprano prides herself are often sadly "tinny." The phonograph, therefore, even in its most perfect form is not the equal of the exquisitely sensitive human ear; and this may partially be accounted for by the fact that the diaphragm in both recorder and reproducer has its own fundamental note which is not in harmony with all other notes, whereas the ear, like the eye, adapts itself to any vibration.

Yet the phonograph has an almost limitless répertoire. It can justly be claimed for it that it is many musical instruments rolled into one. It will reproduce clearly and faithfully an orchestra, an instrumental soloist, the words of a singer, a stump orator, or a stage favourite. Consequently we find it everywhere—at entertainments, in the drawing-room, and even tempting us at the railway station or other places of public resort to part with our superfluous pence. At the London Hippodrome it discourses to audiences of several thousand persons, and in the nursery it delights the possessors of ingeniously-constructed dolls which, on a button being pressed and concealed machinery being brought into action, repeat some well-known childish melody.

It must not be supposed that the phonograph is nothing more than a superior kind of scientific toy. More serious duties than those of mere entertainment have been found for it.

At the last Presidential Election in the States the phonograph was often called upon to harangue large meetings in the interests of the rival candidates, who were perhaps at the time wearing out their voices hundreds of miles away with the same words.

Since the pronunciation of a foreign language is acquired by constant imitation of sounds, the phonograph, instructed by an expert, has been used to repeat words and phrases to a class of students until the difficulties they contain have been thoroughly mastered. The sight of such a class hanging on the lips—or more properly the trumpet—of a phonograph gifted with the true Parisian accent may be common enough in the future.

As a mechanical secretary and substitute for the shorthand writer the phonograph has certainly passed the experimental stage. Its daily use by some of the largest business establishments in the world testify to its value in commercial life. Many firms, especially American, have invested heavily in establishing phonograph establishments to save labour and final expense. The manager, on arriving at his office in the morning, reads his letters, and as the contents of each is mastered, dictates an answer to a phonograph cylinder which is presently removed to the typewriting room, where an assistant, placing it upon her phonograph and fixing the tubes to her ears, types what is required. It is interesting to learn that at Ottawa, the seat of the Canadian Government, phonographs are used for reporting the parliamentary proceedings and debates.

There is therefore a prospect that, though the talking-machine may lose its novelty as an entertainer, its practical usefulness will be largely increased. And while considering the future of the instrument, the thought suggests itself whether we shall be taking full advantage of Mr. Edison's notable invention if we neglect to make records of all kinds of intelligible sounds which have more than a passing interest. If the records were made in an imperishable substance they might remain effective for centuries, due care being taken of them in special depositories owned by the nation. To understand what their value would be to future generations we have only to imagine ourselves listening to the long-stilled thunder of Earl

Chatham, to the golden eloquence of Burke, or the passionate declamations of Mrs. Siddons. And in the narrower circle of family interests how valuable a part of family heirlooms would be the phonograms containing a vocal message to posterity from Grandfather this, or Great-aunt that, whose portraits in the drawing-room album do little more than call attention to the changes in dress since the time when their subjects faced the camera!

Record-Making and Manufacture.—Phonographic records are of two shapes, the cylindrical and the flat, the latter cut with a volute groove continuously diminishing in diameter from the circumference to the centre. Flat records are used in the Gramophone—a reproducing machine only. Their manufacture is effected by first of all making a record on a sheet of zinc coated with a very thin film of wax, from which the sharp steel point moved by the recording diaphragm removes small portions, baring the zinc underneath. The plate is then flooded with an acid solution, which eats into the bared patches, but does not affect the parts still covered with wax. The etching complete, the wax is removed entirely, and a cast or electrotype *negative* record made from the zinc plate. The indentations of the original are in this represented by excrescences of like size; and when the negative block is pressed hard down on to a properly prepared disc of vulcanite or celluloid, the latter is indented in a manner that reproduces exactly the tones received on the "master" record.

Cylindrical records are made in two ways, by moulding or by copying. The second process is extremely simple. The "master" cylinder is placed on a machine which also rotates a blank cylinder at a short distance from and parallel to the first. Over the "master" record passes a reproducing point, which is connected by delicate levers to a cutting point resting on the "blank," so that every movement of the one produces a corresponding movement of the other.

This method, though accurate in its results, is comparatively slow. The *moulding* process is therefore becoming the more general of the two. Edison has recently introduced a most beautiful process for obtaining negative moulds from wax positives. Owing to its shape, a zinc cylinder could not be treated like a flat disc, as, the negative made, it could not be detached without cutting. Edison, therefore, with characteristic perseverance, sought a way of electrotyping the wax, which, being a non-conductor of electricity, would not receive a deposit of metal. The problem was how to deposit on it.

Any one who has seen a Crookes' tube such as is used for X-ray work may have noticed on the glass a black deposit which arises from the flinging off from the negative pole of minute particles of platinum. Edison took advantage of this repellent action; and by enclosing his wax records in a vacuum between two gold poles was able to coat them with an infinitesimally thin skin of pure gold, on which silver or nickel could be easily deposited. The deposit being sufficiently thick the wax was melted out and the surface of the electrotype carefully cleaned. To make castings it was necessary only to pour in wax, which on cooling would shrink sufficiently to be withdrawn. The delicacy of the process may be deduced from the fact that some of the sibilants, or hissing sounds of the voice, are computed to be represented by depressions less than a millionth of an inch in depth, and yet they are most distinctly reproduced! Cylinder records are made in two sizes, 2½ and 5 inches in diameter respectively. The larger size gives the most satisfactory renderings, as the indentations are on a larger scale and therefore less worn by the reproducing point. One hundred turns to the inch is the standard pitch of the thread; but in some records the number is doubled.

Phonographs, Graphophones, and Gramophones are manufactured almost entirely in America, where large factories, equipped with most perfect plant and tools, work day and night to cope with the orders that flow in freely from all sides. One factory alone turns out a thousand machines a day, ranging in value from a few shillings to forty pounds each. Records are made in England on a large scale; and now that the Edison-Bell firm has introduced the unbreakable celluloid form their price will decrease. By means of the Edison electrotyping process a customer can change his record without changing his cylinder. He takes the cylinder to the factory, where it is heated, placed in the mould, and subjected to great pressure which drives the soft celluloid into the mould depressions; and behold! in a few moments "Auld Lang Syne" has become "Home, Sweet Home," or whatever air is desired. Thus altering records is very little more difficult than getting a fresh book at the circulating library.

THE PHOTOGRAPHOPHONE.

This instrument is a phonograph working entirely by means of light and electricity.

The flame of an electric lamp is brought under the influence of sound vibrations which cause its brilliancy to vary at every alteration of pitch or quality.

The light of the flame is concentrated through a lens on to a travelling photographic sensitive film, which, on development in the ordinary way, is found to be covered with dark and bright stripes proportionate in tone to the strength of the light at different moments. The film is then passed between a lamp and a selenium plate connected with an electric circuit and a telephone. The resistance of the selenium to the current varies according to the power of the light thrown upon it. When a dark portion of the film intercepts the light of the lamp the selenium plate offers high resistance; when the light finds its way through a clear part of the film the resistance weakens. Thus the telephone is submitted to a series of changes affecting the "receiver." As in the making of the record speech-vibrations affect light, and the light affects a sensitive film; so in its reproduction the film affects a sensitive selenium plate, giving back to a telephone exactly what it received from the sound vibrations.

One great advantage of Mr. Ruhmer's method is that from a single film any number of records can be printed by photography; another, that, as with the Telegraphone (see below), the same film passed before a series of lamps successively is able to operate a corresponding number of telephones.

The inventor is not content with his success. He hopes to record not merely sounds but even pictures by means of light and a selenium plate.

The Telephonograph.

Having dealt with the phonograph and the telephone separately, we may briefly consider one or two ingenious combinations of the two instruments. The word Telephonograph signifies an apparatus for recording sounds sent from a distance. It takes the place of the human listener at the telephone receiver.

Let us suppose that a Reading subscriber wishes to converse along the wires with a friend in London, but that on ringing up his number he discovers that the friend is absent from his home or office. He is left with the alternative of either waiting till his friend returns, which may cause a serious loss of time, or of dictating his message, a slow and laborious process. This with the ordinary telephonic apparatus. But if the London friend be the possessor of a Telephonograph, the person answering the call-bell can, if desired to do so, switch the wires into connection with it and start the machinery; and in a very short time the message will be stored up for reproduction when the absent friend returns.

The Telephonograph is the invention of Mr. J. E. O. Kumberg. The message is spoken into the telephone transmitter in the ordinary way, and the vibrations set up by the voice are caused to act upon a recording stylus by the impact of the sound waves at the further end of the wires. In this manner a phonogram is produced on the wax cylinder in the house or office of the person addressed, and it may be read off at leisure. A very sensitive transmitter is employed, and if desired the apparatus can be so arranged that by means of a double-channel tube the words spoken are simultaneously conveyed to the telephone and to an ordinary phonograph, which insures that a record shall be kept of any message sent.

The *Telegraphone*, produced by Mr. Valdemar Poulsen, performs the same functions as the telephonograph, but differs from it in being entirely electrical. It contains no waxen cylinder, no cutting-point; their places are taken respectively by a steel wire wound on a cylindrical drum (each turn carefully insulated from its neighbours) and by a very small electro-magnet, which has two delicate points that pass along the wire, one on either side, resting lightly upon it.

As the drum rotates, the whole of the wire passes gradually between the two points, into which a series of electric shocks is sent by the action of the speaker's voice at the further end of the wires. The shocks magnetise the portion of steel wire which acts as a temporary bridge between the two points. At the close of three and a half minutes the magnet has worked from one end of the wire coil to the other; it is then automatically lifted and carried back to the starting-point in readiness for reproduction of the sounds. This is accomplished by disconnecting the telegraphone from the telephone wires and switching it on to an ordinary telephonic earpiece or receiver. As soon as the cylinder commences to revolve a second time, the magnet is influenced by the series of magnetic "fields" in the wires, and as often as it touches a magnetised spot imparts an impulse to the diaphragm of the receiver, which vibrates at the rate and with the same force as the vibrations originally set up in the distant transmitter. The result is a clear and accurate reproduction of the message, even though hours and even days may have elapsed since its arrival.

As the magnetic effects on the wire coil retain their power for a considerable period, the message may be reproduced many times. As soon as the wire-covered drum is required for fresh impressions, the old one is wiped out by passing a permanent magnet along the wire to neutralise the magnetism of the last message.

The Telephonograph

Mr. Poulsen has made an instrument of a different type to be employed for the reception of an unusually lengthy communication. Instead of a wire coil on a cylinder, a ribbon of very thin flat steel spring is wound from one reel on to another across the poles of *two* electro-magnets, which touch the lower side only of the strip. The first magnet is traversed by a continuous current to efface the previous record; the second magnetises the strip in obedience to impulses from the telephone wires. The message complete, the strip is run back, and the magnets connected with receivers, which give out loud and intelligent speech as the strip again traverses them. The Poulsen machine makes the transmission of the same message simultaneously through several telephones an easy matter, as the strip can be passed over a series of electro-magnets each connected with a telephone.

THE TELAUTOGRAPH.

It is a curious experience to watch for the first time the movements of a tiny Telautograph pen as it works behind a glass window in a japanned case. The pen, though connected only with two delicate wires, appears instinct with human reason. It writes in a flowing hand, just as a man writes. At the end of a word it crosses the t's and dots the i's. At the end of a line it dips itself in an inkpot. It punctuates its sentences correctly. It illustrates its words with sketches. It uses shorthand as readily as longhand. It can form letters of all shapes and sizes.

And yet there is no visible reason why it should do what it does. The japanned case hides the guiding agency, whatever it may be. Our ears cannot detect any mechanical motion. The writing seems at first sight as mysterious as that which appeared on the wall to warn King Belshazzar.

In reality it is the outcome of a vast amount of patience and mechanical ingenuity culminating in a wonderful instrument called the Telautograph. The Telautograph is so named because by its aid we can send our autographs, *i.e.* our own particular handwriting, electrically over an indefinite length of wire, as easily as a telegraph clerk transmits messages in

By kind permission of] [*The Telautograph Co.*

The Telautograph. The upper portion is the Receiver, the lower (with cover removed) is the Transmitter.

[*To face p. 72.*

the Morse alphabet. Whatever the human hand does on one telautograph at one end of the wires, that will be reproduced by a similar machine at the other end, though the latter be hundreds of miles away.

The instrument stands about eighteen inches high, and its base is as many inches square. It falls into two parts, the receiver and the transmitter. The receiver is vertical and forms the upright and back portion of the telautograph. At one side of it hangs an ordinary telephone attachment. The transmitter, a sloping desk placed conveniently for the hand, is the front and horizontal portion. The receiver of one station is connected with the transmitter of another station; there being ordinarily no direct communication between the two parts of the same instrument.

An attempt will be made to explain, with the help of a simple diagram, the manner in which the telautograph performs its duties.

These duties are threefold. In the first place, it must reproduce whatever is written on the transmitter. Secondly, it must reproduce only what is *written*, not all the movements of the hand. Thirdly, it must supply the recording pen with fresh paper to write on, and with fresh ink to write with.

In our diagram we must imagine that all the coverings of the telautograph have been cleared away to lay bare the most essential parts of the mechanism. For the sake of simplicity not all the coils, wires, and magnets having functions of their own are represented, and the drawing is not to scale. But what is shown will enable the reader to grasp the general principles which work the machine.

Turning first of all to the transmitter, we have P, a little platform hinged at the back end, and moving up and down very slightly in front, according as pressure is put on to or taken off it by the pencil. Across it a roll of paper is shifted by means of the lever S, which has other uses as well. To the right of P is an electric bell-push, E, and on the left K, another small button.

The pencil is at the junction of two small bars CC′, which are hinged at their other end to the levers AA′. Any motion of the pencil is transmitted by CC′ to AA′, and by them to the arms LL′, the extremities of which, two very small brushes *ZZ′*, sweep along the quadrants RR′. This is the first point to observe, that the position of the pencil decides on which sections of the quadrants these little brushes rest, and consequently how much current is to be sent to the distant station. The quadrants are known technically as rheostats, or current-controllers. Each quadrant is divided into 496 parts, separated from each other by insulating materials, so that current can pass from one to the other only by means of some connecting wire. In our illustration only thirteen divisions are given, for the sake of clearness. The dark lines represent the insulation. WW′ are the very fine wire loops connecting each division of the quadrant with its neighbours. If then a current from the

THE TELAUTOGRAPH

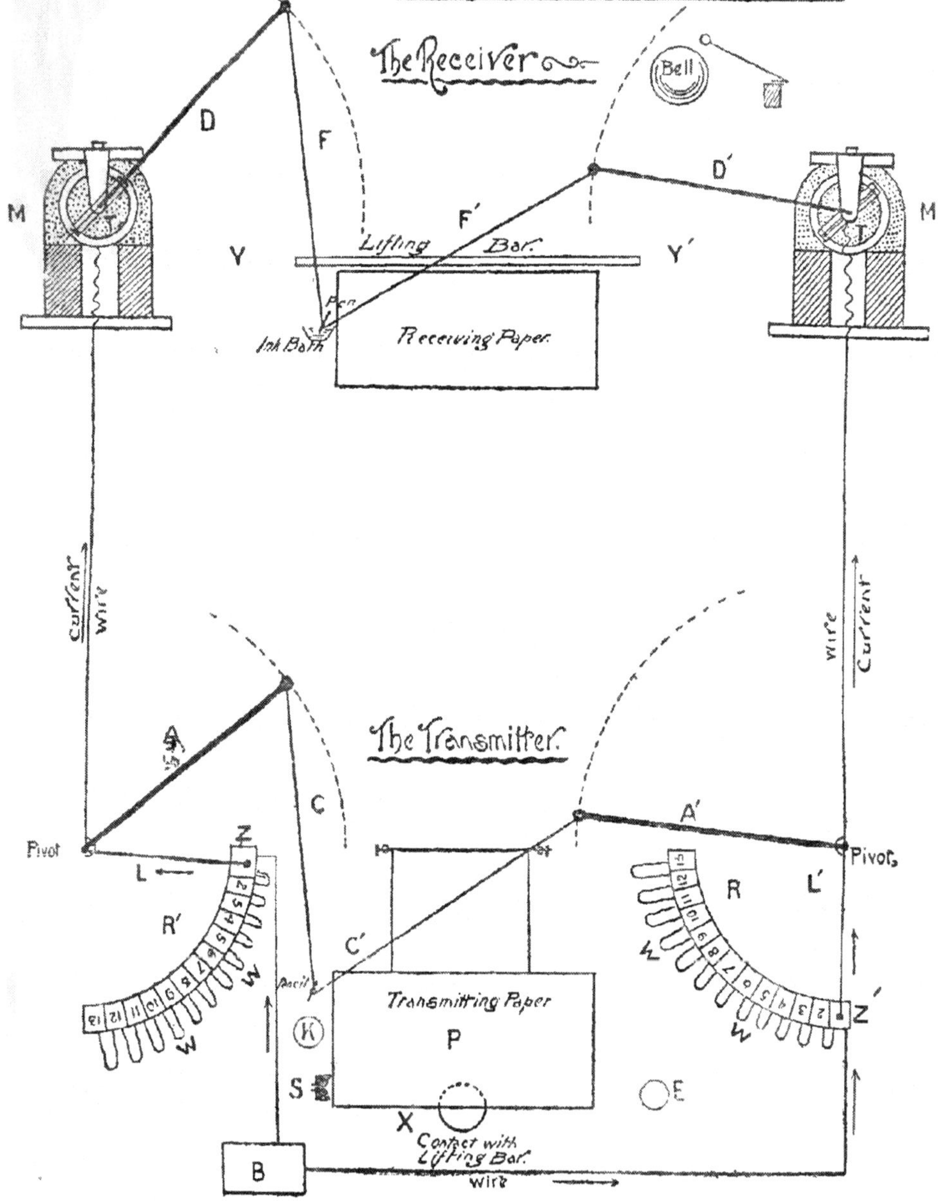

battery B enters the rheostat at division 1 it will have to pass through all these wires before it can reach division 13. The current always enters at 1, but the point of departure from the rheostat depends entirely upon the position of the brushes Z or Z′. If Z happens to be on No. 6 the current will pass through five loops of wire, along the arm L, and so through the main wire to the receiving station; if on No. 13, through twelve loops.

Before going any further we must have clear ideas on the subject of electrical resistance, upon which the whole system of the telautograph is built up. Electricity resembles water in its objection to flow through small passages. It is much harder to pump water through a half-inch pipe than through a one-inch pipe, and the longer the pipe is, whatever its bore, the more work is required. So then, two things affect resistance—*size* of pipe or wire, and *length* of pipe or wire.

The wires WW′ are very fine, and offer very high resistance to a current; so high that by the time the current from battery B has passed through all the wire loops only one-fifteenth or less of the original force is left to traverse the long-distance wire.

The rheostats act independently of one another. As the pencil moves over the transmitting paper, a succession of currents of varying intensity is sent off by each rheostat to the receiving station.

The receiver, to which we must now pay attention, has two arms DD′, and two rods FF′, corresponding

By kind permission of] [*The Telautograph Co.*

An example of the work done by the Telautograph. The upper sketch shows a design drawn on the transmitter; the lower is the same design as reproduced by the receiving instrument, many miles distant.

[*To face p. 76.*

in size with AA′ and CC′ of the transmitter. The arms DD′ are moved up and down by the coils TT′, which turn on centres in circular spaces at the bend of the magnets MM′. The position of these coils relatively to the magnets depend on the strength of the currents coming from the transmitting station. Each coil strains at a small spiral spring until it has reached the position in which its electric force is balanced by the retarding influence of the spring. One of the cleverest things in the telautograph is the adjustment of these coils so that they shall follow faithfully the motions of the rods LL′ in the transmitter.

We are now able to trace the actions of sending a message. The sender first presses the button E to call the attention of some one at the receiving station to the fact that a message is coming, either on the telephone or on the paper. It should be remarked, by-the-bye, that the same wires serve for both telephone and telautograph, the unhooking of the telephone throwing the telautograph out of connection for the time.

He then presses the lever S towards the left, bringing his transmitter into connection with the distant receiver, and also moving a fresh length of paper on to the platform P. With his pencil he writes his message, pressing firmly on the paper, so that the platform may bear down against an electric contact, X. As the pencil moves about the paper the arms CC′ are constantly changing their angles, and the brushes ZZ′ are passing along the segments of the rheostats.

Currents flow in varying intensity away to the coils TT′ and work the arms DD′, the wires FF′, and the pen, a tiny glass tube.

In the perfectly regulated telautograph the arms AA′ and the arms DD′ will move in unison, and consequently the position of the pen must be the same from moment to moment as that of the pencil.

Mr. Foster Ritchie, the clever inventor of this telautograph, had to provide for many things besides mere slavish imitation of movement. As has been stated above, the pen must record only those movements of the pencil which are essential. Evidently, if while the pencil returns to dot an *i* a long line were registered by the pen corresponding to the path of the pencil, confusion would soon ensue on the receiver; and instead of a neatly-written message we should have an illegible and puzzling maze of lines. Mr. Ritchie has therefore taken ingenious precautions against any such mishap. The platen P on being depressed by the pencil touches a contact, X, which closes an electric circuit through the long-distance wires and excites a magnet at the receiving end. That attracts a little arm and breaks another circuit, allowing the bar Y to fall close to the paper. The wires FF′ and the pen are now able to rest on the paper and trace characters. But as soon as the platen P rises, on the removal of the pencil from the transmitting paper, the contact at X is broken, the magnet at the receiver ceases to act, the arm it attracted falls back and sets up a circuit which causes the bar to spring up again and lift the pen. So that unless you are actually pressing the paper with your pencil, the pen is not marking, though it may be moving.

As soon as a line is finished a fresh surface of paper is required at both ends. The operator pushes the lever S sideways, and effects the change mechanically at his end. At the same time a circuit is formed which excites certain magnets at the receiver and causes the shifting forward there also of the paper, and also breaks the *writing* current, so that the pen returns for a moment to its normal position of rest in the inkpot.

It may be asked: If the wires are passing currents to work the writing apparatus, how can they simultaneously affect the lifting-bar, Y? The answer is that currents of two different kinds are used, a direct current for writing, a vibratory current for depressing the lifting-bar. The *direct* current passes from the battery B through the rheostats RR along the wires, through the coils working the arms DD and into the earth at the far end; but the *vibratory* current, changing its direction many times a second and so neutralising itself, passes up one wire and back down the other through the lifting-bar connection without interfering with the direct current.

The message finished, the operator depresses with the point of his pencil the little push-key, K, and connects his receiver with the distant transmitter in readiness for an answer.

The working speed of the telautograph is that of

the writer. If shorthand be employed, messages can be transmitted at the rate of over 100 words per imnute. As regards the range of transmission, successful tests have been made by the postal authorities between Paris and London, and also between Paris and Lyons. In the latter case the messages were sent from Paris to Lyons and back directly to Paris, the lines being connected at Lyons, to give a total distance of over 650 miles. There is no reason why much greater length of line should not be employed.

The telautograph in its earlier and imperfect form was the work of Professor Elisha Gray, who invented the telephone almost simultaneously with Professor Graham Bell. His telautograph worked on what is known as the step-by-step principle, and was defective in that its speed was very limited. If the operator wrote too fast the receiving pen lagged behind the transmitting pencil, and confusion resulted. Accordingly this method, though ingenious, was abandoned, and Mr. Ritchie in his experiments looked about for some preferable system, which should be simpler and at the same time much speedier in its action. After four years of hard work he has brought the rheostat system, explained above, to a pitch of perfection which will be at once appreciated by any one who has seen the writing done by the instrument.

The advantages of the Telautograph over the ordinary telegraphy may be briefly summed up as follows:—

Anybody who can write can use it; the need of skilled operators is abolished.

A record is automatically kept of every message sent.

The person to whom the message is sent need not be present at the receiver. He will find the message written out on his return.

The instrument is silent and so insures secrecy. An ordinary telegraph may be read by sound; but not the telautograph.

It is impossible to tap the wires unless, as is most unlikely, the intercepting party has an instrument in exact accord with the transmitter.

It can be used on the same wires as the ordinary telephone, and since a telephone is combined with it, the subscriber has a double means of communication. For some items of business the telephone may be used as preferable; but in certain cases, the telautograph. A telephone message may be heard by other subscribers; it is impossible to prove the authenticity of such a message unless witnesses have been present at the transmitting end; and the message itself may be misunderstood by reason of bad articulation. But the telautograph preserves secrecy while preventing any misunderstanding. Anything written by it is for all practical purposes as valid as a letter.

We must not forget its extreme usefulness for transmitting sketches. A very simple diagram often explains a thing better than pages of letter-press. The telautograph may help in the detection of criminals, a pictorial presentment of whom can by its means be despatched all over the country in a very short time. And in warfare an instrument flashing back from the advance-guard plans of the country and of the enemy's positions might on occasion prove of the greatest importance.

MODERN ARTILLERY.

THE vast subject of artillery in its modern form, including under this head for convenience' sake not only heavy ordnance but machine-guns and small-arms, can of necessity only be dealt with most briefly in this chapter.

It may therefore be well to take a general survey and to define beforehand any words or phrases which are used technically in describing the various operations.

The employment of firearms dates from a long-distant past, and it is interesting to note that many an improvement introduced during the last century is but the revival of a former invention which only lack of accuracy in tools and appliances had hitherto prevented from being brought into practical usage.

So far back as 1498 the art of *rifling* cannon in straight grooves was known, and a British patent was taken out in 1635 by Rotsipan. The grooves were first made spiral or screwed by Koster of Birmingham about 1620. Berlin possesses a rifled cannon with thirteen grooves dated 1664. But the first recorded uses of such weapons in actual warfare was during Louis Napoleon's Italian campaign in 1859, and two years later by General James of the United States Army.

The system of *breech-loading*, again, is as old as the sixteenth century, and we find a British patent of 1741; while the first United States patent was given in 1811 for a flint-lock weapon.

Magazine guns of American production appeared in 1849 and 1860, but these were really an adaptation of the old matchlock revolvers, said to belong to the period 1480–1500. There is one in the Tower of London credited to the fifteenth century, and a British patent of 1718 describes a well-constructed revolver carried on a tripod and of the dimensions of a modern machine-gun. The inventor gravely explains that he has provided round chambers for round bullets to shoot Christians, and square chambers with square missiles for use against the Turks!

The word "ordnance" is applied to heavy guns of all kinds, and includes guns mounted on fortresses, naval guns, siege artillery, and that for use in the field. These guns are all mounted on stands or carriages, and may be divided into three classes:—

(i.) *Cannon*, or heavy guns.

(ii.) *Howitzers*, for field, mountain, or siege use, which are lighter and shorter than cannon, and designed to throw hollow projectiles with comparatively small charges.

(iii.) *Mortars*, for throwing shells at a great elevation.

The modern long-range guns and improved howitzers have, however, virtually superseded mortars. *Machine-guns* of various forms are comparatively small and light, transportable by hand, and filling a place between cannon and small-arms, the latter term embracing the soldier's personal armament of rifle and pistol or revolver, which are carried in the hand.

A group of guns of the like design are generally given the name of their first inventor, or the place of manufacture : such as the Armstrong gun, the Vickers-Maxim, the Martini-Henry rifle, or the Enfield.

The indifferent use of several expressions in describing the same weapon is, however, rather confusing. One particular gun may be thus referred to :—by its *weight* in tons or cwt., as "the 35-ton gun"; by the weight of its *projectile*, as "a 68-pounder"; by its *calibre*, that is, size of bore, as "the 4-inch gun." Of these the heavier breech-loading (B.-L.) and quick-firing (Q.-F.) guns are generally known by the size of bore; small Q.-F.'s, field-guns, &c., by the weight of projectile. It is therefore desirable to enter these particulars together when making any list of service ordnance for future reference.

No individual gun, whether large or small, is a single whole, but consists of several pieces fastened together by many clever devices.

The principal parts of a cannon are :—

(1) The *chase*, or main tube into which the projectile is loaded ; terminating at one end in the muzzle.

(2) The *breech-piece*, consisting of (*a*) the chamber,

which is bored out for a larger diameter than the chase to contain the firing-charge. (*b*) The *breech-plug*, which is closed before the charge is exploded and screwed tightly into place, sealing every aperture by means of a special device called the "obturator," in order to prevent any gases passing out round it instead of helping to force the projectile forwards towards the muzzle.

The whole length of inside tube is termed the *barrel*, as in a machine-gun, rifle, or sporting-piece, but in the two latter weapons the breech-opening is closed by sliding or springing back the breech-block or bolt into firing position.

Old weapons as a rule were smooth-bored (S.-B.), firing a round missile between which and the barrel a considerable amount of the gases generated by the explosion escaped and caused loss of power, this escape of gas being known as *windage*.

In all modern weapons we use conical projectiles, fitted near the base with a soft copper driving-band, the diameter of which is somewhat larger than that of the bore of the gun, and cut a number of spiral grooves in the barrel. The enormous pressure generated by the explosion of the charge forces the projectile down the bore of the gun and out of the muzzle. The body of the projectile, made of steel or iron, being smaller in diameter than the bore, easily passes through, but the driving-band being of greater diameter, and being composed of soft copper, can only pass down the bore with the projectile by flowing into the grooves, thus preventing any escape of gas, and being forced to follow their twist. It therefore rotates rapidly upon its own longitudinal axis while passing down the barrel, and on leaving the muzzle two kinds of velocity have been imparted to it;—first, a velocity of motion through the air; secondly, a velocity of rotation round its axis which causes it to fly steadily onward in the required direction, *i.e.* a prolongation of the axis of the gun. Thus extreme velocity and penetrating power, as well as correctness of aim, are acquired.

The path of a projectile through the air is called its *trajectory*, and if uninterrupted its flight would continue on indefinitely in a perfectly straight line. But immediately a shot has been hurled from the gun by the explosion in its rear two other natural forces begin to act upon it:—

Gravitation, which tends to bring it to earth.

Air-resistance, which gradually checks its speed.

(Theoretically, a bullet dropped perpendicularly from the muzzle of a perfectly horizontal rifle would reach the ground at the same moment as another bullet fired from the muzzle horizontally, the action of gravity being the same in both cases.)

Its direct, even course is therefore deflected till it forms a curve, and sooner or later it returns to earth, still retaining a part of its velocity. To counteract the attraction of gravity the shot is thrown upwards by elevating the muzzle, care being taken to direct the gun's action to the same height above the object as the force of gravitation would draw the projectile down during the time of flight. The gunner is enabled to give the proper inclination to his piece by means of the *sights;* one of these, near the muzzle, being generally fixed, while that next the breech is adjustable by sliding up an upright bar which is so graduated that the proper *elevation* for any required range is given.

The greater the velocity the flatter is the trajectory, and the more dangerous to the enemy. Assuming the average height of a man to be six feet, all the distance intervening between the point where a bullet has dropped to within six feet of the earth, and the point where it actually strikes is dangerous to any one in that interval, which is called the "danger zone." A higher initial velocity is gained by using stronger firing charges, and a more extended flight by making the projectile longer in proportion to its diameter. The reason why a shell from a cannon travels further than a rifle bullet, both having the same muzzle velocity, is easily explained.

A rifle bullet is, let us assume, three times as long as it is thick; a cannon shell the same. If the shell have ten times the diameter of the bullet, its "nose" will have $10 \times 10 = 100$ times the area of the bullet's nose; but its *mass* will be $10 \times 10 \times 10 = 1000$ times that of the bullet.

In other words, when two bodies are proportional in all their dimensions their air-resistance varies as the square of their diameters, but their mass and consequently their momentum varies as the *cube* of their diameters. The shell therefore starts with a great advantage over the bullet, and may be compared to a "crew" of cyclists on a multicycle all cutting the same path through the air; whereas the bullet resembles a single rider, who has to overcome as much air-resistance as the front man of the "crew" but has not the weight of other riders behind to help him.

As regards the effect of rifling, it is to keep the bullet from turning head over heels as it flies through the air, and to maintain it always point forwards. Every boy knows that a top "sleeps" best when it is spinning fast. Its horizontal rotation overcomes a tendency to vertical movement towards the ground. In like manner a rifle bullet, spinning vertically, overcomes an inclination of its atoms to move out of their horizontal path. Professor John Perry, F.R.S., has illustrated this gyroscopic effect, as it is called, of a whirling body with a heavy flywheel in a case, held by a man standing on a pivoted table. However much the man may try to turn the top from its original direction he will fail as long as its velocity of rotation is high. He may move the top relatively to his body, but the table will turn so as to keep the centre line of the top always pointing in the same direction.

RIFLES.

Up to the middle of last century our soldiers were armed with the flint-lock musket known as "Brown Bess," a smooth-bore barrel ¾-inch in diameter, thirty-nine inches long, weighing with its bayonet over eleven pounds. The round leaden bullet weighed an ounce, and had to be wrapped in a "patch" or bit of oily rag to make it fit the barrel and prevent windage; it was then pushed home with a ramrod on to the powder-charge, which was ignited by a spark passing from the flint into a priming of powder. How little its accuracy of aim could be depended upon, however, is proved by the word of command when advancing upon an enemy, "Wait till you see the whites of their eyes, boys, before you fire!"

In the year 1680 each troop of Life Guards was supplied with eight rifled carbines, a modest allowance, possibly intended to be used merely by those acting as scouts. After this we hear nothing of them until in 1800 the 95th Regiment received a 20-bore muzzle-loading rifle, exchanged about 1835 for the Brunswick rifle firing a spherical bullet, an improvement that more than doubled its effective range. The companies so armed became known as the Rifle Brigade. At last, in 1842, the old flint-lock was superseded for the whole army by the original percussion musket, a smooth-bore whose charge was exploded by a percussion cap made of copper. [That this copper had some commercial value was shown by the rush of "roughs" to Aldershot and elsewhere upon a field-day to collect the split fragments which strewed the ground after the troops had withdrawn.]

Soon afterward the barrel was rifled and an elongated bullet brought into use. This missile was pointed in front, and had a hollowed base so contrived that it expanded immediately the pressure of exploding gases was brought to bear on it, and thus filled up the grooves, preventing any windage. The one adopted by our army in the year 1852 was the production of M. Minié, a Frenchman, though an expanding bullet of English invention had been brought forward several years before.

Meanwhile the Prussians had their famous needle-gun, a breech-loading rifled weapon fired by a needle attached to a sliding bolt; as the bolt is shot forward the needle pierces the charge and ignites the fulminate by friction. This rifle was used in the Prusso-Austrian war of 1866 some twenty years after its first inception, and the French promptly countered it by arming their troops with the Chassepôt rifle, an improved edition of the same principle. A piece which could be charged and fired in any position from five to seven times as fast as the muzzle-loader, which the soldier had to load standing, naturally caused a revolution in the infantry armament of other nations.

The English Government, as usual the last to make a change, decided in 1864 upon using breech-loading rifles. Till a more perfect weapon could be obtained the Enfields were at a small outlay converted into breech-loaders after the plans of Mr. Snider, and were henceforward known as Snider-Enfields. Eventually —as the result of open competition—the Martini-Henry rifle was produced by combining Henry's system of rifling with Martini's mechanism for breech-loading. This weapon had seven grooves with one turn in twenty-two inches, and weighed with bayonet 10 lb. 4 oz. It fired with great accuracy, the trajectory having a rise of only eight feet at considerable distances, so that the bullet would not pass over the head of a cavalry man. Twenty rounds could be fired in fifty-three seconds.

Now in the latter years of the century all these weapons have been superseded by magazine rifles, *i.e.* rifles which can be fired several times without recourse to the ammunition pouch. They differ from the revolver in having only one firing chamber, into which the cartridges are one by one brought by a simple action of the breech mechanism, which also extracts the empty cartridge-case. The bore of these rifles is smaller and the rifling sharper; they therefore shoot straighter and harder than the large bore, and owing to the use of new explosives the recoil is less.

The French *Lebel* magazine rifle was the pioneer of all now used by European nations, though a somewhat similar weapon was familiar to the Americans since 1849, being first used during the Civil War. The Henry rifle, as it was called, afterwards became the Winchester.

The German army rifle is the *Mauser*, so familiar

to us in the hands of the Boers during the South African War—loading five cartridges at once in a case or "clip" which falls out when emptied. The same rifle has been adopted by Turkey, and was used by the Spaniards in the late Spanish-American War.

The Austrian *Mannlicher*, adopted by several continental nations, and the Krag-Jorgensen now used in the north of Europe and as the United States army weapon, resemble the Mauser in most particulars. Each of these loads the magazine in one movement with a clip.

The *Hotchkiss* magazine rifle has its magazine in the stock, holding five extra cartridges pushed successively into loading position by a spiral spring.

Our forces are now armed principally with the *Lee-Enfield*, which is taking the place of the *Lee-Metford* issued a few years ago. These are small-bore rifles of .303 inch calibre, having a detachable box, which is loaded with ten cartridges (Lee-Metford eight) passed up in turn by a spring into the breech, whence, when the bolt is closed, they are pushed into the firing-chamber. The empty case is ejected by pulling back the bolt, and at the same time another cartridge is pressed up from the magazine and the whole process repeated. When the cut-off is used the rifle may be loaded and fired singly, be the magazine full or empty.

The Lee-Enfield has five grooves (Lee-Metford ten), making one complete turn from right to left in every ten inches. It weighs 9 lb. 4 oz., and the barrel is 30.197 inches long. The range averages 3500 yards.

We are now falling into line with other powers by adopting the "clip" form instead of the box for loading. The sealed pattern of the new service weapon is thus provided, and has also been made somewhat lighter and shorter while preserving the same velocity.

We are promised an even more rapid firing rifle than any of these, one in which the recoil is used to work the breech and lock so that it is a veritable automatic gun. Indeed, several continental nations have made trial of such weapons and reported favourably upon them. One lately tried in Italy works by means of gas generated by the explosion passing through a small hole to move a piston-rod. It is claimed that the magazine can hold as many as fifty cartridges and fire up to thirty rounds a minute; but the barrel became so hot after doing this that the trial had to be stopped.

The principal result of automatic action would probably be excessive waste of cartridges by wild firing in the excitement of an engagement. It is to-day as true as formerly that it takes on the average a man's weight of lead to kill him in battle.

To our neighbours across the Channel the credit also belongs of introducing *smokeless powder*, now universally used; that of the Lee-Metford being "cordite." To prevent the bullets flattening on impact they are coated with a hard metal such as nickel and its alloys. If the nose is soft, or split beforehand, a terribly enlarged and lacerated wound is produced; so the Geneva Convention humanely prohibited the use of such missiles in warfare.

Before quitting this part of our subject it is as well to add a few words about *pistols*.

These have passed through much the same process of evolution as the rifle, and have now culminated in the many-shotted *revolver*.

During the period 1480–1500 the match-lock revolver is said to have been brought into use; and one attributed to this date may be seen in the Tower of London.

Two hundred years ago, Richards, a London gunsmith, converted the ancient wheel-lock into the flint-lock; he also rifled his barrel and loaded it at the breech. The Richards weapon was double-barrelled, and unscrewed for loading at the point where the powder-chamber ended; the ball was placed in this chamber in close contact with the powder, and the barrel rescrewed. The bullet being a soft leaden ball, was forced, when the charge was fired, through the rifled barrel with great accuracy of aim.

The percussion cap did not oust the flint-lock till less than a century ago, when many single-barrelled pistols, such as the famous Derringer, were produced; these in their turn were replaced by the revolver which *Colt* introduced in 1836–1850. Smith and Wesson in the early sixties improved upon it by a device for extracting the empty cartridges automatically. Livermore and Russell of the United States invented the "clip," containing several cartridges; but the equally well-known *Winchester* has its cartridges arranged in a tube below the barrel, whence a helical spring feeds them to the breech as fast as they are needed.

At the present time each War Department has its own special service weapon. The German *Mauser* magazine-pistol for officer's use fires ten shots in ten seconds, a slight pressure of the trigger setting the full machinery in motion; the pressure of gas at each explosion does all the rest of the work—extracts and ejects the cartridge case, cocks the hammer, and presses springs which reload and close the weapon, all in a fraction of a second. The *Mannlicher* is of the same automatic type, but its barrel moves to the front, leaving space for a fresh cartridge to come up from the magazine below, while in the Mauser the breech moves to the rear during recoil. The range is half a mile. The cartridges are made up in sets of ten in a case, which can be inserted in one movement.

MACHINE-GUNS.

Intermediate between hand-borne weapons and artillery, and partaking of the nature of both, come the machine-guns firing small projectiles with extraordinary rapidity.

Since the United States made trial of Dr. Gatling's miniature battery in the Civil War (1862–1865), invention has been busy evolving more and more perfect types, till the most modern machine-gun is a marvel of ingenuity and effectiveness.

The *Gatling* machine-gun, which has been much improved in late years by the Accles system of "feed," and is not yet completely out of date, consists of a circular series of ten barrels—each with its own lock—mounted on a central shaft and revolved by a suitable gear. The cartridges are successively fed by automatic actions into the barrels, and the hammers are so arranged that the entire operation of loading, closing the breech, firing and withdrawing the empty cartridge-cases (which is known as their "longitudinal reciprocating motion") is carried on while the locks are kept in constant revolution, along with the barrels and breech, by means of a hand-crank. One man places a feed-case filled with cartridges into the hopper, another turns the crank. As the gun is rotated the cartridges drop one by one from the feed-cases into the grooves of the carrier, and its lock loads and fires each in turn. While the gun revolves further the lock, drawing back, extracts and drops the empty case; it is then ready for the next cartridge.

In action five cartridges are always going through some process of loading, while five empty shells are in different stages of ejection. The latest type, fitted with an electro-motor, will fire at the *rate* of one thousand rounds per minute, and eighty rounds have actually been fired within ten seconds! It is not, however, safe to work these machine-guns so fast, as the cartridges are apt to be occasionally pulled through unfired and then explode among the men's legs. The automatic guns, on the contrary, as they only work by the explosion, are free from any risk of such accidents.

The feed-drums contain 104 cartridges, and can be replaced almost instantly. One drumful can be discharged in $5\frac{1}{4}$ seconds. The small-sized Gatling has a drum-feed of 400 cartridges in sixteen sections of twenty-five each passed up without interruption.

The gun is mounted for use so that it can be pointed at any angle, and through a wide lateral range, without moving the carriage.

The Gardner.—The Gatling, as originally made, was for a time superseded by the *Gardner*, which differed from it in having the barrels (four or fewer in number) fixed in the same horizontal plane. This was worked by a rotatory handle on the side of the gun. The cartridges slid down a feed-case in a column to the barrel, where they were fired by a spring acting on a hammer.

The Nordenfelt.—Mr. Nordenfelt's machine-gun follows this precedent; its barrels—10, 5, 4, 2, or 1 in number—also being arranged horizontally in a strong, rigid frame. Each barrel has its own breech-plug, striker, spring, and extractor, and each fires independently of the rest, so that all are not out of action together. The gun has a swivelled mount easily elevated and trained, and the steel frames take up the force of the discharge. In rapid firing one gunner can work the firing-handle while another lays and alters the direction. The firing is operated by a lever working backwards and forwards by hand, and the gun can be discharged at the rate of 600 rounds per minute.

The Hotchkiss.—The Hotchkiss gun, or revolving cannon, is on a fresh system, that of intermittent rotation of the barrels without any rotation of breech or mechanism. There is only one loading piston, one spring striker, and one extractor for all the barrels. The shock of discharge is received against a massive fixed breech, which distributes it to the whole body.

Like the *Nordenfelt*, however, it can be dismounted and put together again without the need of tools. The above pattern throws 1 lb. projectiles.

The Maxim.—Differing from all these comes the *Maxim* gun, so much in evidence now with both land and sea service. It is made up of two portions :—

(1) *Fixed:* a barrel-casing, which is also a water-jacket, and breech-casing.

(2) *Recoiling:* a barrel and two side plates which carry lock and crank.

This recoiling portion works inside the fixed.

The gun is supplied with ammunition by a belt holding 250 cartridges passing through a feed-block on the top. Its mechanism is worked *automatically;* first by the explosion of the charge, which causes the barrel to recoil backwards and extends a strong spring which, on reasserting itself, carries it forwards again. The recoiling part moves back about an inch, and this recoil is utilised by bringing into play mechanism which extracts the empty cartridge-case, and on the spring carrying the barrel forward again moves a fresh one into position. Under the barrel casing is the ejector tube through which the empty cartridge-cases are ejected from the gun.

The rate of fire of the Maxim gun is 600 rounds per minute. Deliberate fire means about 70 rounds per minute; rapid fire will explode 450 rounds in the same time. As the barrel becomes very hot in use the barrel-casing contains seven pints of water to keep it cool. About 2000 rounds can be fired at short intervals; but in continuous firing the water boils after some 600 rounds, and needs replenishing after about 1000. A valved tube allows steam, but not water to escape.

The operator works this gun by pressing a firing-lever or button. After starting the machine he merely sits behind the shield, which protects him from the enemy, directing it, as it keeps on firing automatically so long as the bands of cartridges are supplied and a finger held on the trigger or button. By setting free a couple of levers with his left hand, and pressing his shoulder against the padded shoulder-piece, he is able to elevate or depress, or train the barrel horizontally, without in any way interfering with the hail of missiles.

We use two sizes, one with .45 bore for the Navy, which takes an all-lead bullet weighing 480 grains, and the other with .303 bore, the ordinary nickel-coated rifle bullet for the Army. But as the Maxim gun can be adapted to every rifle-calibre ammunition it is patronised by all governments.

The gun itself weighs 56 lbs., and is mounted for use in various ways: on a tripod, a field stand, or a field carriage with wheels. This carriage has sixteen boxes of ammunition, each containing a belt of 250 cartridges, making 4000 rounds altogether. Its total weight is about half a ton, so that it can be drawn by one horse, and it is built for the roughest cross-country work. A little machine, which can be fixed to the wheel, recharges the belts with cartridges by the working of a handle.

For ships the Maxim is usually mounted on the ordinary naval cone mount, or it can be clamped to the bulwark of the deck or the military "top" on the mast.

But there is a most ingenious form of parapet mounting, known as the garrison mount, which turns the Maxim into a "disappearing gun," and can be used equally well for fortress walls or improvised entrenchments. The gun is placed over two little wheels on which it can be run along by means of a handle pushed behind in something the fashion of a lawn-mower. Arrived at its destination, the handle, which is really a rack, is turned downwards, and on twisting one of the wheels the gun climbs it by means of a pinion-cog till it points over the wall, to which hooks at the end of two projecting bars firmly fix it, the broadened end of the handle being held by its weight to the ground. It is locked while in use, but a few turns of the wheel cause it to sink out of sight in as many seconds.

The rifle-calibre guns may also be used as very light horse artillery to accompany cavalry by being mounted on a "galloping carriage" drawn by a couple of horses, and with two seats for the operators. The carriage conveys 3000 rounds, and the steel-plated seats turn up and form shields during action.

It is interesting to notice that an extra light form of the gun is made which may be carried strapped on an infantryman's back and fired from a tripod. Two of these mounted on a double tricycle can be propelled at a good pace along a fairly level road, and the riders dismounting have, in a few moments, a valuable little battery at their disposal.

The *Pom-pom*, of which we have heard so much in the late war, is a large edition of the Maxim automatic system with some differences in the system. Its calibre is 1½ inches. Instead of bullets it emits explosive shells 1 lb. in weight, fitted with percussion fuses which burst them into about twelve or fourteen pieces. The effective range is up to 2000 yards, and it will carry to 4000 yards. An improved *Pom-pom* recently brought out hurls a 1¼ lb. shell with effect at a mark 3000 yards away, and as far as 6000 yards before its energy is entirely exhausted. The muzzle velocity of this weapon is 2350 feet a second as against the 1800 feet of the older pattern. They both fire 300 rounds a minute.

The *Colt* automatic gun is an American invention whose automatic action is due to explosion of the charge, not to recoil. The force by which the motions of firing, extracting, and loading are performed is derived from the powder-gases, a portion of which—passing through a small vent in the muzzle—acts by means of a lever on the mechanism of the gun.

This is also in two parts: (*a*) *barrel*, attached to (*b*) breech-casing, in which gear for charging, firing, and ejecting is contained. The barrel, made of a strong alloy of nickel, has its cartridges fed in by means of belts coiled in boxes attached to the breech-casing, the boxes moving with the latter so that the movements of the gun do not affect it. These boxes contain 250 cartridges each and are easily replaced.

The feed-belt is inserted, and the lever thrown down and moved backward—once by hand—as far as it will go; this opens the breech and passes the first cartridge from the belt to the carrier. The lever is then released and the spring causes it to fly forward, close the vent, and transfer the cartridge from the carrier to the barrel, also compressing the mainspring and opening and closing the breech.

On pulling the trigger the shot is fired, and after the bullet has passed the little vent, but is not yet out of the muzzle, the force of the expanding gas, acting through the vent on the piston, sets a gas-lever in operation which acts on the breech mechanism, opens breech, ejects cartridge-case, and feeds another cartridge into the carrier. The gas-lever returning forces the cartridge home in the barrel and closes and locks the breech.

The hammer of the gun acts as the piston of an air-pump, forcing a strong jet of air into the chamber, and through the barrel, thus removing all unburnt powder, and thoroughly cleansing it. The metal employed is strong enough to resist the heaviest charge of nitro-powder, and the accuracy of its aim is not disturbed by the vibrations of rapid fire. It does not heat fast, so has no need of a water-jacket, any surplus heat being removed by a system of radiation.

The bore is made of any rifle calibre for any small-arm ammunition, and is fitted with a safety-lock. For our own pieces we use the Lee-Metford cartridges. Four hundred shots per minute can be fired.

The gun consists altogether of ninety-four pieces, but the working-pieces, *i.e.* those only which need be separated for cleaning, &c., when in the hands of the artilleryman, are less than twenty. It can be handled in action by one man, the operation resembling that of firing a pistol.

The machine weighs 40 lbs., and for use by cavalry or infantry can be mounted on the *Dundonald Galloping Carriage.* The ammunition-box, containing 2000 rounds ready for use, carries the gun on its upper side, and is mounted on a strong steel axle. A pole with a slotted end is inserted into a revolving funnel on the bend of the shaft, the limbering-up being completed by an automatic bolt and plug.

The gun-carriage itself is of steel, with hickory wheels and hickory and steel shafts, detachable at will. The simple harness suits any saddled cavalry horse, and the shafts work in sockets behind the rider's legs. Its whole weight with full load of ammunition is under four hundredweight.

HEAVY ORDNANCE.

As with rifles and the smaller forms of artillery, so also with heavy ordnance, the changes and improvements within the last fifty years have been greater than those made during the course of all the previous centuries.

These changes have affected alike not only the materials from which a weapon is manufactured, the relative size of calibre and length of bore, the fashion of mounting and firing, but also the form and weight of the projectile, the velocity with which it is thrown, and even the substances used in expelling it from the gun.

Compare for a moment the old cast-iron muzzle-loaders, stubby of stature, which Wellington's bronzed veterans served with round cannon balls, well packed in greasy clouts to make them fit tight, or with shell and grape shot, throughout the hard-fought day of Waterloo, from a distance which the chroniclers measure by *paces*, so near stood the opposing ranks to one another.

Or stand in imagination upon one of Nelson's

stately men-o'-war and watch the grimy guns' crews, eight or ten to each, straining on the ropes. See the still smoking piece hauled inboard, its bore swabbed out to clean and cool it, then recharged by the muzzle; home go powder, wad, and the castor full of balls or the chain shot to splinter the enemy's masts, rammed well down ere the gun is again run out through the port-hole. Now the gunner snatches the flaming lintstock and, signal given, applies it to the powder grains sprinkled in the touch-hole. A salvo of fifty starboard guns goes off in one terrific broadside, crashing across the Frenchman's decks at such close quarters that in two or three places they are set on fire by the burning wads. Next comes a cry of "Boarders!' and the ships are grappled as the boarding-party scrambles over the bulwarks to the enemy's deck, a brisk musket-fire from the crowded rigging protecting their advance; meanwhile the larboard guns, with their simultaneous discharge, are greeting a new adversary.

Such was war a century ago. Compare with it the late South African Campaign where the range of guns was estimated in *miles*, and after a combat lasting from morn to eve, the British general could report: "I do not think we have seen a gun or a Boer all day."

The days of hand-to-hand fighting have passed, the mêlée in the ranks may be seen no more; in a few years the bayonet may be relegated to the limbo of the coat-of-mail or the cast-iron culverin. Yet the modern battle-scene bristles with the most death-dealing weapons which the ingenuity of man has ever constructed. The hand-drawn machine-gun discharges in a couple of minutes as many missiles as a regiment of Wellington's infantry, with a speed and precision undreamt of by him. The quick-firing long-range naval guns now in vogue could annihilate a fleet or destroy a port without approaching close enough to catch a glimpse of the personnel of their opponents. The deadly torpedo guards our waterways more effectually than a squadron of ships.

All resources of civilisation have been drawn upon, every triumph of engineering secured, to forge such weapons as shall strike the hardest and destroy the most pitilessly. But strange and unexpected the result! Where we counted our battle-slain by thousands we now mourn over the death of hundreds; where whole regiments were mown down our ambulances gather wounded in scattered units. Here is the bright side of modern war.

The muzzle-loading gun has had its day, a very long day and a successful one. Again and again it has reasserted itself and ousted its rivals, but at last all difficulties of construction have been surmounted and the breech-loader has "come to stay."

However, our services still contain a large number of muzzle-loading guns, many of them built at quite a recent period, and adapted as far as possible to modern requirements. So to these we will first turn our attention.

The earliest guns were made of cast-iron, but this being prone to burst with a large charge, bronze, brass, and other tougher materials were for a long time employed. Most elaborately chased and ornamented specimens of these old weapons are to be seen in the Tower, and many other collections.

In the utilitarian days of the past century cheapness and speed in manufacture were more sought after than show. Iron was worked in many new ways to resist the pressure of explosion.

Armstrong of Elswick conceived the idea of building up a barrel of *coiled* iron by joining a series of short welded cylinders together, and closing them by a solid forged breech-piece. Over all, again, wrought-iron coils were shrunk. Subsequently he tried a solid forged-iron barrel bored out to form a tube. Neither make proving very satisfactory, steel tubes were next used, but were too expensive and uncertain at that stage of manufacture. Again coiled iron was called into requisition, and Mr. Frazer of the Royal Gun Factory introduced a system of double and triple coils which was found very successful, especially when a thin steel inner tube was substituted for the iron one (1869).

All these weapons were rifled, so that there was of necessity a corresponding difference in the projectile employed. Conical shells being used, studs were now placed on the body of the shell to fit into the rifling grooves, which were made few in number and deeply cut. This was apt to weaken the bore of the gun; but on the other hand many studs to fit into several shallow grooves weakened the cover of the shells.

Various modifications were tried, and finally a gas-check which expands into the grooves was placed at the base of the shell.

The muzzle-loader having thus been turned into a very efficient modern weapon the next problem to be solved was how to throw a projectile with sufficient force to penetrate the iron and steel armour-plates then being generally applied to war-ships. "Build larger guns" was the conclusion arrived at, and presently the arsenals of the Powers were turning out mammoth weapons up to 100 tons, and even 110 tons in weight with a calibre of 16 inches and more for their huge shells. Then was the mighty 35-ton "Woolwich Infant" born (1872), and its younger but still bigger brothers, 81 tons, 16-inch bore, followed by the Elswick 100-ton giants, some of which were mounted on our defences in the Mediterranean. But the fearful concussion of such enormous guns when fixed in action on board ship injured the superstruction, and even destroyed the boats, and the great improvements made in steel both for guns and armour soon led to a fresh revolution. Henceforward instead of mounting a few very heavy guns we have preferred to trust to the weight of metal projected by an increased number of smaller size, but much higher velocity. And these guns are the quick-firing breech-loaders.

The heaviest of our up-to-date ordnance is of moderate calibre, the largest breech-loaders being 12-inch, 10-inch, and 9.2-inch guns. But the elaborateness of its manufacture is such that one big gun takes nearly as long to "build up" as the ship for which it is destined. Each weapon has to pass through about sixteen different processes :—

(1) The solid (or hollow) ingot is *forged.*

(2) *Annealed,* to get rid of strains.

(3) It is placed horizontally on a lathe and *rough-turned.*

(4) *Rough-bored* in a lathe.

(5) *Hardened.* Heated to a high temperature and plunged, while hot, into a bath of rape oil kept cold by a water-bath. It cools slowly for seven to eight hours, being moved about at intervals by a crane. This makes the steel more elastic and tenacious.

(6) *Annealed, i.e.* reheated to 900° Fahr. and slowly cooled. Siemens' pyrometer is used in these operations.

(7) *Tested* by pieces cut off.

(8) *Turned* and *bored* for the second time.

(9) Carefully turned again for *shrinkage.* Outer coil expanded till large enough to fit easily over inner. Inside, set up vertically in a pit, has outside lowered on to it, water and gas being applied to make all shrink evenly. Other projections, hoops, rings, &c., also shrunk on.

(10) Finish—*bored* and *chambered.*

(11) *Broached,* or very fine bored, perhaps *lapped* with lead and emery.

(12) *Rifled* horizontally in a machine.

(13) Prepared for breech fittings.

(14) Taken to the Proof Butts for trial.

(15) Drilled for sockets, sights, &c. Lined and engraved. Breech fittings, locks, electric firing gear, &c., added. Small adjustments made by filing.

(16) *Browned* or *painted.*

When worn the bore can be lined with a new steel tube.

These lengthy operations completed, our gun has still to be *mounted* upon its field-carriage, naval cone, or disappearing mounting, any of which are complicated and delicately-adjusted pieces of mechanism, the product of much time and labour, which we have no space here to describe.

Some account of the principal parts of these guns has already been given, but the method by which the breech is closed remains to be dealt with.

It will be noticed that though guns now barely reach half the weight of the monster muzzle-loaders, they are even more effective. Thus the 46-ton (12-inch) gun hurls an 850-lb. projectile with a velocity of 2750 foot-seconds, and uses a comparatively small charge. The famous "81-ton" needed a very big charge for its 1700-lb. shell, and had little more than half the velocity and no such power of penetration. This change has been brought about by using a slower-burning explosive very powerful in its effects; enlarging the chamber to give it sufficient air space, and lengthening the chase of the gun so that every particle of the powder-gas may be brought into action before the shot leaves the muzzle. This system and the substitution of steel for the many layers of welded iron, makes our modern guns long and slim in comparison with the older ones.

To resist the pressure of the explosion against the breech end, a tightly-fitting breech-plug must be employed. The most modern and ingenious is the Welin plug, invented by a Swedish engineer. The ordinary interrupted screw breech-plug has three parts of its circumference plane and the other three parts "threaded," or grooved, to screw into corresponding grooves in the breech; thus only half of the circumference is engaged by the screw. Mr. Welin has cut steps on the plug, three of which would be threaded to one plane segment, each locking with its counterpart in the breech. In this case there are three segments engaged to each one left plane, and the strength of the screw is almost irresistible. The plug, which is hinged at the side, has therefore been shortened by one-third, and is light enough to swing clear with one touch of the handwheel that first rotates and unlocks it.

The method of firing is this: The projectile lifted (by hydraulic power on a ship) into the loading tray is swung to the mouth of the breech and pushed into the bore. A driving-band attached near its base is so notched at the edges that it jams the shell closely and prevents it slipping back if loaded at a high angle of elevation. The powder charge being placed in the chamber the breech-plug is now swung-to and turned till it locks close. The vent-axial or inner part of this breech-plug (next to the charge), which is called from its shape the "mushroom-head," encloses between its head and the screw-plug the de Bange obturator, a flat canvas pad of many layers soaked with mutton fat tightly packed between discs of tin. When the charge explodes, the mushroom-head—forced back upon the pad—compresses it till its edges bulge against the tube and prevent any escape of gas breechwards.

The electric spark which fires the charge is passed in from outside by means of a minute and ingenious apparatus fitted into a little vent or tube in the mushroom-head. As the electric circuit cannot be completed till the breech-plug is screwed quite home there is now no more fear of a premature explosion than of double loading. If the electric gear is disordered the gun can be fired equally well and safely by a percussion tube.

This description is of a typical large gun, and may be applied to all calibres and also to the larger quick-firers. The mechanism as the breech is swung open again withdraws the empty cartridge. So valuable has de Bange's obturator proved, however, that guns up to the 6-inch calibre now have the powder charge thrown into the chamber in bags, thus saving the weight of the metal tubes hitherto necessary.

Of course several types of breech-loading guns are used in the Service, but the above are the most modern.

The favourite mode of construction at the present time is the wire-wound barrel, the building up of which is completed by covering the many layers of wire with an outer tube or jacket expanded by heat before it is slipped on in order that it may fit closely when cold. A previous make, without wire, is strengthened by rings or hoops also shrunk on hot.

The quick-firers proper are of many sizes, 8-inch, 7.5-inch, 6-inch, 4.7-inch, 4-inch, and 3-inch (12-pounders). The naval type is as a rule longer and lighter than those made for the rough usage of field campaigning and have a much greater range. There are also smaller quick-firers, 3-pounders and 6-pounders with bore something over 1-inch and 2-inch (Nordenfelt, Hotchkiss, Vickers-Maxim). Some of the high velocity 12-pounders being employed as garrison guns along with 6-inch and 4.7-inch, and the large calibre howitzers.

We still use howitzer batteries of 5-inch bore in the field and in the siege-train, all being short, rifled, breech-loading weapons, as they throw a heavy shell with smallish charges at a high angle of elevation, but cover a relatively short distance. A new pattern of 8-inch calibre is now under consideration.

It is interesting to contrast the potencies of some of these guns, all of which use cordite charges.

Calibre.	Charge.	Weight of Shot.	Muzzle Velocity in Foot Seconds.	Number of Rounds per Minute.
12 inch	207 lbs.	850 lbs.	2750	1
8 "	52 "	210 "	2750	5
6 "	25 "	100 "	2775	8
4.7 "	9 "	45 "	2600	12
3 "	2 lbs. 9 oz.	12.5 "	2600	20

The Simms armour-clad motor-car for coast defence. Maxim guns and Pom-pom in action.

[To face p. 114.

Heavy Ordnance

In the armament of our fine Navy guns are roughly distributed as follows :—81-ton, 13½-inch, and superseded patterns of machine-guns such as Gatling's Gardner's, and Nordenfelt's, besides a few surviving muzzle-loaders, &c., are carried only by the oldest battleships.

The first-class battleships are chiefly supplied with four 12-inch guns in barbettes, twelve 6-inch as secondary batteries, and a number of smaller quick-firers on the upper decks and in the fighting tops, also for use in the boats, to which are added several Maxims.

The first-class cruisers have 9.2 as their largest calibre, with a lessened proportion of 6-inch, &c. Some of the newest bear only 7½ or 6-inch guns as their heaviest ordnance ; like the second-class cruisers which, however, add several 4.7's between these and their small quick-firers.

Vessels of inferior size usually carry nothing more powerful than the 4.7.

All are now armed with torpedo tubes.

These same useful little quick-firers and machine-guns have been the lethal weapons which made the armoured trains so formidable. Indeed, there seems no limit to their value both for offence and defence, for the battle chariot of the ancient Briton has its modern successor in the Simms' motor war car lately exhibited at the Crystal Palace. This armour-plated movable fort is intended primarily for coast defence, but can work off beaten tracks over almost any sort of country. It is propelled at the rate of nine miles an hour by a 16-horse-power motor, carrying all its own fuel, two pom-poms, two small Maxims, and 10,000 rounds of ammunition, besides the necessary complement of men and searchlights for night use, &c., &c.

The searchlight, by the way, has taken the place of all former inventions thrown from guns, such as ground-light balls, or parachute lights with a time-fuse which burst in the air and remained suspended, betraying the enemy's proceedings.

In like manner the linked chain and "double-headed" shot, the "canister"—iron balls packed in thin iron or tin cylinders which would travel about 350 yards—the "carcasses" filled with inflammable composition for firing ships and villages, are as much out of date as the solid round shot or cannon-ball. Young Shrapnell's invention a century ago of the form of shell that bears his name, a number of balls arranged in a case containing also a small bursting-charge fired either by percussion or by a time-fuse, has practically replaced them all. Thrown with great precision of aim its effective range is now up to 5000 yards. A 15-pounder shrapnell shell, for instance, contains 192 bullets, and covers several hundred yards with the scattered missiles flying with extreme velocity.

Common shell, from 2½ to 3 calibres long, contains an explosive only. Another variety is segment shell, made of pieces built up in a ring with a bursting charge in the centre which presently shatters it.

The Palliser shell has a marvellous penetrating power when used against iron plates. But, *mirabile dictu!* experiments tried within the past few months prove that a soft cap added externally enables a projectile to pierce with ease armour which had previously defied every attack.

EXPLOSIVES.

Half a century ago gunpowder was still the one driving power which started the projectile on its flight. It is composed of some 75 parts of saltpetre or nitrate of potash, 15 parts of carefully prepared charcoal, and 10 parts of sulphur. This composition imprisons a large amount of oxygen for combustion and is found to act most successfully when formed into rather large prismatic grains.

On the abolition of the old flint-lock its place was taken by a detonating substance enclosed in a copper cap, and some time later inventors came forward with new and more powerful explosives to supersede the use of gunpowder.

By treating cotton with nitric and sulphuric acid reaction *gun-cotton* was produced; and a year later glycerine treated in the same manner became known to commerce as *nitro-glycerine.* This liquid form being inconvenient to handle, some inert granular substance such as infusorial earth was used to absorb the nitro-glycerine, and *dynamite* was the result.

The explosion of gun-cotton was found to be too

sudden and rapid for rifles or cannon; it was liable to burst the piece instead of blowing out the charge. In order to lessen the rapidity of its ignition ordinary cotton was mixed with it, or its threads were twisted round some inert substance.

When repeating-rifles and machine-guns came into general use a smokeless powder became necessary. Such powders as a rule contain nitro-cellulose (gun-cotton) or nitro-glycerine, or both. These are combined into a plastic, gluey composition, which is then made up into sticks or pellets of various shapes, and usually of large size to lessen the extreme rapidity of their combustion. Substances such as tan, paraffin, starch, bran, peat, &c., &c., and many mineral salts, are used in forming low explosives from high ones.

To secure complete combustion some of the larger pellets are made with a central hole, or even pierced by many holes, so that the fire penetrates the entire mass and carries off all its explosive qualities.

Our *cordite* consists of nitro-glycerine dissolving di-nitro cellulose by the acid of a volatile solvent and a mineral jelly or oil. This compound is semi-fluid, and being passed like macaroni through round holes in a metal plate it forms strings or cords of varying size according to the diameter of the holes. Hence the name, cordite.

Many experiments in search of more powerful explosives resulted in an almost universal adoption of picric acid as the base. This acid is itself produced by the action of nitric acid upon carbolic acid, and each nation has its own fashion of preparing it for artillery.

The French began with *mélinite* in 1885, this being a mixture of picric acid and gun-cotton.

The composition of *lyddite* (named from its place of manufacture, Lydd, in Kent) is a jealously-guarded British secret. This substance was first used in 5-inch howitzers during the late Soudan campaign, playing a part in the bombardment of Omdurman. The effect of the 50-lb. lyddite shells upon the South African kopjes is described as astounding. When the yellow cloud had cleared away trees were seen uprooted, rocks pulverised, the very face of the earth had changed.

Several attempts have been made to utilise dynamite for shells, some of the guns employing compressed air as their motive power. The United States some years ago went to great expense in setting up for this purpose heavy pneumatic plant, which has recently been disposed of as too cumbrous. Dudley's "Aërial Torpedo" gun discharged a 13-lb. shell containing explosive gelatine, gun-cotton, and fulminate of mercury by igniting the small cordite charge in a parallel tube, through a vent in which the partially cooled gases acted on the projectile in the barrel. This was rotated in the air by inclined blades on a tailpiece, as the barrel could not be rifled for fear of the heat set up by friction. Some guns actuated on much the same principle are said to have been used with effect in the Hispano-American war. Mr. Hudson Maxim with his explosive "maximite" claims to throw half a ton of dynamite about a mile, and a one-ton shell to half that distance.

But even these inventors are outstripped by Professor Birkeland, who undertakes to hurl a projectile weighing two tons from an iron tube coiled with copper wire down which an electric current is passed; thus doing away entirely with the need of a firing-charge.

In the Gun Factory.

Let us pay a visit to one of our gun factories and get some idea of the multiform activities necessary to the turning out complete of a single piece of ordnance or a complicated machine-gun. We enter the enormous workshop, glazed as to roof and sides, full of the varied buzz and whirr and clank of the machinery. Up and down the long bays stand row upon row of lathes, turning, milling, polishing, boring, rifling—all moving automatically, and with a precision which leaves nothing to be desired. The silent attendants seem to have nothing in their own hands, they simply watch that the cutting does not go too far, and with a touch of the guiding handles regulate the pace or occasionally insert a fresh tool. The bits used in these processes are self-cleaning, so the machinery is never clogged; and on the ground lie little heaps of brass chips cut away by the minute milling tools; or in other places it is bestrewn with shavings of brass and steel which great chisels peel off as easily as a carpenter shaves a deal board.

Here an enormous steel ingot, forged solid, heated again and again in a huge furnace and beaten by steam-hammers, or pressed by hydraulic power between each heating till it is brought to the desired size and shape, is having its centre bored through by a special drill which takes out a solid core. This operation is termed "trepanning," and is applied to guns not exceeding eight inches; those of larger calibre being rough-bored on a lathe, and mandrils placed in them during the subsequent forgings. The tremendous heat generated during the boring processes —we may recall how Benjamin Thompson made water boil by the experimental boring of a cannon— is kept down by streams of soapy water continually pumped through and over the metal. We notice this flow of lubricating fluid in all directions, from oil dropping slowly on to the small brass-milling machines to this fountain-play of water which makes a pleasant undertone amidst the jangle of the machines. But these machines are less noisy than we anticipated; in their actual working they emit scarcely the slightest sound. What strikes us more than the supreme exactness with which each does its portion of the work, is the great deliberateness of its proceeding. All the hurry and bustle is above us, caused by the driving-bands from the engine, which keeps the whole machinery of the shed in motion. Suddenly, with harsh creakings, a great overhead crane comes jarring along the bay, drops a chain, grips up a gun-barrel, and, handling this mass of many tons' weight as easily as we should lift a walking-stick, swings it off to undergo another process of manufacture.

We pass on to the next lathe where a still larger forging is being turned externally, supported on specially devised running gear, many different cutters acting upon it at the same time, so that it is gradually assuming the tapering, banded appearance familiar to us in the completed state.

We turn, fairly bewildered, from one stage of manufacture to another. Here is a gun whose bore is being "chambered" to the size necessary for containing the firing charge. Further along we examine a more finished weapon in process of preparation to receive the breech-plug and other fittings. Still another we notice which has been "fine-bored" to a beautifully smooth surface but is being improved yet more by "lapping" with lead and emery powder.

In the next shed a marvellous machine is rifling the interior of a barrel with a dexterity absolutely uncanny, for the tool which does the rifling has to be rotated in order to give the proper "twist" at the same moment as it is advancing lengthwise down the bore. The grooves are not made simultaneously but as a rule one at a time, the distance between them being kept by measurements on a prepared disc.

Now we have reached the apparatus for the wire-wound guns, a principle representing the *ne plus ultra* of strength and durability hitherto evolved.

The rough-bored gun is placed upon a lathe which revolves slowly, drawing on to it from a reel mounted at one side a continuous layer of steel ribbon about a quarter of an inch wide. On a 12-inch gun there is wound some 117 miles of this wire! fourteen layers of it at the muzzle end and seventy-five at the breech end. Heavy weights regulate the tension of the wire, which varies for each layer, the outermost being at the lowest tension, which will resist a pressure of over 100 tons to the square inch.

We next enter the division in which the gun cradles and mounts are prepared, where we see some of the heaviest work carried out by electric dynamos, the workman sitting on a raised platform to keep careful watch over his business.

Passing through this with interested but cursory inspection of the cone mountings for quick-firing naval guns, some ingenious elevating and training gear and a field carriage whose hydraulic buffers merit closer examination, we come to the shell department where all kinds of projectiles are manufactured. Shrapnel in its various forms, armour-piercing shells, forged steel or cast-iron, and small brass cartridges for the machine-guns may be found here; and the beautifully delicate workmanship of the fuse arrangements attracts our admiration. But we may not linger; the plant for the machine-guns themselves claim our attention.

Owing to the complexity and minute mechanism of these weapons almost a hundred different machines are needed, some of the milling machines taking a large selection of cutters upon one spindle. Indeed, in many parts of the works one notices the men changing their tools for others of different size or application. Some of the boring machines work two barrels at the same time, others can drill three barrels or polish a couple simultaneously. But there are hundreds of minute operations which need to be done separately, down to the boring of screw holes and cutting the groove on a screw-head. Many labourers are employed upon the lock alone. And every portion is gauged correctly to the most infinitesimal fraction, being turned out by the thousand, that every separate item may be interchangeable among weapons of the same make.

Look at the barrel which came grey and dull from its first turning now as it is dealt with changing into bright silver. Here it is adjusted upon the hydraulic rifling machine which will prepare it to carry the small-arm bullet (.303 inch). That one of larger calibre is rifled to fire a small shell. Further on, the barrels and their jackets are being fitted together and the different parts assembled and screwed up. We have not time to follow the perfect implement to its mounting, nor to do more than glance at those howitzers and the breech mechanism of the 6-inch quick-firers near which our guide indicates piles of flat cases to keep the de Bange obturators from warping while out of use. For the afternoon is waning and the foundry still unvisited.

In the Gun Factory

To reach it we pass through the smith's shop and pause awhile to watch a supply of spanners being roughly stamped by an immense machine out of metal plates and having their edges tidied off before they can be further perfected. A steam-hammer is busily engaged in driving mandrils of increasing size through the centre of a red-hot forging. The heat from the forges is tremendous, and though it is tempered by a spray of falling water we are glad to escape into the next shed.

Here we find skilled workmen carefully preparing moulds by taking in sand the exact impression of a wooden dummy. Fortunately we arrive just as a series of casts deeply sunk in the ground are about to be made. Two brawny labourers bear forward an enormous iron crucible, red-hot from the furnace, filled with seething liquid—manganese bronze, we are told—which, when an iron bar is dipped into it, throws up tongues of beautiful greenish-golden flame. The smith stirs and clears off the scum as coolly as a cook skims her broth! Now it is ready, the crucible is again lifted and its contents poured into a large funnel from which it flows into the moulds beneath and fills them to the level of the floor. At each one a helper armed with an iron bar takes his stand and stirs again to work up all dross and air-bubbles to the surface before the metal sets—a scene worthy of a painter's brush.

And so we leave them.

DIRIGIBLE TORPEDOES.

THE history of warlike inventions is the history of a continual see-saw between the discovery of a new means of defence and the discovery of a fresh means of attack. At one time a shield is devised to repel a javelin; at another a machine to hurl the javelin with increased violence against the shield; then the shield is reinforced by complete coats of mail, and so on. The ball of invention has rolled steadily on into our own times, gathering size as it rolls, and bringing more and more startling revolutions in the art of war. To-day it is a battle between the forces of nature, controllable by man in the shape of "high explosives," and the resisting power of metals tempered to extreme toughness.

At present it looks as if, on the sea at least, the attack were stronger than the defence. Our warships may be cased in the hardest metal several inches thick until they become floating forts, almost impregnable to the heaviest shells. They may be provided with terrible engines able to give blow for blow, and be manned with the stoutest hearts in the world. And yet, were a sea-fight in progress, a blow, crushing and resistless, might at any time come upon the vessel from a quarter whence, even though suspected, its coming might escape notice—below the waterline. Were it possible to case an ironclad from deck to keel in foot-thick plating, the metal would crumple like a biscuit-box under the terrible impact of the torpedo.

This destructive weapon is an object of awe not so much from what it has done as from what it can do. The instances of a torpedo shivering a vessel in actual warfare are but few. Yet its moral effect must be immense. Even though it may miss its mark, the very fact of its possible presence will, especially at night-time, tend to keep the commanding minds of a fleet very much on the stretch, and to destroy their efficiency. A torpedo knows no half measures. It is either entirely successful or utterly useless. Its construction entails great expense, but inasmuch as it can, if directed aright, send a million of the enemy's money and a regiment of men to the bottom, the discharge of a torpedo is, after all, but the setting of a sprat to catch a whale.

The aim of inventors has been to endow the dirigible torpedo, fit for use in the open sea, with such qualities that when once launched on its murderous course it can pursue its course in the required direction without external help. The difficulties to be overcome in arriving at a serviceable weapon have been very great owing to the complexity of the problem. A torpedo cannot be fired through water like a cannon shell through air. Water, though yielding, is incompressible, and offers to a moving body a resistance increasing with the speed of that body. Therefore the torpedo must contain its own motive power and its own steering apparatus, and be in effect a miniature submarine vessel complete in itself. To be out of sight and danger it must travel beneath the surface and yet not sink to the bottom; to be effective it must possess great speed, a considerable sphere of action, and be able to counteract any chance currents it may meet on its way.

Among purely automobile torpedoes the Whitehead is easily first. After thirty years it still holds the lead for open sea work. It is a very marvel of ingenious adaptation of means to an end, and as it has fulfilled most successfully the conditions set forth above for an effective projectile it will be interesting to examine in some detail this most valuable weapon.

In 1873 one Captain Lupuis of the Austrian navy experimented with a small fireship which he directed along the surface of the sea by means of ropes and guiding lines. This fireship was to be loaded with explosives which should ignite immediately on coming into collision with the vessel aimed at. The Austrian Government declared his scheme unworkable in its crude form, and the Captain looked about for some one to help him throw what he felt to be a sound idea into a practical shape. He found the man he wanted in Mr. Whitehead, who was at that time manager of an engineering establishment at Fiume. Mr. Whitehead fell in enthusiastically with his proposition, at once discarded the complicated system of guiding ropes, and set to work to solve the problem on his own lines. At the end of two years, during which he worked in secret, aided only by a trusted mechanic and a boy, his son, he constructed the first torpedo of the type that bears his name. It was made of steel, was fourteen inches in diameter, weighed 300 lbs., and carried eighteen pounds of dynamite as explosive charge. But its powers were limited. It could attain a rate of but six knots an hour under favourable conditions, and then for a short distance only. Its conduct was uncertain. Sometimes it would run along the surface, at others make plunges for the bottom. However, the British Government, recognising the importance of Mr. Whitehead's work, encouraged him to perfect his instrument, and paid him a large sum for the patent rights. Pattern succeeded pattern, until comparative perfection was reached.

Described briefly, the Whitehead torpedo is cigar-shaped, blunt-nosed and tapering gradually towards the tail, so following the lines of a fish. Its length is twelve times its diameter, which varies in different patterns from fourteen to nineteen inches. At the fore end is the striker, and at the tail are a couple of three-bladed screws working on one shaft in opposite directions, to economise power and obviate any tendency of the torpedo to travel in a curve; and two sets of rudders, the one horizontal, the other vertical. The latest form of the torpedo has a speed of twenty-nine knots and a range of over a thousand yards.

The torpedo is divided into five compartments by watertight steel bulkheads. At the front is the *explosive head,* containing wet gun-cotton, or some other explosive. The "war head," as it is called, is detachable, and for practice purposes its place is taken by a dummy-head filled with wood to make the balance correct.

Next comes the *air chamber,* filled with highly-compressed air to drive the engines; after it the *balance chamber,* containing the apparatus for keeping the torpedo at its proper depth; then the *engine-room;* and, last of all, the *buoyancy chamber,* which is air-tight and prevents the torpedo from sinking at the end of its run.

To examine the compartments in order:—

In the very front of the torpedo is the pistol and primer-charge for igniting the gun-cotton. Especial care has been taken over this part of the mechanism, to prevent the torpedo being as dangerous to friends as to foes. The pistol consists of a steel plug sliding in a metal tube, at the back end of which is the fulminating charge. Until the plug is driven right in against this charge there can be no explosion. Three precautions are taken against this happening prematurely. In the first place, there is on the forward end of the plug a thread cut, up which a screw-fan travels as soon as it strikes the water. Until the torpedo has run forty-five feet the fan has not reached the end of its travel, and the plug consequently cannot be driven home. Even when the plug is quite free only a heavy blow will drive it in, as a little copper pin has to be sheared through by the impact. And before the screw can unwind at all, a safety-pin must be withdrawn at the moment of firing. So that a torpedo is harmless until it has passed outside the zone of danger to the discharging vessel.

The detonating charge is thirty-eight grains of fulminate of mercury, and the primer-charge consists of six one-ounce discs of dry gun-cotton contained in a copper cylinder, the front end of which is connected with the striker-tube of the pistol. The fulminate, on receiving a blow, expands 2500 times, giving a violent shock to the gun-cotton discs, which in turn explode and impart a shock to the main charge, 200 lbs. of gun-cotton.

The *air chamber* is made of the finest compressed steel, or of phosphor-bronze, a third of an inch thick. When ready for action this chamber has to bear a pressure of 1350 lbs. to the square inch. So severe is the compression that in the largest-sized torpedoes the air in this chamber weighs no less than 63 lbs. The air is forced in by very powerful pumps of a special design. Aft of this chamber is that containing the stop-valve and steering-gear. The stop-valve is a species of air-tap sealing the air chamber until the torpedo is to be discharged. The valve is so arranged that it is impossible to insert the torpedo into the firing-tube before the valve has been opened, and so brought the air chamber into communication with the starting-valve, which does not admit air to the engines till after the projectile has left the tube.

The *steering apparatus* is undoubtedly the most ingenious of the many clever contrivances packed into a Whitehead torpedo. Its function is to keep the torpedo on an even keel at a depth determined before the discharge. This is effected by means of two agencies, a swinging weight, and a valve which is driven in by water pressure as the torpedo sinks. When the torpedo points head downwards the weight swings forward, and by means of connecting levers brings the horizontal rudders up. As the torpedo rises the weight becomes vertical and the rudder horizontal. This device only insures that the torpedo shall travel horizontally. The valve makes it keep its proper depth by working in conjunction with the pendulum. The principle, which is too complicated for full description, is, put briefly, a tendency of the valve to correct the pendulum whenever the latter swings too far. Lest the pendulum should be violently shaken by the discharge there is a special controlling gear which keeps the rudders fixed until the torpedo has proceeded a certain distance, when the steering mechanism is released. The steering-gear does not work directly on the rudder. Mr. Whitehead found in his earlier experiments that the pull exerted by the weight and valve was not sufficient to move the rudders against the pressure of the screws. He therefore introduced a beautiful little auxiliary engine, called the servo-motor, which is to the torpedo what the steam steering-gear is to a ship. The servo-motor, situated in the *engine-room*, is only four inches long, but the power it exerts by means of compressed air is so great that a pressure of half an ounce exerted by the steering-gear produces a pull of 160 lbs. on the rudders.

The engines consist of three single-action cylinders, their cranks working at an angle of 120° to one another, so that there is no "dead" or stopping point in their action. They are very small, but, thanks to the huge pressure in the air chamber, develop nearly thirty-one horse-power. Lest they should "race," or revolve too quickly, while passing from the tube to the water and do themselves serious damage, they are provided with a "delay action valve," which is opened by the impact of the torpedo against the water. Further, lest the air should be admitted to the cylinders at a very high pressure gradually decreasing to zero, a "reducing valve" or governor is added to keep the engines running at a constant speed.

Whitehead torpedoes are fired from tubes above or below the waterline. Deck tubes have the advantage of being more easily aimed, but when loaded they are a source of danger, as any stray bullet or shell from an enemy's ship might explode the torpedo with dire results. There is therefore an increasing preference for submerged tubes. An ingenious device is used for aiming the torpedo, which makes allowances for the speed of the ship from which it is fired, the speed of the ship aimed at, and the speed of the torpedo itself. When the moment for firing arrives, the officer in charge presses an electric button, which sets in motion an electric magnet fixed to the side of the tube. The magnet releases a heavy ball which falls and turns the "firing rod." Compressed air or a powder discharge is brought to bear on the rear end of the torpedo, which, if submerged, darts out from the vessel's side along a guiding bar, from which it is released at both ends simultaneously, thus avoiding the great deflection towards the stern which would occur were a broadside torpedo not held at the nose till the tail is clear. This guiding apparatus enables a torpedo to leave the side of a vessel travelling at high speed almost at right angles to the vessel's path.

It will be easily understood that a Whitehead torpedo is a costly projectile, and that its value—£500 or more—makes the authorities very careful of its welfare. During practice with "blank" torpedoes a "Holmes light" is attached. This light is a canister full of calcium phosphide to which water penetrates through numerous holes, causing gas to be thrown off and rise to the surface, where, on meeting with the oxygen of the air, it bursts into flame and gives off dense volumes of heavy smoke, disclosing the position of the torpedo by night or day.

At Portsmouth are storehouses containing upwards of a thousand torpedoes. Every torpedo is at intervals taken to pieces, examined, tested, and put together again after full particulars have been taken down on paper. Each steel "baby" is kept bright and clean, coated with a thin layer of oil, lest a single spot of rust should mar its beauty. An interesting passage from Lieutenant G. E. Armstrong's book on "Torpedoes and Torpedo Vessels" will illustrate the scrupulous exactness observed in all things relating to the torpedo depôts: "As an example of the care with which the stores are kept it may be mentioned that a particular tiny pattern of brass screw which forms part of the torpedo's mechanism and which is valued at about twopence-halfpenny per gross, is never allowed to be a single number wrong. On one occasion, when the stocktaking took place, it was found that instead of 5000 little screws being accounted for by the man who was told off to count them, there were only 4997. Several foolscap letters were written and exchanged over these three small screws, though their value was not more than a small fraction of a farthing."

The classic instance of the effectiveness of this type of torpedo is the battle of the Yalu, fought between the Japanese and Chinese fleets in 1894. The Japanese had been pounding their adversaries for hours with their big guns without producing decisive results. So they determined upon a torpedo attack, which was delivered early in the morning under cover of darkness, and resulted in the destruction of a cruiser, the *Ting Yuen.* The next night a second incursion of the Japanese destroyers wrecked another cruiser, the *Lai Yuen,* which sunk within five minutes of being struck; sank the *Wei Yuen,* an old wooden vessel used as a training-school; and blew a large steam launch out of the water on to an adjacent wharf. These hits "below the belt" were too much for the Chinese, who soon afterwards surrendered to their more scientific and better equipped foes.

If a general naval war broke out to-day most nations would undoubtedly pin their faith to the Whitehead torpedo for use in the open sea, now that its accuracy has been largely increased by the gyroscope, a heavy flywheel attachment revolving rapidly at right angles to the path of the torpedo, and rendering a change of direction almost impossible.

For harbour defence the Brennan or its American rival, the Sims-Edison, might be employed. They are both torpedoes dirigible from a fixed base by means of connecting wires. The presence of these wires constitutes an obstacle to their being of service in a fleet action.

The Brennan is used by our naval authorities. It is the invention of a Melbourne watchmaker. Being a comparatively poor man, Mr. Brennan applied to the Colonial Government for grants to aid him in the manufacture and development of his torpedo, and he was supplied with sufficient money to perfect it. In 1881 he was requested by our Admiralty to bring his invention to England, where it was experimented upon, and pronounced so efficient for harbour and creek defence that at the advice of the Royal Engineers Mr. Brennan was paid large sums for his patents and services.

The Brennan torpedo derives its motive power from a very powerful engine on shore, capable of developing 100 horse-power, with which it is connected by stout piano wires. One end of these wires is wound on two reels inside the torpedo, each working a screw; the other end is attached to two winding drums driven at high velocity by the engine on shore. As the drums wind in the wire the reels in the torpedo revolve; consequently, the harder the torpedo is pulled back the faster it moves forward, liked a trained trotting mare. The steering of the torpedo is effected by alterations in the relative speeds of the drums, and consequently of the screws. The drums run loose on the engine axle, and are thrown in or out of gear by means of a friction-brake, so that their speed can be regulated without altering the pace of the engines. Any increase in the speed of one drum causes a corresponding decrease in the speed of the other. The torpedo can be steered easily to right or left within an arc of forty degrees on each side of straight ahead; but when once launched it cannot be retrieved except by means of a boat. Its path is marked by a Holmes light, described above. It has a 200-lb. gun-cotton charge, and is fitted with an apparatus for maintaining a proper depth very similar to that used in the Whitehead torpedo.

The Sims-Edison torpedo differs from the Brennan in its greater obedience to orders and in its motive power being electrically transmitted through a single connecting cable. It is over thirty feet in length and two feet in diameter. Attached to the torpedo proper by rods is a large copper float, furnished with balls to show the operator the path of the torpedo. The torpedo itself is in four parts: the explosive head; the magazine of electric cables, which is paid out as the torpedo travels; the motor room; and the compartment containing the steering-gear. The projectile has a high speed and long range—over four thousand yards. It can twist and turn in any direction, and, if need be, be called to heel. Like the Brennan, it has the disadvantage of a long trailing wire, which could easily become entangled; and it might be put out of action by any damage inflicted on its float by the enemy's guns. But it is likely to prove a very effective harbour-guard if brought to the test.

In passing to the Orling-Armstrong torpedo we enter the latest phase of torpedo construction. Seeing the disadvantages arising from wires, electricians have sought a means of controlling torpedoes without any tangible connection. Wireless telegraphy showed that such a means was not beyond the bounds of possibility. Mr. Axel Orling, a Swede, working in concert with Mr. J. T. Armstrong, has lately proved that a torpedo can be steered by waves of energy transmitted along rays of light, or perhaps it would be more correct to say along shafts of a form of X-rays.

Mr. Orling claims for his torpedo that it is capable of a speed of twenty-two knots or more an hour; that it can be called to heel, and steered to right or left at will; that as long as it is in sight it is controllable by rays invisible to the enemy; that not merely one, but a number of torpedoes can be directed by the same beams of light; that, as it is submerged, it would, even if detected, be a bad mark for the enemy's guns.

The torpedo carries a shaft which projects above the water, and bears on its upper end a white disc to receive the rays and transmit them to internal motors to be transmuted into driving power. The rod also carries at night an electric light, shaded on the enemy's side, but rendering the whereabouts of the torpedo very visible to the steerer.

Mr. Orling's torpedo acts throughout in a cruelly calculating manner. Before its attack a ship would derive small advantage from a crinoline of steel netting; for the large torpedo conceals in its head a smaller torpedo, which, as soon as the netting is struck, darts out and blasts an opening through which its longer brother, after a momentary delay, can easily follow. The netting penetrated, the torpedo has yet to strike twice before exploding. On the first impact, a pin, projecting from the nose, is driven in to reverse the engines, and at the same time a certain nut commences to travel along a screw. The nut having worked its way to the end of the thread, the head of the torpedo fills slowly through a valve, giving it a downward slant in front. The engines are again reversed and the nut again travels, this time bringing the head of the torpedo up, so as to strike the vessel at a very effective angle from below.

This torpedo has passed beyond the experimental

stage. It is reported that by command of the Swedish Government, to whom Mr. Orling offered his invention, and of the King, who takes a keen interest in the ideas of his young countryman, a number of experiments were some time ago carried out in the Swedish rivers. Torpedoes were sent 2½ miles, directed as desired, and made to rise or sink—all this without any tangible connection. The Government was sufficiently satisfied with the result to take up the patents, as furnishing a cheap means of defending their coasts.

Mr. Orling has described what he imagines would happen in case of an attack on a position protected by his ingenious creations. "Suppose that I had twelve torpedoes hidden away under ten feet of water in a convenient little cove, and that I was directed to annihilate a hostile fleet just appearing above the horizon. Before me, on a little table perhaps, I should have my apparatus; twelve buttons would be under my fingers. Against each button there would be a description of the torpedo to which it was connected; it would tell me its power of destruction, and the power of its machinery, and for what distance it would go. On each button, also, would be indicated the time that I must press it to release the torpedoes. Well now, I perceive a large vessel in the van of the approaching fleet. I put my fingers on the button which is connected with my largest and most formidable weapon. I press the button—perhaps for twelve seconds. The torpedo is pushed forward from its fastenings by a special spring, a small pin is extracted from it, and immediately the motive machinery is set in motion, and underneath the water goes my little agent of destruction, and there is nothing to tell the ship of its doom. I place my hand on another button, and according to the time I press it I steer the torpedo; the rudder answers to the rays, and the rays answer to the will of my mind."[1]

If this torpedo acts fully up to its author's expectations, naval warfare, at least as at present conducted, will be impossible. There appears to be no reason why this torpedo should not be worked from shipboard; and we cannot imagine that hostile ships possessing such truly infernal machines would care to approach within miles of one another, especially if the submarine be reinforced by the aërial torpedo, different patterns of which are in course of construction by Mr. Orling and Major Unge, a brother Swede. The Orling type will be worked by the new rays, strong enough to project it through space. Major Unge's will depend for its motive power upon a succession of impulses obtained by the ignition of a slow-burning gas, passing through a turbine in the rear of the torpedo. The inventor hopes for a range of at least six miles.

What defence would be possible against such missiles? Liable to be shattered from below, or shivered from above, the warship will be placed at an ever-increasing disadvantage. Its size will only

[1] *Pearson's Magazine.*

render it an easier mark; its strength, bought at the expense of weight, will be but the means of insuring a quicker descent to the sea's bottom. Is it not probable that sea-fights will become more and more matters of a few terrible, quickly-delivered blows? Human inventions will hold the balance more and more evenly between nations of unequal size, first on sea, then on land, until at last, as we may hope, even the hottest heads and bravest hearts will shrink from courting what will be less war than sheer annihilation, and war, man's worst enemy, will be itself annihilated.

SUBMARINE BOATS.

THE introduction of torpedoes for use against an enemy's ships below the waterline has led by natural stages to the evolution of a vessel which may approach unsuspected close enough to the object of attack to discharge its missile effectively. Before the search-light was adopted a night surprise gave due concealment to small craft; but now that the gloom of midnight can be in an instant flooded with the brilliance of day a more subtle mode of attack becomes necessary.

Hence the genesis of the submarine or submersible boat, so constructed as to disappear beneath the sea at a safe distance from the doomed ship, and when its torpedo has been sped to retrace its invisible course until outside the radius of destruction.

To this end many so-called submarine boats have been invented and experimented with during recent years. The idea is an ancient one revived, as indeed are the large proportion of our boasted modern discoveries.

Aristotle describes a vessel of this kind (a diving-bell rather than a boat, however), used in the siege of Tyre more than two thousand years ago; and also refers to the divers being provided with an air-tube, "like the trunk of an elephant," by means of which they drew a fresh supply of air from above the surface—a contrivance adopted in more than one of our modern submarines. Alexander the Great is said to have employed divers in warfare; Pliny speaks of an ingenious diving apparatus, and Bacon refers to air-tubes used by divers. We even find traces of weapons of offence being employed. Calluvius is credited with the invention of a submarine gun for projecting Greek fire.

The Bishop of Upsala in the sixteenth century gives a somewhat elaborate description of certain leather skiffs or boats used to scuttle ships by attacking them from beneath, two of which he claims to have personally examined. In 1629 we read that the Barbary corsairs fixed submarine torpedoes to the enemy's keel by means of divers.

As early as 1579 an English gunner named William Bourne patented a submarine boat of his own invention fitted with leather joints, so contrived as to be made smaller or larger by the action of screws, ballasted with water, and having an air-pipe as mast. The Campbell-Ash submarine tried in 1885 was on much the same principle.

Cornelius van Drebbel, an ingenious Dutchman who settled in England before 1600, produced certain submersible vessels and obtained for them the patronage of two kings. He claims to have discovered a means of re-oxygenating the foul air and so enabling his craft to remain a long time below water; whether

The "Holland" Submarine Boat.

[*To face p.* 144.

this was done by chemical treatment, compressed air, or by surface tubes no record remains. Drebbel's success was such that he was allowed to experiment in the Thames, and James I. accompanied him on one of his sub-aquatic journeys. In 1626 Charles I. gave him an order to make "boates to go under water," as well as "water mines, water petards," &c., presumably for the campaign against France, but we do not hear of these weapons of destruction being actually used upon this occasion.

These early craft seem to have been generally moved by oars working in air-tight leather sockets; but one constructed at Rotterdam about 1654 was furnished with a paddle-wheel.

Coming now nearer to our own times, we find that an American called Bushnell had a like inspiration in 1773, when he invented his famous "Turtles," small, upright boats in which one man could sit, submerge himself by means of leather bottles with the mouths projecting outside, propel himself with a small set of oars and steer with an elementary rudder. An unsuccessful attempt was made to blow up the English fleet with one of these "Turtles" carrying a torpedo, but the current proved too strong, and the missile exploded at a harmless distance, the operator being finally rescued from an unpremeditated sea-trip! Bushnell was the author of the removable safety-keel now uniformly adopted.

Soon afterwards another New Englander took up the running, Fulton—one of the cleverest and least appreciated engineers of the early years of the nineteenth century. His *Nautilus*, built in the French dockyards, was in many respects the pattern for our own modern submarines. The cigar-shaped copper hull, supported by iron ribs, was twenty-four feet four inches long, with a greatest diameter of seven feet. Propulsion came from a wheel, rotated by a hand winch, in the centre of the stern; forward was a small conning-tower, and the boat was steered by a rudder. There was a detachable keel below; and fitted into groves on the top were a collapsible mast and sail for use on the surface of the water. An anchor was also carried externally. In spite of the imperfect materials at his disposal Fulton had much success. At Brest he took a crew of three men twenty-five feet down, and on another day blew up an old hulk. In the Seine two men went down for twenty minutes and steered back to their starting-point under water. He also put in air at high pressure and remained submerged for hours. But France, England, and his own country in turn rejected his invention; and, completely discouraged, he bent his energies to designing boat engines instead.

In 1821 Captain Johnson, also an American, made a submersible vessel 100 feet long, designed to fetch Napoleon from St. Helena, travelling for the most part upon the surface. This expedition never came off.

Two later inventions, by Castera and Payerne, in 1827 and 1846 respectively, were intended for more peaceful objects. Being furnished with diving-chambers, the occupants could retrieve things from the bottom of the sea; Castera providing his boat with an air-tube to the surface.

Bauer, another inventor, lived for some years in England under the patronage of Prince Albert, who supplied him with funds for his experiments. With Brunel's help he built a vessel which was indiscreetly modified by the naval authorities, and finally sank and drowned its crew. Going then to Russia he constructed sundry submarines for the navy; but was in the end thrown over, and, like Fulton, had to turn himself to other employment.

The fact is that up to this period the cry for a practical submarine to use in warfare had not yet arisen, or these inventions would have met with a far different reception. Within the last half century all has changed. America and France now rival each other in construction, while the other nations of Europe look on with intelligent interest, and in turn make their contributions towards solving the problem of under-wave propulsion.

America led the way during the Civil War blockades in 1864, when the *Housatonic* was sunk in Charleston harbour, and damage done to other ships. But these experimental torpedo-boats were clumsy contrivances compared with their modern successors, for they could only carry their destructive weapon at the end of a spar projecting from the bows—to be exploded upon contact with the obstacle, and probably involve the aggressor in a common ruin. So nothing more was done till the perfecting of the Whitehead torpedo (see Dirigible Torpedoes) gave the required impetus to fresh enterprise.

France, experimenting in the same direction, produced in 1889 Goubet's submarine, patent of a private inventor, who has also been patronised by other navies. These are very small boats, the first, 16½ feet long, carrying a crew of two or three men. *Goubet No.* 2, built in 1899, is 26¼ feet long, composed of several layers of gun-metal united by strong screw-bolts, and so able to resist very great pressure. They are egg- or spindle-shaped, supplied with compressed air, able to sink and rise by rearrangement of water-ballast. Reservoirs in the hull are gradually filled for submersion with water, which is easily expelled when it is desired to rise again. If this system goes wrong a false keel of thirty-six hundredweight can be detached and the boat springs up to the surface. The propulsive force is electricity, which works the driving-screw at the rear, and the automobile torpedo is discharged from its tube by compressed air.

"By the aid of an optical tube, which a pneumatic telescopic apparatus enables the operator to thrust above the surface and pull down in a moment, the captain of the *Goubet* can, when near the surface, see what is going on all round him. This telescope has a system of prisms and lenses which cause the image of the sea-surface to be deflected down to the eye of the observer below.

"Fresh air for the crew is provided by reservoirs of oxygen, and accumulations of foul air can be expelled by means of a small pump. Enough fresh air can be compressed into the reservoirs to last the crew for a week or more."

The *Gymnote*, laid down in 1898, is more than double the size of the *Goubet;* it is cigar-shaped, 29 feet long by 6 feet diameter, with a displacement of thirty tons. The motive power is also electricity stored in accumulators for use during submersion, and the speed expected—but not realised—was to be ten knots.

Five years later this type was improved upon in the *Gustave Zédé*, the largest submarine ever yet designed. This boat, built of phosphor-bronze, with a single screw, measures 131 feet in length and has a displacement of 266 tons; she can contain a crew of nine officers and men, carries three torpedoes — though with one torpedo tube instead of two—has a lightly armoured conning-tower, and is said to give a surface speed of thirteen knots and to make eight knots when submerged. At a trial of her powers made in the presence of M. Lockroy, Minister of Marine, she affixed an unloaded torpedo to the battleship *Magenta* and got away unobserved. The whole performance of the boat on that occasion was declared to be most successful. But its cost proved excessive considering the small radius of action obtainable, and a smaller vessel of the same type, the *Morse* (118 × 9 feet), is now the official size for that particular class.

In 1896 a competition was held and won by the submersible *Narval* of M. Laubeuf, a craft shaped much like the ordinary torpedo-boat. On the surface or awash the *Narval* works by means of a Brulé engine burning oil fuel to heat its boilers; but when submerged for attack with funnel shut down is driven by electric accumulators. She displaces 100 odd tons and is provided with four Dzewiecki torpedo tubes. Her radius of action, steaming awash, is calculated at some 250 miles, or seventy miles when proceeding under water at five knots an hour. This is the parent of another class of boats designed for offensive tactics, while the *Morse* type is adapted chiefly for coast and harbour defence. The French navy includes altogether thirty submarine craft, though several of these are only projected at present, and none have yet been put to the practical tests of actual warfare—the torpedoes used in experimenting being, of course, blank.

Meanwhile in America experiments have also been proceeding since 1887, when Mr. Holland of New York produced the vessel that bears his name. This, considerably modified, has now been adopted as model by our Navy Department, which is building some half-dozen on very similar lines. Though it is not easy to get any definite particulars concerning French submarines Americans are less reticent, and we have graphic accounts of the *Holland* and her offspring from those who have visited her.

These vessels, though cigar-shaped liked most others, in some respects resemble the *Narval*, being intended

An interior view of the "Holland." The large pendulum on the right actuates mechanism to keep the Submarine at the required depth below the surface.

[*To face p.* 150.

for long runs on the surface, when they burn oil in a four-cylinder gasolene engine of 160 horse-power. Under water they are propelled by an electric water-proof motor of seventy horse-power, and proceed at a pace of seven knots per hour. There is a super-structure for deck, with a funnel for the engine and a small conning-tower protected by 4-inch armour. The armament carried comprises five 18-inch White-head torpedoes, 11 feet 8 inches long. One hundred and twenty tons is the displacement, including tank capacity for 850 gallons of gasolene; the full length is 63 feet 4 inches, with a beam of 11 feet 9 inches.

The original Holland boat is thus described by an adventurous correspondent who took a trip in her[1]: "The *Holland* is fifty-three feet long, and in its widest part it is 10¼ feet in diameter. It has a displacement of seventy-four tons, and what is called a reserve buoyancy of 2½ tons which tends to make it come to the surface.

"The frames of the boat are exact circles of steel. They are set a little more than a foot apart. They diminish gradually in diameter from the centre of the boat to the bow and stern. On the top of the boat a flat superstructure is built to afford a walking plat-form, and under this are spaces for exhaust pipes and for the external outfit of the boat, such as ropes and a small anchor. The steel plates which cover the frame are from one-half to three-eighths of an inch in thickness.

[1] *Pearson's Magazine.*

"From what may be called the centre of the boat a turret extends upwards through the superstructure for about eighteen inches. It is two feet in diameter, and is the only means of entrance to the boat. It is the place from which the boat is operated. At the stern is an ordinary three-bladed propeller and an ordinary rudder, and in addition there are two horizontal rudders—"diving-rudders" they are called—which look like the feet of a duck spread out behind as it swims along the water.

"From the bow two-thirds of the way to the stern there is a flooring, beneath which are the storage batteries, the tank for the gasolene, and the tanks which are filled with water for submerging; in the last one-third of the boat the flooring drops away, and the space is occupied by the propelling machinery.

"There are about a dozen openings in the boat, the chief being three Kingston valves, by means of which the submerging tanks are filled or emptied. Others admit water to pressure gauges, which regulate or show the depth of the vessel under water. There are twelve deadlights in the top and sides of the craft. To remain under water the boat must be kept in motion, unless an anchor is used.

"It can be steered to the surface by the diving rudders, or sent flying to the top through emptying the storage tanks. If it strikes bottom, or gets stuck in the mud, it can blow itself loose by means of its compressed air. It cannot be sunk unless pierced above the flooring. It has a speed capacity of from eight to ten knots either on the surface or under water.

"It can go 1500 miles on the surface without renewing its supply of gasolene. It can go fully forty knots under water without coming to the surface, and there is enough compressed air in the tanks to supply a crew with fresh air for thirty hours, if the air is not used for any other purpose, such as emptying the submerging tanks. It can dive to a depth of twenty feet in eight seconds.

"The interior is simply packed with machinery. As you climb down the turret you are confronted with it at once. There is a diminutive compass which must be avoided carefully by the feet. A pressure gauge is directly in front of the operator's eye as he stands in position. There are speaking-tubes to various parts of the boat, and a signal-bell to the engine-room.

"As the operator's hands hang by his sides, he touches a wheel on the port side, by turning which he steers the little vessel, and one on the starboard side, by turning which he controls the diving machinery. After the top is clamped down the operator can look out through plate-glass windows, about one inch wide and three inches long, which encircle the turret.

"So long as the boat is running on the surface these are valuable, giving a complete view of the surroundings if the water is smooth. After the boat goes beneath the surface, these windows are useless; it is impossible to see through the water. Steering must be done by compass; until recently considered an impossible task in a submarine boat. A tiny electric light in the turret shows the operator the direction in which he is going, and reveals the markings on the depth gauges. If the boat should pass under an object, such as a ship, a perceptible shadow would be noticed through the deadlights, but that is all. The ability to see fishes swimming about in the water is a pleasant fiction.

"The only clear space in the body of the boat is directly in front of the bench on which the man in the turret is standing. It is where the eighteen-inch torpedo-tube, and the eight and five-eighths inch aërial gun are loaded.

"Along the sides of this open space are six compressed-air tanks, containing thirty cubic feet of air at a pressure of 2000 lbs. to a square inch. Near by is a smaller tank, containing three cubic feet of air at a fifty pounds pressure. A still smaller tank contains two cubic feet of air at a ten pounds pressure. These smaller tanks supply the compressed air which, with the smokeless powder, is used in discharging the projectiles from the boat.

"Directly behind the turret, up against the roof on the port side, is the little engine by which the vessel is steered; it is worked by compressed air. Fastened to the roof on the starboard side is the diving-engine, with discs that look as large as dinner-plates stood on end. These discs are diaphragms on which the water-pressure exerts an influence, counteracting certain springs which are set to keep the diving rudders at a given pitch, and thus insuring an immersion of an exact depth during a run.

"At one side is a cubic steel box—the air compressor; and directly in the centre of this part of the boat is a long pendulum, just as there is in the ordinary torpedo, which, by swinging backwards and forwards as the boat dives and rises, checks a tendency to go too far down, or to come up at too sharp an angle. On the floor are the levers which, when raised and moved in certain directions, fill or empty the submerging tanks. On every hand are valves and wheels and pipes in such apparent confusion as to turn a layman's head.

"There are also pumps in the boat, a ventilating apparatus, and a sounding contrivance, by means of which the channel is picked out when running under water. This sounding contrivance consists of a heavy weight attached to a piano wire passing from a reel out through a stuffing-box in the bottom. There are also valves which release fresh air to the crew, although in ordinary runs of from one-half to one hour this is not necessary, the fresh air received from the various exhausts in the boat being sufficient to supply all necessities in that length of time."

Another submersible of somewhat different design is the production of the Swedish inventor, Mr. Nordenfelt. This boat is 9½ metres in length, and has a displacement of sixty tons. Like the *Goubet* it sinks only in a horizontal position, while the *Holland* plunges downward at a slight angle. On the surface a steam-engine of 100 horse-power propels it, and when the funnel is closed down and the vessel submerges itself, the screws are still driven by superheated steam from the large reservoir of water boiling at high pressure which maintains a constant supply, three circulation pumps keeping this in touch with the boiler. The plunge is accomplished by means of two protected screws, and when they cease to move the reserve buoyancy of the boat brings it back to the surface. It is steered by a rudder which a pendulum regulates. The most modern of these boats is of English manufacture, built at Barrow, and tried in Southampton Water.

The vessels hitherto described should be termed submersible rather than submarine, as they are designed to usually proceed on the surface, and submerge themselves only for action when in sight of the enemy.

American ingenuity has produced an absolutely unique craft to which the name submarine may with real appropriateness be applied, for, sinking in water 100 feet deep, it can remain below and run upon three wheels along the bottom of the sea. This is the *Argonaut*, invented by Mr. Simon Lake of Baltimore, and its main portion consists of a steel framework of cylindrical form which is surmounted by a flat, hollow steel deck. During submersion the deck is filled with water and thus saved from being crushed by outside pressure as well as helping to sink the craft.

When moving on the surface it has the appearance of an ordinary ship, with its two light masts, a small conning-tower on which is the steering-wheel, bowsprit, ventilators, a derrick, suction-pump, and two anchors. A gasolene engine of special design is used for both surface and submerged cruising under ordinary circumstances, but in time of war storage batteries are available. An electric dynamo supplies light to the whole interior, including a 4000 candle-power searchlight in the extreme bow which illuminates the pathway while under water.

On the boat being stopped and the order given to submerge, the crew first throw out sounding lines to make sure of the depth. They then close down external openings, and retreat into the boat through the conning-tower, within which the helmsman takes his stand, continuing to steer as easily as when outside. The valves which fill the deck and submersion tanks are opened, and the *Argonaut* drops gently to the floor of the ocean. The two apparent masts are in reality 3-inch iron pipes which rise thirty feet or more above the deck, and so long as no greater depth is attained, they supply the occupants with fresh air and let exhausted gases escape, but close automatically when the water reaches their top.

Once upon the bottom of the sea this versatile submarine begins its journey as a tricycle. It is furnished with a driving-wheel on either side, each of which is 6½ feet in diameter and weighs 5000 lbs.; and is guided by a third wheel weighing 2000 lbs.

journalled in the rudder. On a hard bottom or against a strong tide the wheels are most effective owing to their weight, but in passing through soft sand or mud the screw propeller pushes the boat along, the driving-wheels running "loose." In this way she can travel through even waist-deep mud, the screw working more strongly than on the surface, because it has such a weight of water to help it, and she moves more easily uphill.

In construction the *Argonaut* is shaped something like a huge cigar, her strong steel frames, spaced twenty inches apart, being clad with steel plates $\frac{3}{8}$-inch thick double riveted over them. Great strength is necessary to resist the pressure of superincumbent water, which at a depth of 100 feet amounts to 44 lbs. per square inch.

Originally she was built 36 feet long, but was subsequently lengthened by some 20 odd feet, and has 9 feet beam. She weighs fifty-seven tons when submerged. A false section of keel, 4000 lbs. in weight, can on emergency be instantly released from inside; and two downhaul weights, each of 1000 lbs., are used as an extra precaution for safety when sinking in deep water.

The interior is divided into various compartments, the living quarters consisting of the cabin, galley, operating chamber and engine-room. There are also a division containing stores and telephone, the intermediate, and the divers' room. The "operating" room contains the levers, handwheels, and other mechanism by which the boat's movements are governed. A water gauge shows her exact depth below the surface; a dial on either side indicates any inclination from the horizontal. Certain levers open the valves which admit water to the ballast-tanks in the hold; another releases the false keel; there is a cyclometer to register the wheel travelling, and other gauges mark the pressure of steam, speed of engines, &c.

A compass in the conning-tower enables the navigator to steer a true course whether above or below the surface. This conning-tower, only six feet high, rises above the centre of the living quarters, and is of steel with small windows in the upper part. Encircling it to about three-quarters of its height is a reservoir for gasolene, which feeds into a smaller tank within the boat for consumption. The compressed air is stored in two Mannesmann steel reservoirs which have been tested to a pressure of 4000 lbs. per square inch. This renews the air-supply for the crew when the *Argonaut* is long below, and also enables the diving operations to be carried on.

The maximum speed at which the *Argonaut* travels submerged is five knots an hour, and when she has arrived at her destination—say a sunken coal steamer—the working party pass into the "intermediate" chamber, whose air-tight doors are then closed. A current of compressed air is then turned on until the air is equal in pressure to that in the divers' room. The doors of this close over indiarubber to be air and water-tight; one communicates with the "intermediate," the other is a trap which opens downwards into the sea. Through three windows in the prow those remaining in the room can watch operations outside within a radius varying according to the clearness of the water. The divers assume their suits, to the helmets of which a telephone is attached, so arranged that they are able to talk to each other as well as to those in the boat. They are also provided with electric lamps, and a brilliant flood of light streams upon them from the bows of the vessel. The derrick can be used with ease under water, and the powerful suction-pump will "retrieve" coal from a submerged vessel into a barge above at the rate of sixty tons per hour.

It will thus be seen how valuable a boat of this kind may be for salvage operations, as well as for surveying the bottom of harbours, river mouths, sea coasts, and so on. In war time it can lay or examine submarine mines for harbour defence, or, if employed offensively, can enter the enemy's harbour with no chance of detection, and there destroy his mines or blow up his ships with perfect impunity.

To return the *Argonaut* to the surface it is only necessary to force compressed air into the space below the deck and the four tanks in the hold. Her buoyancy being thus gradually restored she rises slowly and steadily till she is again afloat upon the water, and steams for land.

We have now glanced briefly at some of the most

The "Holland" Submarine in the last stages of submersion.

[*To face p.* 160.

interesting attempts—out of many dozens—to produce a practicable submarine vessel in bygone days; and have inquired more closely into the construction of several modern designs; among these the *Holland* has received especial attention, as that is the model adopted by our Admiralty, and our own new boats only differ in detail from their American prototype. But before quitting this subject it will be well to consider what is required from the navigating engineer, and how far present invention has supplied the demand.

The perfect submarine of fiction was introduced by Jules Verne, whose *Nautilus* remains a masterpiece of scientific imagination. This marvellous vessel ploughed the seas with equal power and safety, whether on the surface or deeply sunk beneath the waves, bearing the pressure of many atmospheres. It would rest upon the ocean floor while its inmates, clad in diving suits, issued forth to stroll amid aquatic forests and scale marine mountains. It gathered fabulous treasures from pearl beds and sunken galleons; and could ram and sink an offending ship a thousand times its size without dinting or loosening a plate on its own hull. No weather deflected its compass, no movement disturbed its equilibrium. Its crew followed peacefully and cheerfully in their spacious cabins a daily round of duties which electric power and automatic gear reduced to a minimum. Save for the misadventure of a shortened air-supply when exploring the Polar pack, and the clash of human passions, Captain

Nemo's guests would have voyaged in a floating paradise.

Compare with this entrancing creation the most practical vessels of actual experiment. They are small, blind craft, groping their way perilously when below the surface, the steel and electrical machinery sadly interfering with any trustworthy working of their compass, and the best form of periscope hitherto introduced forming a very imperfect substitute for ordinary vision.

Their speed, never very fast upon the surface, is reduced by submersion to that of the oldest and slowest gunboats. Their radius of action is also circumscribed—that is, they cannot carry supplies sufficient to go a long distance, deal with a hostile fleet, and then return to headquarters without replenishment.

Furthermore, there arise the nice questions of buoyancy combined with stability when afloat, of sinking quickly out of sight, and of keeping a correct balance under water. The equilibrium of such small vessels navigating between the surface and the bottom is extremely sensitive; even the movements to and fro of the crew are enough to imperil them. To meet this difficulty the big water-ballast tanks, engines and accumulators are necessarily arranged at the bottom of the hull, and a pendulum working a helm automatically is introduced to keep it longitudinally stable.

To sink the boat, which is done by changing the

angle of the propeller in the *Goubet* and some others, and by means of horizontal rudders and vanes in the *Nordenfelt* and *Holland*, it must first be most accurately balanced, bow and stern exactly in trim. Then the boat must be put into precise equilibrium with the water—*i.e.* must weigh just the amount of water displaced. For this its specific gravity must be nearly the same as that of the water (whether salt or fresh), and a small accident might upset all calculations. Collision, even with a large fish, could destroy the steering-gear, and a dent in the side would also tend to plunge it at once to destruction.

Did it escape these dangers and succeed in steering an accurate course to its goal, we have up to now little practical proof that the mere act of discharging its torpedo—though the weight of the missile is intended to be automatically replaced immediately it drops from the tube—may not suffice to send the vessel either to bottom or top of the sea. In the latter case it would be within the danger zone of its alarmed enemy and at his mercy, its slow speed (even if uninjured) leaving it little chance of successful flight.

But whatever the final result, one thing is certain, that—untried as it is—the possible contingency of a submarine attack is likely to shake the *morale* of an aggressive fleet.

"When the first submarine torpedo-boat goes into action," says Mr. Holland, "she will bring us face to face with the most perplexing problem ever met in warfare. She will present the unique spectacle, when used in attack, of a weapon against which there is no defence. . . . You can send nothing against the submarine boat, not even itself. . . . You cannot see under water, hence you cannot fight under water. Hence you cannot defend yourself against an attack under water except by running away."

This inventor is, however, an enthusiast about the future awaiting the submarine as a social factor. His boat has been tested by long voyages on and below water with complete success. The *Argonaut* also upon one occasion travelled a thousand miles with five persons, and proved herself "habitable, seaworthy, and under perfect control."

Mr. Holland confidently anticipates in the near future a Channel service of submerged boats run by automatic steering-gear upon cables stretched from coast to coast, and eloquently sums up its advantages.

The passage would be always practicable, for ordinary interruptions such as fog and storms cannot affect the sea depths.

An even temperature would prevail summer and winter, the well-warmed and lighted boats being also free from smoke and spray.

No nauseating smells would proceed from the evenly-working electric engines. No motion cause sea-sickness, no collision be apprehended—as each line would run on its own cable, and at its own specified depth, a telephone keeping it in communication with shore.

In like manner a service might be plied over lake bottoms, or across the bed of wide rivers whose surface is bound in ice. Such is the submarine boat as hitherto conceived for peace or war—a daring project for the coming generation to justify.

ANIMATED PICTURES.

HAS it ever occurred to the reader to ask himself why rain appears to fall in streaks though it arrives at earth in drops? Or why the glowing end of a charred stick produces fiery lines if waved about in the darkness? Common sense tells us the drop and the burning point cannot *be* in two places at one and the same time. And yet apparently we are able to see both in many positions simultaneously.

This seeming paradox is due to "persistence of vision," a phenomenon that has attracted the notice of scientific men for many centuries. Persistence may be briefly explained thus:—

The eye is extremely sensitive to light, and will, as is proved by the visibility of the electric spark, lasting for less than the millionth part of a second, *receive* impressions with marvellous rapidity.

But it cannot get rid of these impressions at the same speed. The duration of a visual impression has been calculated as one-tenth to one-twenty-first of a second. The electric spark, therefore, appears to last much longer than it really does.

Hence it is obvious that if a series of impressions follow one another more rapidly than the eye can free itself of them, the impressions will overlap, and one of four results will follow.

(*a*) *Apparently uninterrupted presence* of an image if the same image be repeatedly represented.

(*b*) *Confusion*, if the images be all different and disconnected.

(*c*) *Combination*, if the images of two or a very few objects be presented in regular rotation.

(*d*) *Motion*, if the objects be similar in all but one part, which occupies a slightly different portion in each presentation.

In connection with (*c*) an interesting story is told of Sir J. Herschel by Charles Babbage :—[1]

"One day Herschel, sitting with me after dinner, amusing himself by spinning a pear upon the table, suddenly asked whether I could show him the two sides of a shilling at the same moment. I took out of my pocket a shilling, and holding it up before the looking-glass, pointed out my method. 'No,' said my friend, 'that won't do;' then spinning my shilling upon the table, he pointed out his method of seeing both sides at once. The next day I mentioned the anecdote to the late Dr. Fitton, who a few days after brought me a beautiful illustration of the principle. It consisted of a round disc of card suspended between two pieces of sewing silk. These threads being held between the finger and thumb of each hand, were

[1] Quoted from Mr. Henry V. Hopwood's "Living Pictures," to which book the author is indebted for much of his information in this chapter.

then made to turn quickly, when the disc of card, of course, revolved also. Upon one side of this disc of card was painted a bird, upon the other side an empty bird-cage. On turning the thread rapidly the bird appeared to have got inside the cage. We soon made numerous applications, as a rat on one side and a trap on the other, &c. It was shown to Captain Kater, Dr. Wollaston, and many of our friends, and was, after the lapse of a short time, forgotten. Some months after, during dinner at the Royal Society Club, Sir Joseph Banks being in the chair, I heard Mr. Barrow, then secretary to the Admiralty, talking very loudly about a wonderful invention of Dr. Paris, the object of which I could not quite understand. It was called the Thaumatrope, and was said to be sold at the Royal Institution, in Albemarle Street. Suspecting that it had some connection with our unnamed toy I went next morning and purchased for seven shillings and sixpence a thaumatrope, which I afterwards sent down to Slough to the late Lady Herschel. It was precisely the thing which her son and Dr. Fitton had contributed to invent, which amused all their friends for a time, and had then been forgotten."

The *thaumatrope*, then, did nothing more than illustrate the power of the eye to weld together a couple of alternating impressions. The toys to which we shall next pass represent the same principle working in a different direction towards the production of the living picture.

Now, when we see a man running (to take an instance) we see the *same* body and the same legs continuously, but in different positions, which merge insensibly the one into the other. No method of reproducing that impression of motion is possible if only *one* drawing, diagram, or photograph be employed.

A man represented with as many legs as a centipede would not give us any impression of running or movement; and a blur showing the positions taken successively by his legs would be equally futile. Therefore we are driven back to a *series* of pictures, slightly different from one another; and in order that the pictures may not be blurred a screen must be interposed before the eye while the change from picture to picture is made. The shorter the period of change, and the greater the number of pictures presented to illustrate a single motion, the more realistic is the effect. These are the general principles which have to be observed in all mechanism for the production of an illusory effect of motion. The persistence of vision has led to the invention of many optical toys, the names of which, in common with the names of most apparatus connected with the living picture, are remarkable for their length. Of these toys we will select three for special notice.

In 1833 Plateau of Ghent invented the *phenakistoscope*, "the thing that gives one a false impression of reality"—to interpret this formidable word. The phenakistoscope is a disc of card or metal round the edge of which are drawn a succession of pictures showing a man or animal in progressive positions. Between every two pictures a narrow slit is cut. The disc is mounted on an axle and revolved before a mirror, so that a person looking through the slits see one picture after another reflected in the mirror.

The *zoetrope*, or Wheel of Life, which appeared first in 1860, is a modification of the same idea. In this instrument the pictures are arranged on the inner side of a hollow cylinder revolving on a vertical axis, its sides being perforated with slits above the pictures. As the slit in both cases caused distortion M. Reynaud, a Frenchman, produced in 1877 the *praxinoscope*, which differed from the zoetrope in that the pictures were not seen directly through slits, but were reflected by mirrors set half-way between the pictures and the axis of the cylinder, a mirror for every picture. Only at the moment when the mirror is at right angles to the line of sight would the picture be visible. M. Reynaud also devised a special lantern for projecting praxinoscope pictures on to a screen.

These and other somewhat similar contrivances, though ingenious, had very distinct limitations. They depended for their success upon the inventiveness and accuracy of the artist, who was confined in his choice of subject; and could, owing to the construction of the apparatus, only represent a small series of actions, indefinitely repeated by the machine. And as a complete action had to be crowded into a few pictures, the changes of position were necessarily abrupt.

To make the living picture a success two things were needed; some method of securing a very rapid series of many pictures, and a machine for reproducing the series, whatever its length. The method was found in photography, with the advance of which the living picture's progress is so closely related, that it will be worth while to notice briefly the various improvements of photographic processes. The old-fashioned Daguerreotype process, discovered in 1839, required an exposure of half-an-hour. The introduction of wet collodion reduced this tax on a sitter's patience to ten seconds. In 1878 the dry plate process had still further shortened the exposure to one second; and since that date the silver-salt emulsions used in photography have had their sensitiveness to light so much increased, that clear pictures can now be made in one-thousandth of a second, a period minute enough to arrest the most rapid movements of animals.

By 1878, therefore, instantaneous photography was ready to aid the living picture. Previously to that year series of photographs had been taken from posed models, without however extending the choice of subjects to any great extent. But between 1870 and 1880 two men, Marey and Muybridge, began work with the camera on the movements of horses. Marey endeavoured to produce a series of pictures round the edge of one plate with a single lens and repeated exposures.[1] Muybridge, on the other hand, used a series of cameras. He erected a long white background parallel to which were stationed the cameras at equal distances. The shutters of the cameras were connected to threads laid across the interval between the background and the cameras in such a manner that a horse driven along the track snapped them at regular intervals, and brought about successive exposures. Muybridge's method was carried on by Anschütz, a German, who in 1899 brought out his electrical Tachyscope, or "quick-seer." Having secured his negatives he printed off transparent positives on glass, and arranged these last round the circumference of a large disc rotating in front of a screen, having in it a hole the size of the transparencies. As each picture came opposite the hole a Geissler tube was momentarily lit up behind it by electrical contact, giving a fleeting view of one phase of a horse's motion.

The introduction of the ribbon film in or about 1888 opened much greater possibilities to the living picture than would ever have existed had the glass plate been retained. It was now comparatively easy to take a long series of pictures; and accordingly we find Messrs. Friese-Greene and Evans exhibiting in 1890 a camera capable of securing three hundred exposures in half a minute, or ten per second.

[1] A very interesting article in the May, 1902, issue of *Pearson's Magazine* deals with the latest work of Professor Marey in the field of the photographic representation of the movements of men birds, and quadrupeds.

The next apparatus to be specially mentioned is Edison's Kinetoscope, which he first exhibited in England in 1894. As early as 1887 Mr. Edison had tried to produce animated pictures in a manner analogous to the making of a sound-record on a phonograph (see p. 56). He wrapped round a cylinder a sheet of sensitized celluloid which was covered, after numerous exposures, by a spiral line of tiny negatives. The positives made from these were illuminated in turn by flashes of electric light. This method was, however, entirely abandoned in the perfected kinetoscope, an instrument for viewing pictures the size of a postage stamp, carried on a continuously moving celluloid film between the eye of the observer and a small electric lamp. The pictures passed the point of inspection at the rate of forty-six per second (a rate hitherto never approached), and as each picture was properly centred a slit in a rapidly revolving shutter made it visible for a very small fraction of a second. Holes punched at regular intervals along each side of the film engaged with studs on a wheel, and insured a regular motion of the pictures. This principle of a perforated film has been used by nearly all subsequent manufacturers of animatographs.

To secure forty-six negatives per second Edison invented a special exposure device. Each negative would have but one-forty-sixth of a second to itself, and that must include the time during which the fresh surface of film was being brought into position before the lens. He therefore introduced an intermittent gearing, which jerked the film forwards forty-six times per second, but allowed it to remain stationary for nine-tenths of the period allotted to each picture. During the time of movement the lens was covered by the shutter. This principle of exposure has also been largely adopted by other inventors. By its means weak negatives are avoided, while pictures projected on to a screen gain greatly in brilliancy and steadiness.

The capabilities of a long flexible film-band having been shown by Edison, he was not long without imitators. Phantoscopes, Bioscopes, Photoscopes, and many other instruments followed in quick succession. In 1895 Messrs. Lumière scored a great success with their Cinematograph, which they exhibited at Marseilles and Paris; throwing the living picture as we now know it on to a screen for a large company to see. This camera-lantern opens the era of commercial animated-photography. The number of patents taken out since 1895 in connection with living-picture machines is sufficient proof that inventors have either found in this particular branch of photography a peculiar fascination, or have anticipated from it a substantial profit.

A company known as the Mutoscope and Biograph Company has been formed for the sole object of working the manufacture and exhibition of the living picture on a great commercial scale. The present company is American, but there are subsidiary allied companies in many parts of the world, including the British Isles, France, Italy, Belgium, Germany, Austria, India, Australia, South Africa. The part that the company has played in the development of animated photography will be easily understood from the short account that follows.

The company controls three machines, the Mutograph, or camera for making negatives; the Biograph, or lantern for throwing pictures on to the screen; and the Mutoscope, a familiar apparatus in which the same pictures may be seen in a different fashion on the payment of a penny.

Externally the Mutograph is remarkable for its size, which makes it a giant of its kind. The complete apparatus weighs, with its accumulators, several hundreds of pounds. It takes a very large picture, as animatograph pictures go—two by two-and-a-half inches, which, besides giving increased detail, require less severe magnification than is usual with other films. The camera can make up to a hundred exposures per second, in which time *twenty-two* feet of film will have passed before the lens.

The film is so heavy that were it arrested bodily during each exposure and then jerked forward again, it might be injured. The mechanism of the mutograph, driven at regular speed by an electric motor, has been so arranged as to halt only that part of the film which is being exposed, the rest moving forward continuously. The exposed portion, together with the next surface, which has accumulated in a loop behind it, is dragged on by two rollers that are in contact with the film during part only of their revolutions. Thus the jerky motion is confined to but a few inches of the film, and even at the highest speeds the camera is peculiarly free from vibration.

An exposed mutograph film is wound for development round a skeleton reel, three feet in diameter and seven long, which rotates in a shallow trough containing the developing solution. Development complete, the reel is lifted from its supports and suspended over a succession of other troughs for washing, fixing, and final washing. When dry the negative film is passed through a special printing frame in contact with another film, which receives the positive image for the biograph. The difficulty of handling such films will be appreciated to a certain extent even by those whose experience is confined to the snaky behaviour of a short Kodak reel during development.

The Mutoscope Company's organisation is as perfect as its machinery. It has representatives in all parts of the world. Wherever stirring events are taking place, whether in peace or war, a mutograph operator will soon be on the spot with his heavy apparatus to secure pictures for world-wide exhibition. It need hardly be said that great obstacles, human and physical, have often to be overcome before a film can be exposed; and considerable personal danger encountered. We read that an operator, despatched to Cuba during the Spanish-American War was left three days and nights without food or water to guard his precious instruments, the party that had landed him having suddenly put to sea on sighting a Spanish cruiser. Another is reported to have had a narrow escape from being captured at sea by the Spaniards after a hot chase. It is also on record that a mutograph set up in Atlantic City to take a procession of fire-engines was charged and shattered by one of the engines; that the operators were flung into the crowd: and that nevertheless the box containing the exposed films was uninjured, and on development yielded a very sensational series of pictures lasting to the moment of collision.

The Mutoscope Company owns several thousand series of views, none probably more valuable than those of his Holiness the Pope, who graciously gave Mr. W. K. Dickson five special sittings, during which no less than 17,000 negatives were made, each one of great interest to millions of people throughout the world.

The company spares neither time nor money in its endeavour to supply the public with what will prove acceptable. A year's output runs into a couple of hundred miles of film. As much as 700 feet is sometimes expended on a single series, which may be worth anything up to £1000.

The energy displayed by the operators is often marvellous. To take instances. The Derby of 1898 was run at 3.20 P.M. At ten o'clock the race was run again by Biograph on the great sheet at the

Palace Theatre. On the home-coming of Lord Kitchener from the Soudan Campaign, a series of photographs was taken at Dover in the afternoon and exhibited the same evening! Or again, to consider a wider sphere of action, the Jubilee Procession of 1897 was watched in New York ten days after the event; two days later in Chicago; and in three more the films were attracting large audiences in San Francisco, 5000 miles from the actual scene of the procession!

One may easily weary of a series of single views passed slowly through a magic-lantern at a lecture or entertainment. But when the Biograph is flashing its records at lightning speed there is no cause for dulness. It is impossible to escape from the fascination of *movement*. A single photograph gives the impression of mere resemblance to the original; but a series, each reinforcing the signification of the last, breathes life into the dead image, and deludes us into the belief that we see, not the representation of a thing, but the thing itself. The bill of fare provided by the Biograph Company is varied enough to suit the most fastidious taste. Now it is the great Naval Review off Spithead, or President Faure shooting pheasants on his preserves near Paris. A moment's pause and then the magnificent Falls of Niagara foam across the sheet; Maxim guns fire harmlessly; panoramic scenes taken from locomotives running at high velocity unfold themselves to the delighted spectators, who feel as if they really were speeding over open country, among towering rocks, or plunging into the darkness of a tunnel. Here is an express approaching with all the quiver and fuss of real motion, so faithfully rendered that it seems as if a catastrophe were imminent; when, snap! we are transported a hundred miles to watch it glide into a station. The doors open, passengers step out and shake hands with friends, porters bustle about after luggage, doors are slammed again, the guard waves his flag, and the carriages move slowly out of the picture. Then our attention is switched away to the 10-inch disappearing gun, landing and firing at Sandy Hook. And next, as though to show that nothing is beneath the notice of the biograph, we are perhaps introduced to a family of small pigs feeding from a trough with porcine earnestness and want of manners.

It must not be thought that the Living Picture caters for mere entertainment only. It serves some very practical and useful ends. By its aid the movements of machinery and the human muscles may be studied in detail, to aid a mechanical or medical education. It furnishes art schools with all the poses of a living model. Less serious pursuits, such as dancing, boxing, wrestling and all athletic sports and exercise, will find a use for it. As an advertising medium it stands unrivalled, and we shall owe it a deep debt of gratitude if it ultimately supplants the flaring posters that disfigure our towns and desecrate our landscapes. Not so long since, the directors of the Norddeutscher-

Lloyd Steamship Company hired the biograph at the Palace Theatre, London, to demonstrate to anybody who cared to witness a very interesting exhibition that their line of vessels should always be used for a journey between England and America.

The Living Picture has even been impressed into the service of the British Empire to promote emigration to the Colonies. Three years ago Mr. Freer exhibited at the Imperial Institute and in other places in England a series of films representing the 1897 harvest in Manitoba. Would-be emigrants were able to satisfy themselves that the great Canadian plains were fruitful not only on paper. For could they not see with their own eyes the stately procession of automatic "binders" reaping, binding, and delivering sheaves of wheat, and puffing engines threshing out the grain ready for market? A far preferable method this to the bogus descriptions of land companies such as lured poor Chuzzlewit and Mark Tapley into the deadly swamps of "Eden."

Again, what more calculated to recruit boys for our warships than the fine Polytechnic exhibition known as "Our Navy"? What words, spoken or printed, could have the effect of a series of vivid scenes truthfully rendered, of drills on board ship, the manning and firing of big guns, the limbering-up of smaller guns, the discharge of torpedoes, the headlong rush of the "destroyers"?

The Mutoscope, to which reference has been made above, may be found in most places of public entertainment, in refreshment bars, on piers, in exhibitions, on promenades. A penny dropped into a slot releases a handle, the turning of which brings a series of pictures under inspection. The pictures, enlarged from mutograph films, are mounted in consecutive order round a cylinder, standing out like the leaves of a book. When the cylinder is revolved by means of the handle the picture cards are snapped past the eye, giving an effect similar to the lifelike projections on a biograph screen. From 900 to 1000 pictures are mounted on a cylinder.

The advantages of the mutoscope—its convenient size, its simplicity, and the ease with which its contents may be changed to illustrate the topics and events of the day—have made the animated photograph extremely popular. It does for vision what the phonograph does for sound. In a short time we shall doubtless be provided with handy machines combining the two functions and giving us double value for our penny.

The real importance and value of animated photography will be more easily estimated a few years hence than to-day, when it is still more or less of a novelty. The multiplication of illustrated newspapers and magazines points to a general desire for pictorial matter to help down the daily, weekly, or monthly budget of news, even if the illustrations be imaginative products of Fleet Street rather than faithful to fact. The reliable living picture (we except the "set-scene") which "holds up a mirror to nature," will be a companion rather than a rival of journalism, following hard on the description in print of an event that has taken place under the eye of the recording camera. The zest with which we have watched during the last two years biographic views of the embarkation and disembarkation of troops, of the transport of big guns through drifts and difficult country, and of the other circumstances of war, is largely due to the descriptions we have already read of the things that we see on the screen. And, on the other hand, the impression left by a series of animated views will dwell in our memories long after the contents of the newspaper columns have become confused and jumbled. It is therefore especially to be hoped that photographic records will be kept of historic events, such as the Jubilee, the Queen's Funeral, King Edward's Coronation, so that future generations may, by the turning of a handle, be brought face to face with the great doings of a bygone age.

THE GREAT PARIS TELESCOPE

A TELESCOPE so powerful that it brings the moon apparently to within thirty-five miles of the earth; so long that many a cricketer could not throw a ball from one end of it to the other; so heavy that it would by itself make a respectable load for a goods train; so expensive that astronomically-inclined millionaires might well hesitate to order a similar one for their private use.

Such is the huge Paris telescope that in 1900 delighted thousands of visitors in the French Exposition, where, among the many wonderful sights to be seen on all sides, it probably attracted more notice than any other exhibit. This triumph of scientific engineering and dogged perseverance in the face of great difficulties owes its being to a suggestion made in 1894 to a group of French astronomers by M. Deloncle. He proposed to bring astronomy to the front at the coming Exposition, and to effect this by building a refracting telescope that in size and power should completely eclipse all existing instruments and add a new chapter to the "story of the heavens."

To the mind unversed in astronomy the telescope appeals by the magnitude of its dimensions, in the same way as do the Forth Bridge, the Eiffel Tower, the Big Wheel, the statue of Liberty near New York harbour, the Pyramids, and most human-made "biggest on records."

At the time of M. Deloncle's proposal the largest refracting telescope was the Yerkes' at William's Bay, Wisconsin, with an object-glass forty inches in diameter; and next to it the 36-inch Lick instrument on Mount Hamilton, California, built by Messrs. Alvan Clark of Cambridgeport, Massachusetts. Among reflecting telescopes the prior place is still held by Lord Rosse's, set up on the lawn of Birr Castle half a century ago. Its speculum, or mirror, weighing three tons, lies at the lower end of a tube six feet across and sixty feet long. This huge reflector, being mounted in meridian, moves only in a vertical direction. A refracting telescope is one of the ordinary pocket type, having an object-lens at one end and an eyepiece at the other. A reflector, on the other hand, has no object-lens, its place being taken by a mirror that gathers the rays entering the tube and reflects them back into the eyepiece, which is situated nearer the mouth end of the tube than the mirror itself.

Each system has its peculiar disadvantages. In reflectors the image is more or less distorted by "spherical aberration." In refractors the image is approximately perfect in shape, but liable to "chromatic aberration," a phenomenon especially noticeable in cheap telescopes and field-glasses, which often show objects fringed with some of the colours of the spectrum. This defect arises from the different refrangibility of different light rays. Thus, violet rays come to a focus at a shorter distance from the lens than red rays, and when one set is in focus to the eye the other must be out of focus. In carefully-made and expensive instruments compound lenses are used, which by the employment of different kinds of glass bring all the colours to practically the same focus, and so do away with chromatic aberration.

To reduce colour troubles to a *minimum* M. Deloncle proposed that the object-lens should have a focal distance of about two hundred feet, since a long focus is more easily corrected than a short one, and a diameter of over fifty-nine inches. The need for so huge a lens arises out of the optical principles of a refractor. The rays from an object—a star, for instance—strike the object-glass at the near end, and are bent by it into a converging beam, till they all meet at the focus. Behind the focus they again separate, and are caught by the eyepiece, which reduces them to a parallel beam small enough to enter the pupil. We thus see that though the unaided eye gathers only the few rays that fall directly from the object on to the pupil, when helped by the telescope it receives the concentrated rays falling on the whole area of the object-glass; and it would be sensible of a greatly increased brightness had not this light to be redistributed over the image, which is the object magnified by the eyepiece. Assuming the aperture of the pupil to be one-tenth of an inch, and the object to be magnified a hundred times, the object-lens should have a hundred times the diameter of the pupil to render the image as bright as the object itself. If the lens be five instead of ten inches across, a great loss of light results, as in the high powers of a microscope, and the image loses in distinctness what it gains in size.

As M. Deloncle meant his telescope to beat all records in respect of magnification, he had no choice but to make a lens that should give proportionate illumination, and itself be of unprecedented size.

At first M. Deloncle met with considerable opposition and ridicule. Such a scheme as his was declared to be beyond accomplishment. But in spite of many prophecies of ultimate failure he set to work, entrusting the construction of the various portions of his colossal telescope to well-tried experts. To M. Gautier was given the task of making all the mechanical parts of the apparatus; to M. Mantois the casting of the giant lenses; to M. Despret the casting of the huge mirror, to which reference will be made immediately.

The first difficulty to be encountered arose from the sheer size of the instrument. It was evidently impossible to mount such a leviathan in the ordinary way. A tube, 180 feet long, could not be made rigid enough to move about and yet permit careful observation of the stars. Even supposing that it were satisfactorily mounted on an "equatorial foot" like smaller glasses, how could it be protected from wind and weather? To cover it, a mighty dome, two hundred feet or more in diameter, would be required; a dome exceeding by over seventy feet the cupola of St. Peter's, Rome; and this dome must revolve easily on its base at a pace of about fifty feet an hour, so that the telescope might follow the motion of the heavenly bodies.

The constructors therefore decided to abandon any idea of making a telescope that could be moved about and pointed in any desired direction. The alternative course open to them was to fix the telescope itself rigidly in position, and to bring the stars within its field by means of a mirror mounted on a massive iron frame—the two together technically called a siderostat. The mirror and its support would be driven by clockwork at the proper sidereal rate. The siderostat principle had been employed as early as the eighteenth century, and perfected in recent years by Léon Foucault, so that in having recourse to it the builders of the telescope were not committing themselves to any untried device.

In days when the handling of masses of iron, and the erection of huge metal constructions have become matters of everyday engineering life, no peculiar difficulty presented itself in connection with the metal-work of the telescope. The greatest possible care was of course observed in every particular. All joints and bearings were adjusted with an extraordinary accuracy; and all the cylindrical moving parts of the siderostat verified till they did not vary from perfect cylindricity by so much as one twenty-five-thousandth of an inch!

The tube of the telescope, 180 feet long, consisted of twenty-four sections, fifty-nine inches in diameter, bolted together and supported on seven massive iron pillars. It weighed twenty-one tons. The siderostat, twenty-seven feet high, and as many in length, weighed forty-five tons. The lower portion, which was fixed firmly on a bed of concrete, had on the top a tank filled with quicksilver, in which the mirror and its frame floated. The quicksilver supported nine-tenths of the weight, the rest being taken by the levers used to move the mirror. Though the total weight of the mirror and frame was thirteen tons, the quicksilver offered so little resistance that a pull of a few pounds sufficed to rotate the entire mass.

The real romance of the construction of this huge telescope centres on the making of the lenses and mirror. First-class lenses for all photographic and optical purposes command a very high price on account of the care and labour that has to be expended on their production; the value of the glass being trifling by comparison. Few, if any, trades require greater mechanical skill than that of lens-making; the larger the lens the greater the difficulties it presents, first in the casting, then in the grinding, last of all in the polishing. The presence of a single air-bubble in the molten glass, the slightest irregularity of surface in the polishing may utterly

Reproduced by the permission of] [*Proprietors of "Knowledge"*

destroy the value of a lens otherwise worth several thousands of pounds.

The object-glass of the great telescope was cast by M. Mantois, famous as the manufacturer of large lenses. The glass used was boiled and reboiled many times to get rid of all bubbles. Then it was run into a mould and allowed to cool very gradually. A whole month elapsed before the breaking of a mould, when the lens often proved to be cracked on the surface, owing to the exterior having cooled faster than the interior and parted company with it. At last, however, a perfect cast resulted.

M. Despret undertook the even more formidable task of casting the mirror at his works at Jeumont, North France. A special furnace and oven, capable of containing over fifteen tons of molten glass, had to be constructed. The mirror, 6½ feet in diameter and eleven inches thick, absorbed 3¾ tons of liquid glass; and so great was the difficulty of cooling it gradually, that out of the twenty casts eighteen were failures.

The rough lenses and mirror having been ground to approximate correctness in the ordinary way, there arose the question of polishing, which is generally done by one of the most sensitive and perfect instruments existing—the human hand. In this case, owing to the enormous size of the objects to be treated, hand work would not do. The mere hot touch of a workman would raise on the glass a tiny protuberance, which would be worn level with the rest of the surface by the polisher, and on the cooling of the part would leave a depression, only 1-75,000 of an inch deep, perhaps, but sufficient to produce distortion, and require that the lens should be ground down again, and the whole surface polished afresh.

M. Gautier therefore polished by machinery. It proved a very difficult process altogether, on account of frictional heating, the rise of temperature in the polishing room, and the presence of dust. To insure success it was found necessary to warm all the polishing machinery, and to keep it at a fixed temperature.

At the end of almost a year the polishing was finished, after the lenses and mirror had been subjected to the most searching tests, able to detect irregularities not exceeding 1-250,000 of an inch. M. Gautier applied to the mirror M. Foucault's test, which is worth mentioning. A point of light thrown by the mirror is focused through a telescope. The eyepiece is then moved inwards and outwards so as to throw the point out of focus. If the point becomes a luminous circle surrounded by concentric rings, the surface throwing the light point is perfectly plane or smooth. If, however, a pushing-in shows a vertical flattening of the point, and a pulling-out a horizontal flattening, that part is concave; if the reverse happens, convexity is the cause.

For the removal of the mirror from Jeumont to Paris a special train was engaged, and precautions were taken rivalling those by which travelling Royalty is guarded. The train ran at night without stopping, and at a constant pace, so that the vibration of the glass atoms might not vary. On arriving at Paris, the mirror was transferred to a ponderous waggon, and escorted by a body of men to the Exposition buildings. The huge object-lens received equally careful treatment.

The telescope was housed at the Exhibition in a long gallery pointing due north and south, the siderostat at the north end. At the other, the eyepiece, end, a large amphitheatre accommodated the public assembled to watch the projection of stellar or lunar images on to a screen thirty feet high, while a lecturer explained what was visible from time to time. The images of the sun and moon as they appeared at the primary focus in the eyepiece measured from twenty-one to twenty-two inches in diameter, and the screen projections were magnified from these about thirty times superficially.

The eyepiece section consisted of a short tube, of the same breadth as the main tube, resting on four wheels that travelled along rails. Special gearing moved this truck-like construction backwards and forwards to bring a sharp focus into the eyepiece or on to a photographic plate. Focusing was thus easy enough when once the desired object came in view; but the observer being unable to control the siderostat, 250 feet distant, had to telephone directions to an assistant stationed near the mirror whenever he wished to examine an object not in the field of vision.

By the courtesy of the proprietors of the *Strand*

Magazine we are allowed to quote M. Deloncle's own words describing his emotions on his first view through the giant telescope :—

"As is invariably the case, whenever an innovation that sets at nought old-established theories is brought forward, the prophecies of failure were many and loud, and I had more than a suspicion that my success would cause less satisfaction to others than to myself. Better than any one else I myself was cognisant of the unpropitious conditions in which my instrument had to work. The proximity of the river, the dust raised by hundreds of thousands of trampling feet, the trepidation of the soil, the working of the machinery, the changes of temperature, the glare from the thousands of electric lamps in close proximity—each of these circumstances, and many others of a more technical nature, which it would be tedious to enumerate, but which were no less important, would have been more than sufficient to make any astronomer despair of success even in observatories where all the surroundings are chosen with the utmost care.

"In regions pure of calm and serene air large new instruments take months, more often years, to regulate properly.

"In spite of everything, however, I still felt confident. Our calculations had been gone over again and again, and I could see nothing that in my opinion warranted the worst apprehensions of my kind critics.

"It was with ill-restrained impatience that I waited

for the first night when the moon should show herself in a suitable position for being observed; but the night arrived in due course.

"Everything was in readiness. The movable portion of the roof of the building had been slid back, and the mirror of the siderostat stood bared to the sky.

"In the dark, square chamber at the other end of the instrument, 200 feet away, into which the eyepiece of the instrument opened, I had taken my station with two or three friends. An attendant at the telephone stood waiting at my elbow to transmit my orders to his colleague in charge of the levers that regulated the siderostat and its mirror.

"The moon had risen now, and her silvery glory shone and sparkled in the mirror.

"'A right declension,' I ordered.

"The telephone bell rang in reply. 'Slowly, still slower; now to the left—enough; again a right declension—slower; stop now—very, very slowly.'

"On the ground-glass before our eyes the moon's image crept up from one corner until it had overspread the glass completely. And there we stood in the centre of Paris, examining the surface of our satellite with all its craters and valleys and bleak desolation.

"I had won the day."

PHOTOGRAPHING THE INVISIBLE.

Most of us are able to recognise when we see them shadowgraphs taken by the aid of the now famous X-rays. They generally represent some part of the structure of men, beasts, birds, or fishes. Very dark patches show the position of the bones, large and small; lighter patches the more solid muscles clinging to the bony framework; and outside these again are shadowy tracts corresponding to the thinnest and most transparent portions of the fleshy envelope.

In an age fruitful as this in scientific marvels, it often takes some considerable time for the public to grasp the full importance of a fresh discovery. But when, in 1896, it was announced that Professor Röntgen of Würzburg had actually taken photographs of the internal organs of still living creatures, and penetrated metal and other opaque substances with a new kind of ray, great interest was manifested throughout the civilised world. On the one hand the "new photography" seemed to upset popular ideas of opacity; on the other it savoured strongly of the black art, and, by its easy excursions through the human body, seemed likely to revolutionise medical and surgical methods. At first many strange ideas about the X-rays got afloat, attributing to them powers which would have surprised even their modest discoverer. It was also thought that the records were made in a camera after the ordinary manner of photography, but as a matter of fact Röntgen used neither lens nor camera, the operation being similar to that of casting a shadow on a wall by means of a lamp. In X-radiography a specially constructed electrically-lit glass tube takes the place of the lamp, and for the wall is substituted a sensitised plate. The object to be radiographed is merely inserted between them, its various parts offering varying resistance to the rays, so that the plate is affected unequally, and after exposure may be developed and printed from in the usual way. Photographs obtained by using X-rays are therefore properly called shadowgraphs or skiagraphs.

The discovery that has made Professor Röntgen famous is, like many great discoveries, based upon the labours of other men in the same field. Geissler, whose vacuum tubes are so well known for their striking colour effects, had already noticed that electric discharges sent through very much rarefied air or gases produced beautiful glows. Sir William Crookes, following the same line of research, and reducing with a Sprengel air-pump the internal pressure of the tubes to $\frac{1}{1000000}$ of an atmosphere, found that a luminous glow streamed from the cathode, or negative pole, in a straight line, heating and rendering phosphorescent anything that it met.

Crookes regarded the glow as composed of "radiant matter," and explained its existence as follows. The airy particles inside the tube, being few in number, are able to move about with far greater freedom than in the tightly packed atmosphere outside the tube. A particle, on reaching the cathode, is repelled violently by it in a straight line, to "bombard" another particle, the walls of the tube, or any object set up in its path, the sudden arrest of motion being converted into light and heat.

By means of special tubes he proved that the "radiant matter" could turn little vanes, and that the flow continued even when the terminals of the shocking-coil were *outside* the glass, thus meeting the contention of Puluj that the radiant matter was nothing more than small particles of platinum torn from the terminals. He also showed that, when intercepted, radiant matter cast a shadow, the intercepting object receiving the energy of the bombardment; but that when the obstruction was removed the hitherto sheltered part of the glass wall of the tube glowed with a brighter phosphorescence than the part which had become "tired" by prolonged bombardment. Experiments further revealed the fact that the shaft of "Cathode rays" could be deflected by a magnet from their course, and that they affected an ordinary photographic plate exposed to them.

In 1894 Lenard, a Hungarian, and pupil of the famous Hertz, fitted a Crookes' tube with a "window" of aluminium in its side replacing a part of the glass, and saw that the course of the rays could be traced through the outside air. From this it was evident that something else than matter must be present in the shaft of energy sent from the negative terminal of the tube, as there was no direct communication between the interior and the exterior of the tube to account for the external phosphorescence. Whatever was the nature of the rays he succeeded in making them penetrate and impress themselves on a sensitised plate enclosed in a metal box.

Then in 1896 came Röntgen's great discovery that the rays from a Crookes' tube, after traversing the *glass*, could pierce opaque matter. He covered the tube with thick cardboard, but found that it would still cast the shadows of books, cards, wood, metals, the human hand, &c., on to a photographic plate even at the distance of some feet. The rays would also pass through the wood, metal, or bones in course of time; but certain bodies, notably metals, offered a much greater resistance than others, such as wood, leather, and paper. Professor Röntgen crowned his efforts by showing that a skeleton could be "shadowgraphed" while its owner was still alive.

Naturally everybody wished to know not only what the rays could do, but what they were. Röntgen, not being able to identify them with any known rays, took refuge in the algebraical symbol of the unknown quantity and dubbed them X-rays. He discovered this much, however, that they were invisible to the eye under ordinary conditions; that they travelled in straight lines only, passing through a prism, water, or other refracting bodies without turning aside from their path; and that a magnet exerted no power over them. This last fact was sufficient of itself to prevent their confusion with the radiant matter "cathode rays" of the tube. Röntgen thought, nevertheless, that they might be the cathode rays transmuted in some manner by their passage through the glass, so as to resemble in their motion sound-waves, *i.e.* moving straight forward and not swaying from side to side in a series of zig-zags. The existence of such ether waves had for some time before been suspected by Lord Kelvin.

Other authorities have other theories. We may mention the view that X represents the ultra-violet rays of the spectrum, caused by vibrations of such extreme rapidity as to be imperceptible to the human eye, just as sounds of extremely high pitch are inaudible to the ear. This theory is to a certain extent upheld by the behaviour of the photographic plate, which is least affected by the colours of the spectrum at the red end and most by those at the violet end. A photographer is able to use red or orange light in his dark room because his plates cannot "see" them, though he can; whereas the reverse would be the case with X-rays. This ultra-violet theory claims for X-rays a rate of ether vibration of trillions of waves per second.

An alternative theory is to relegate the rays to the gap in the scale of ether-waves between heat-waves and light-waves. But this does not explain any more satisfactorily than the other the peculiar phenomenon of non-refraction.

The apparatus employed in X-photography consists of a Crookes' tube of a special type, a powerful shocking or induction coil, a fluorescent screen and photographic plates and appliances for developing, &c., besides a supply of high-pressure electricity derived from the main, a small dynamo or batteries.

A Crookes' tube is four to five inches in diameter, globular in its middle portion, but tapering away towards each end. Through one extremity is led a platinum wire, terminating in a saucer-shaped platinum plate an inch or so across. At the focus of this, the negative terminal, is fixed a platinum plate at an angle to the path of the rays so as to deflect them through the side of the tube. The positive terminal penetrates the glass at one side. The tube contains, as we have seen, a very tiny residue of air. If this were entirely exhausted the action of the tube would cease; so that some tubes are so arranged that when rarefaction becomes too high the passage of an electrical current through small bars of chemicals, whose ends project through the sides of the tube, liberates gas from the bars in sufficient quantity to render the tube active again.

When the Ruhmkorff induction coil is joined to the electric circuit a series of violent discharges of great rapidity occur between the tube terminals, resembling in their power the discharge of a Leyden jar, though for want of a dense atmosphere the brilliant spark has been replaced by a glow and brush-light in the tube. The coil is of large dimensions, capable of passing a spark across an air-gap of ten to twelve inches. It will perhaps increase the reader's respect for X-rays to learn that a coil of proper size contains upwards of thirteen miles of wire; though indeed this quantity is nothing in comparison with the 150 miles wound on the huge inductorium formerly exhibited at the London Polytechnic.

If we were invited to an X-ray demonstration we should find the operator and his apparatus in a darkened room. He turns on the current and the darkness is broken by a velvety glow surrounding the negative terminal, which gradually extends until the whole tube becomes clothed in a green phosphorescence. A sharply-defined line athwart the tube separates the shadowed part behind the receiving plate at the negative focus—now intensely hot—from that on which the reflected rays fall directly.

One of us is now invited to extend a hand close to the tube. The operator then holds on the near side of the hand his fluorescent screen, which is nothing more than a framework supporting a paper smeared on one side with platino-cyanide of barium, a chemical that, in common with several others, was discovered by Salvioni of Perugia to be sensitive to the rays and able to make them visible to the human eye. The value of the screen to the X-radiographer is that of the ground-glass plate to the ordinary photographer, as it allows him to see exactly what things are before the sensitised plate is brought into position, and in fact largely obviates the necessity for making a permanent record.

The screen shows clearly and in full detail all the bones of the hand—so clearly that one is almost irresistibly drawn to peep behind to see if a real hand is there. One of us now extends an arm and the screen shows us the *ulna* and the *radius* working round each other, now both visible, now one obscuring the other. On presenting the body to the course of the rays a remarkable shadow is cast on to the screen. The spinal column and the ribs; the action of the heart and lungs are seen quite distinctly. A deep breath causes the movement of a dark mass—the liver. There is no privacy in presence of the rays. The enlarged heart, the diseased lung, the ulcerated liver betrays itself at once. In a second of time the phosphorescent screen reveals what might baulk medical examination for months.

If a photographic slide containing a dry-plate be substituted for the focusing-screen, the rays soon penetrate any covering in which the plate may be wrapped to protect it from ordinary light rays. The process of taking a shadowgraph may therefore be conducted in broad daylight, which is under certain conditions a great advantage, though the sensitiveness of plates exposed to Röntgen rays entails special care being taken of them when they are not in use. In the early days of X-radiography an exposure of some minutes was necessary to secure a negative, but now, thanks to the improvements in the tubes, a few seconds is often sufficient.

The discovery of the X-rays is a great discovery, because it has done much to promote the noblest possible cause, the alleviation of human suffering. Not everybody will appreciate a more rapid mode of telegraphy, or a new method of spinning yarn, but the dullest intellect will give due credit to a scientific process that helps to save life and limb. Who among us is not liable to break an arm or leg, or suffer from internal injuries invisible to the eye? Who among us therefore should not be thankful on reflecting that, in event of such a mishap, the X-rays will be at hand to show just what the trouble is, how to deal with it, and how far the healing advances day by day? The X-ray apparatus is now as necessary for the proper equipment of a hospital as a camera for that of a photographic studio.

It is especially welcome in the hospitals which accompany an army into the field. Since May 1896 many a wounded soldier has had reason to bless the patient work that led to the discovery at Würzburg. The Greek war, the war in Cuba, the Tirah campaign, the Egyptian campaign, and the war in South Africa, have given a quick succession of fine opportunities for putting the new photography to the test. These is now small excuse for the useless and agonising probings that once added to the dangers and horrors of the military hospital. Even if the X-ray equipment, by reason of its weight, cannot conveniently be kept at the front of a rapidly moving army, it can be set up in the "advanced" or "base" hospitals, whither the wounded are sent after a first rough dressing of their injuries. The medical staff there subject their patients to the searching rays, are able to record the exact position of a bullet or shell-fragment, and the damage it has done; and by promptly removing the intruder to greatly lessen its power to harm.

The Röntgen ray has added to the surgeon's armoury a powerful weapon. Its possibilities are not yet fully known, but there can be no doubt that it marks a new epoch in surgical work. And for this reason Professor Röntgen deserves to rank with Harvey, the discoverer of the blood's circulation; with Jenner, the father of vaccination; and with Sir James Young Simpson, the first doctor to use chloroform as an anæsthetic.

PHOTOGRAPHY IN THE DARK.

Strange as it seems to take photographs with invisible rays, it is still stranger to be able to affect sensitised plates without apparently the presence of any kind of rays.

Professor W. J. Russell, Vice-President of the Royal Society of London, has discovered that many substances have the power of impressing their outlines automatically on a sensitive film, if the substance be placed in a dark cupboard in contact with, or very close to a dry-plate.

After some hours, or it may be days, development of the plate will reveal a distinct impression of the body in question. Dr. Russell experimented with wood, metal, leaves, drawings, printed matter, lace. Zinc proved to be an unusually active agent. A plate of the metal, highly polished and then ruled with patterns, had at the end of a few days imparted a record of every scratch and mark to the plate. And not only will zinc impress itself, but it affects substances which are not themselves active, throwing shadowgraphs on to the plate. This was demonstrated with samples of lace, laid between a plate and a small sheet of bright zinc; also with a skeleton leaf. It is curious that while the interposition of thin films of celluloid, gutta-percha, vegetable parchment, and gold-beater's skin—all inactive—between the zinc and the plate has no obstructive effect, a plate of thin glass counteracts the action of the zinc. Besides zinc, nickel, aluminium, pewter, lead, and tin among the metals influence a sensitised plate. Another totally different substance, printer's ink, has a similar power ; or at least some printer's ink, for Professor Russell found that different samples varied greatly in their effects. What is especially curious, the printed matter on *both sides* of a piece of newspaper appeared on the plate, and that the effect proceeded from the ink and not from any rays passing from beyond it is proved by the fact that the type came out *dark* in the development, whereas if it had been a case of shadowgraphy, the ink by intercepting rays would have produced *white* letters. Professor Russell has also shown that modern writing ink is incapable of producing an impression unaided, but that on the other hand paper written on a hundred years ago or a printed book centuries old will, with the help of zinc, yield a picture in which even faded and uncertain characters appear quite distinctly. This opens the way to a practical use of the discovery, in the deciphering of old and partly obliterated manuscripts.

A very interesting experiment may be made with that useful possession—a five-pound note. Place the note printed side next to the plate, and the printing appears dark ; but insert the note between a zinc sheet and the plate, its back being this time towards the sensitised surface, and the printing appears *white;* and the zinc, after contact with the printed side, will itself yield a picture of the inscription as though it had absorbed some virtue from the note!

As explanation of this paradoxical dark photography—or whatever it is—two theories may be advanced. The one—favoured by Professor Russell—is that all "active" substances give off *vapours* able to act on a photographic plate. In support of this may be urged the fact that the interposition of glass prevents the making of dark pictures. But on the other hand it must be remembered that celluloid and sheet-gelatine, also air-tight substances, are able to store up light and to give it out again. It is well known among photographers that to allow sunlight to fall on the inside of a camera is apt to have a "fogging" effect on a plate that is exposed in the camera afterwards, though the greatest care be taken to keep all external light from the plate. But here the glass again presents a difficulty, for if this were a case of reflected light, glass would evidently be *less* obstructive than opaque vegetable parchment or gutta-percha

SOLAR MOTORS.

ONE day George Stephenson and a friend stood watching a train drawn by one of his locomotives.

"What moves that train?" asked Stephenson.

"The engine," replied his friend.

"And what moves the engine?"

"The steam."

"And what produces the steam?"

"Coal."

"And what produces coal?"

This last query nonplussed his friend, and Stephenson himself replied, "The sun."

The "bottled sunshine" that drove the locomotive was stored up millions of years ago in the dense forests then covering the face of the globe. Every day vegetation was built by the sunbeams, and in the course of ages this growth was crushed into fossil form by the pressure of high-piled rock and débris. To-day we cast "black diamonds" into our grates and furnaces, to call out the warmth and power that is a legacy from a period long prior to the advent of fire-loving man, often forgetful of its real source.

We see the influence of the sun more directly in the motions of wind and water. Had not the sun's action deposited snow and rain on the uplands of the world, there would be no roaring waterfall, no rushing torrent, no smooth-flowing stream. But for the sun heating the atmosphere unequally, there would not be that rushing of cool air to replace hot which we know as wind.

We press Sol into our service when we burn fuel; our wind-mills and water-mills make him our slave. Of late years many prophets have arisen to warn us that we must not be too lavish of our coal; that the time is not so far distant, reckoning by centuries, when the coal-seams of the world will be worked out and leave our descendants destitute of what plays so important a part in modern life. Now, though waste is unpardonable, and the care for posterity praiseworthy, there really seems to be no good reason why we should alarm ourselves about the welfare of the people of the far future. Even if coal fails, the winds and the rivers will be there, and the huge unharnessed energy of the tides, and the sun himself is ready to answer appeals for help, if rightly shaped. He does not demand the prayers of Persian fire-worshippers, but rather the scientific gathering of his good gifts.

Place your hand on a roof lying square to the summer sun, and you will find it too hot for the touch. Concentrate a beam of sunshine through a small burning-glass. How fierce is the small glowing focal spot that makes us draw our hands suddenly away! Suppose now a large glass many feet across bending several square yards of sun rays to a point, and at that point a boiler. The boiler would develop steam, and the steam might be led into cylinders and forced to drudge for us.

Do many of us realise the enormous energy of a hot summer's day? The heat falling in the tropics on a single square foot of the earth's surface has been estimated as the equivalent of one-third of a horse-power. The force of Niagara itself would on this basis be matched by the sunshine streaming on to a square mile or so. A steamship might be propelled by the heat that scorches its decks.

For many centuries inventors have tried to utilise this huge waste power. We all know how, according to the story, Archimedes burnt up the Roman ships besieging his native town, Syracuse, by concentrating on them the sun heat cast from hundreds of mirrors. This story is less probable than interesting as a proof that the ancients were aware of the sun's power. The first genuine solar machine was the work of Ericsson, the builder of the *Monitor*. He focused sun heat on a boiler, which gave the equivalent of one horse-power for every hundred square feet of mirrors employed. This was not what engineers would call a "high efficiency," a great deal of heat being wasted, but it led the way to further improvements.

In America, especially in the dry, arid regions, where fuel is scarce and the sun shines pitilessly day after day, all the year round, sun-catchers of various types have been erected and worked successfully.

Dr. William Calver, of Washington, has built in the barren wastes of Arizona huge frames of mirrors, travelling on circular rails, so that they may be brought to face the sun at all hours between sunrise and sunset. Dr. Calver employs no less than 1600 mirrors. As each of these mirrors develops 10–15 degrees of heat it is obvious, after an appeal to simple arithmetic, that the united efforts of these reflectors should produce the tremendous temperature 16,000–24,000 degrees, which, expressed comparatively, means the paltry 90 degrees in the shade beneath which we grow restive multiplied hundreds of times. Hitherto the greatest known heat had been that of the arc of the electric lamp, in which the incandescent particles between pole and pole attain 6000 degrees Fahrenheit.

The combined effect of the burning mirrors is irresistible. They can, we are told, in a few moments reduce Russian iron to the consistency of warmed wax, though it mocks the heat of many blast-furnaces. They will bake bricks twenty times as rapidly as any kiln, and the bricks produced are not the friable blocks which a mason chips easily with his trowel, but bodies so hard as to scratch case-hardened steel.

There are at work in California sun-motors of another design. The reader must imagine a huge conical lamp-shade turned over on to its smaller end, its inner surface lined with nearly 1800 mirrors 2 feet long and 3 inches broad, the whole supported on a light iron framework, and he will have a good idea of the apparatus used on the Pasadena ostrich farm. The machine is arranged *in meridian*, that is, at right angles to the path of the sun, which it follows all day long by the agency of clockwork. In the focus of the mirrors is a boiler, 13 feet 6 inches long, coated with black, heat-absorbing substances. This boiler holds over 100 gallons of water, and being fed automatically will raise steam untended all the day through. The steam is led by pipes to an engine working a pump, capable of delivering 1400 gallons per minute.

The cheapness of the apparatus in proportion to its utility is so marked that, in regions where sunshine is almost perpetual, the solar motor will in time become as common as are windmills and factory chimneys elsewhere. If the heat falling on a few square yards of mirror lifts nearly 100,000 gallons of water an hour, there is indeed hope for the Sahara, the Persian Desert, Arabia, Mongolia, Mexico, Australia. That is to say, if the water under the earth be in these parts as plentiful as the sunshine above it. The effect of water on the most unpromising soil is marvellous. Already in Algeria the French have reclaimed thousands of square miles by scientific irrigation. In Australia huge artesian wells have made habitable for man and beast millions of acres that were before desert.

It is only a just retribution that the sun should be harnessed and compelled to draw water for tracts to which he has so long denied it. The sun-motor is only just entering on its useful career, and at present we can but dream of the great effects it may have on future civilisation. Yet its principle is so simple, so scientific, and so obvious, that it is easy to imagine it at no far distant date a dangerous rival to King Coal himself. To quarry coal from the bowels of the earth and transform it into heat, is to traverse two sides of a triangle, the third being to use the sunshine of the passing hour.

LIQUID AIR.

AMONG common phenomena few are more interesting than the changes undergone by the substance called water. Its usual form is a liquid. Under the influence of frost it becomes hard as iron, brittle as glass. At the touch of fire it passes into unsubstantial vapour.

This transformation illustrates the great principle that the form of every substance in the universe is a question of heat. A metal transported from the earth to the sun would first melt and then vaporise; while what we here know only as vapours would in the moon turn into liquids.

We notice that, as regards bulk, the most striking change is from liquid to gaseous form. In steam the atoms and molecules of water are endowed with enormous repulsive vigour. Each atom suddenly shows a huge distaste for the company of its neighbours, drives them off, and endeavours to occupy the largest possible amount of private space.

Now, though we are accustomed to see water-atoms thus stirred into an activity which gives us the giant steam as servant, it has probably fallen to the lot of but few of us to encounter certain gaseous substances so utterly deprived of their self-assertiveness as to collapse into a liquid mass, in which shape they are quite strangers to us. What gaseous body do we know better than the air we breathe? and what should we less expect to be reducible to the consistency of water? Yet science has lately brought prominently into notice that strange child of pressure and cold, Liquid Air; of which great things are prophesied, and about which many strange facts may be told.

Very likely our readers have sometimes noticed a porter uncoupling the air-tube between two railway carriages. He first turns off the tap at each end of the tube, and then by a twist disconnects a joint in the centre. At the moment of disconnection what appears to be a small cloud of steam issues from the joint. This is, however, the result of cold, not heat, the tube being full of highly-compressed air, which by its sudden expansion develops cold sufficient to freeze any particles of moisture in the surrounding air.

Keep this in mind, and also what happens when you inflate your cycle-tyre. The air-pump grows hotter and hotter as inflation proceeds: until at last, if of metal, it becomes uncomfortably warm. The heat is caused by the forcing together of air-molecules, and inasmuch as all force produces heat, your strength is transformed into warmth.

In these two operations, compression and expansion, we have the key to the creation of liquid air—the great power, as some say, of to-morrow.

By kind permission of] [*The Liquid Air Co.*

Suppose we take a volume of air and squeeze it into $\frac{1}{100}$ of its original space. The combativeness of the air-atoms is immensely increased. They pound each other frantically, and become very hot in the process. Now, by cooling the vessel in which they are, we rob them of their energy. They become quiet, but they are much closer than before. Then imagine that all of a sudden we let them loose again. The life is gone out of them, their heat has departed, and on separating they shiver grievously. In other words, the heat contained by the $\frac{1}{100}$ volume is suddenly compelled to "spread itself thin" over the whole volume: result—intense cold. And if this air be brought to bear upon a second vessel filled likewise with compressed air, the cold will be even more intense, until at last the air-atoms lose all their strength and collapse into a liquid.

Liquid air is no new thing. Who first made it is uncertain. The credit has been claimed for several people, among them Olzewski, a Pole, and Pictet, a Swiss. As a mere laboratory experiment the manufacture of liquid air in small quantities has been known for twenty years or more. The earlier process was one of terrific compression alone, actually forcing the air molecules by sheer strength into such close contact that their antagonism to one another was temporarily overcome. So expensive was the process that the first ounce of liquid air is estimated to have cost over £600!

In order to make liquid air an article of commerce

the most important condition was a wholesale decrease in cost of production. In 1857 C. W. Siemens took out a patent for making the liquid on what is known as the regenerative principle, whereby the compressed air is chilled by expanding a part of it. Professor Dewar—a scientist well known for his researches in the field of liquid gases—had in 1892 produced liquid air by a modification of the principle at comparatively small cost; and other inventors have since then still further reduced the expense, until at the present day there appears to be a prospect of liquid air becoming cheap enough to prove a dangerous rival to steam and electricity.

A company, known as the Liquid Air, Power and Automobile Company, has established large plants in America and England for the manufacture of the liquid on a commercial scale. The writer paid a visit to their depôt in Gillingham Street, London, where he was shown the process by Mr. Hans Knudsen, the inventor of much of the machinery there used. The reader will doubtless like to learn the "plain, unvarnished truth" about the creation of this peculiar liquid, and to hear of the freaks in which it indulges—if indeed those may be called freaks which are but obedience to the unchanging laws of Nature.

On entering the factory the first thing that strikes the eye and ear is the monstrous fifty horse-power gas-engine, pounding away with an energy that shakes the whole building. From its ponderous flywheels great leather belts pass to the compressors, three in number, by which the air, drawn from outside the building through special purifiers, is subjected to an increasing pressure. Three dials on the wall show exactly what is going on inside the compressors. The first stands at 90 lbs. to the square inch, the second at 500, and the third at 2200, or rather less than a ton pressure on the area of a penny! The pistons of the low-pressure compressor is ten inches in diameter, but that of the high pressure only two inches, or $\frac{1}{25}$ of the area, so great is the resistance to be overcome in the last stage of compression.

Now, if the cycle-pump heats our hands, it will be easily understood that the temperature of the compressors is very high. They are water-jacketed like the cylinders of a gas-engine, so that a circulating stream of cold water may absorb some of the heat. The compressed air is passed through spiral tubes winding through large tanks of water which fairly boils from the fierceness of the heat of compression.

When the air has been sufficiently cooled it is allowed to pass into a small chamber, expanding as it goes, and from the small into a larger chamber, where the cold of expansion becomes so acute that the air-molecules collapse into liquid, which collects in a special receptacle. Arrangements are made whereby any vapour rising from the liquid passes through a space outside the expansion-chambers, so that it helps to cool the incoming air and is not wasted.

The liquid-air tank is inside a great wooden case, carefully protected from the heat of the atmosphere by non-conducting substances. A tap being turned, a rush of vapour shoots out, soon followed by a clear, bluish liquid, which is the air we breathe in a fresh guise.

A quantity of it is collected in a saucepan. It simmers at first, and presently boils like water on a fire. The air-heat is *by comparison* so great that the liquid cannot resist it, and strives to regain its former condition.

You may dip your finger into the saucepan—if you withdraw it again quickly—without hurt. The cushion of air that your finger takes in with it protects you against harm—for a moment. But if you held it in the liquid for a couple of seconds you would be minus a digit. Pour a little over your coat sleeve. It flows harmlessly to the ground, where it suddenly expands into a cloud of chilly vapour.

Put some in a test tube and cork it up. The cork soon flies out with a report—the pressure of the boiling air drives it. Now watch the boiling process. The nitrogen being more volatile—as it boils at a lower temperature than oxygen—passes off first, leaving the pure, blue oxygen. The temperature of this liquid is over 312 degrees below zero (as far below the temperature of the air we breathe as the temperature of molten lead is above it!). A tumbler of liquid oxygen dipped into water is soon covered with a coating of ice, which can be detached from the tumbler and itself used as a cup to hold the liquid. If a bit cf steel wire be now twisted round a lighted match and the whole dipped into the cup, the steel flares fiercely and fuses into small pellets; which means that an operation requiring 3000 degrees Fahrenheit has been accomplished in a liquid 300 degrees below zero!

Liquid air has curious effects upon certain substances. It makes iron so brittle that a ladle immersed for a few moments may be crushed in the hands; but, curiously enough, it has a toughening effect on copper and brass. Meat, eggs, fruit, and all bodies containing water become hard as steel and as breakable as glass. Mercury is by it congealed to the consistency of iron; even alcohol, that can brave the utmost Arctic cold, succumbs to it. The writer was present when some thermometers, manufactured by Messrs. Negretti and Zambra, were tested with liquid air. The spirit in the tubes rapidly descended to 250 degrees below zero, then sank slowly, and at about 260 degrees froze and burst the bulb. The measuring of such extreme temperatures is a very difficult matter in consequence of the inability of spirit to withstand them, and special apparatus, registering cold by the shrinkage of metal, must be used for testing some liquid gases, notably liquid hydrogen, which is so much colder than liquid air that it actually freezes it into a solid ice form!

For handling and transporting liquid gases glass receptacles with a double skin from which all air has been exhausted are employed. The surrounding vacuum is so perfect an insulator that a "Dewar bulb" full of liquid air scarcely cools the hand, though the intervening space is less than an inch. This fact is hard to square with the assertion of scientific men that our atmosphere extends but a hundred or two miles from the earth's surface, and that the recesses of space are a vacuum. If it were so, how would heat reach us from the sun, ninety-two millions of miles away?

One use at least for liquid air is sufficiently obvious. As a refrigerating agent it is unequalled. Bulk for bulk its effect is of course far greater than that of ice; and it has this advantage over other freezing compounds, that whereas slow freezing has a destructive effect upon the tissues of meat and fruit, the instantaneous action of liquid air has no bad results when the thing frozen is thawed out again. The Liquid Air Company therefore proposes erecting depôts at large ports for supplying ships, to preserve the food, cool the cabins in the tropics, and, we hope, to alleviate some of the horrors of the stokehold.

Liquid air is already used in medical and surgical science. In surgery it is substituted for anæsthetics, deadening any part of the body on which an operation has to be performed. In fever hospitals, too, its cooling influence will be welcomed; and liquid oxygen takes the places of compressed oxygen for reviving the flickering flame of life. It will also prove invaluable for divers and submarine boats.

In combination with oil and charcoal liquid air, under the name of "oxyliquit," becomes a powerful blasting agent. Cartridges of paper filled with the oil and charcoal are provided with a firing primer. When everything is ready for the blasting the cartridges are dropped into a vessel full of liquid air, saturated, placed in position, and exploded. Mr. Knudsen assured the writer that oxyliquit is twice as powerful as nitro-glycerine, and its cost but one-third of that of the other explosive. It is also safer to handle, for in case of a misfire the cartridge becomes harmless in a few minutes, after the liquid air has evaporated.

But the greatest use will be found for liquid air when it exerts its force less violently. It is the result of power; its condition is abnormal; and its return to its ordinary state is accompanied by a great development of energy. If it be placed in a closed vessel it is capable of exerting a pressure of 12,000 lbs. to the square inch. Its return to atmospheric condition may be regulated by exposing it more or less to the heat of the atmosphere. So long as it remains liquid it represents so much *stored force*, like the electricity stored in accumulators. The Liquid Air Company have at their Gillingham Street depôt a neat little motor car worked by liquid air. A copper reservoir, carefully protected, is filled with the liquid, which is by mechanical means squirted into coils, in which it rapidly expands, and from them passes to the cylinders. A charge of eighteen gallons will move the car forty miles at an average pace of twelve miles an hour, without any of the noise, dirt, smell, or vapour inseparable from the employment of steam or petroleum. The speed of the car is regulated by the amount of liquid injected into the expansion coils.

We now come to the question of cost—the unromantic balance in which new discoveries are weighed and many found wanting. The storage of liquid air is feasible for long periods. (A large vacuum bulb filled and exposed to the atmosphere had some of the liquid still unevaporated at the end of twenty-two days.) But will it be too costly for ordinary practical purposes now served by steam and electricity? The managers of the Liquid Air Company, while deprecating extravagant prophecies about the future of their commodity, are nevertheless confident that it has "come to stay." With the small 50 horse-power plant its production costs upwards of one shilling a gallon, but with much larger plant of 1000 horse-power they calculate that the expenses will be covered and a profit left if they retail it at but one penny the gallon. This great reduction in cost arises from the economising of "waste energy." In the first place the power of expansion previous to the liquefaction of the compressed air will be utilised to work motors. Secondly, the heat of the cooling tanks will be turned to account, and even the "exhaust" of a motor would be cold enough for ordinary refrigerating. It is, of course, impossible to get more out of a thing than has been put into it; and liquid air will therefore not develop even as much power as was required to form it. But its handiness and cleanliness strongly recommend it for many purposes, as we have seen; and as soon as it is turned out in large quantities new uses will be found for it. Perhaps the day will come when liquid-air motors will replace the petrol car, and in every village we shall see hung out the sign, "Liquid air sold here." As the French say, "*Qui vivra verra.*"

HORSELESS CARRIAGES.

A BODY of enterprising Manchester merchants, in the year 1754, put on the road a "flying coach," which, according to their special advertisement, would, "however incredible it may appear, actually, barring accidents, arrive in London in four and a half days after leaving Manchester." According to the Lord Chancellor of the time such swift travelling was considered dangerous as well as wonderful—the condition of the roads might well make it so—and also injurious to health. "I was gravely advised," he says, "to stay a day in York on my journey between Edinburgh and London, as several passengers who had gone through without stopping had died of apoplexy from the rapidity of the motion."

As the coach took a fortnight to pass from the Scotch to the English capital, at an average pace of between three and four miles an hour, it is probable that the Chancellor's advisers would be very seriously indisposed by the mere sight of a motor-car whirling along in its attendant cloud of dust, could they be resuscitated for the purpose. And we, on the other hand, should prefer to get out and walk to "flying" at the safe speed of their mail coaches.

By kind permission of] [*The Speedwell Motor Co.*

Horseless Carriages

The improvement of highroads, and road-making generally, accelerated the rate of posting. In the first quarter of the nineteenth century an average of ten or even twelve miles an hour was maintained on the Bath Road. But that pace was considered inadequate when the era of the "iron horse" commenced, and the decay of stage-driving followed hard upon the growth of railways. What should have been the natural successor of the stage-coach was driven from the road by ill-advised legislation, which gave the railroads a monopoly of swift transport, which has but lately been removed.

The history of the steam-coach, steam-carriage, automobile, motor-car—to give it its successive names—is in a manner unique, showing as it does, instead of steady development of a practical means of locomotion, a sudden and decisive check to an invention worthy of far better treatment than it received. The compiler of even a short survey of the automobile's career is obliged to divide his account into two main portions, linked together by a few solitary engineering achievements.

The first period (1800–1836), will, without any desire to arrogate for England more than her due or to belittle the efforts of any other nations, be termed the English period, since in it England took the lead, and produced by far the greatest number of steam-carriages. The second (1870 to the present day) may, with equal justice, be styled the Continental period, as witnessing the great developments made in automobilism by French, German, Belgian, and American engineers: England, for reasons that will be presently noticed, being until quite recently too heavily handicapped to take a part in the advance.

Historical.—It is impossible to discover who made the first self-moving carriage. In the sixteenth century one Johann Haustach, a Nuremberg watch-maker, produced a vehicle that derived its motive power from coiled springs, and was in fact a large edition of our modern clockwork toys. About the same time the Dutch, and among them especially one Simon Stevin, fitted carriages with sails, and there are records of a steam-carriage as early as the same century.

But the first practical, and at least semi-successful, automobile driven by internal force was undoubtedly that of a Frenchman, Nicholas Joseph Cugnot, who justly merits the title of father of automobilism. His machine, which is to-day one of the most treasured exhibits in the Paris Museum of Arts and Crafts, consisted of a large carriage, having in front a pivoted platform bearing the machinery, and resting on a solid wheel, which propelled as well as steered the vehicle. The boiler, of stout riveted copper plates, had below it an enclosed furnace, from which the flames passed upwards through the water through a funnel. A couple of cylinders, provided with a simple reversing gear, worked a ratchet that communicated motion to the driving-wheel. This carriage did not travel beyond a very slow walking pace, and

Cugnot therefore added certain improvements, after which (1770) it reached the still very moderate speed of four miles an hour, and distinguished itself by charging and knocking down a wall, a feat that is said to have for a time deterred engineers from developing a seemingly dangerous mode of progression.

Ten years later Dallery built a steam car, and ran it in the streets of Amiens—we are not told with what success ; and before any further advance had been made with the automobile the French Revolution put a stop to all inventions of a peaceful character among our neighbours.

In England, however, steam had already been recognised as the coming power. Richard Trevethick, afterwards to become famous as a railroad engineer, built a steam motor in 1802, and actually drove it from Cambourne to Plymouth, a distance of ninety miles. But instead of following up this success, he forsook steam-carriages for the construction of locomotives, leaving his idea to be expanded by other men, who were convinced that a vehicle which could be driven over existing roads was preferable to one that was helpless when separated from smooth metal rails. Between the years 1800 and 1836 many steam vehicles for road traffic appeared from time to time, some, such as David Gordon's (propelled by metal legs pressing upon the ground), strangely unpractical, but the majority showing a steady improvement in mechanical design.

As it will be impossible, without writing a small

book, to name all the English constructors of this period, we must rest content with the mention of the leading pioneers of the new locomotion.

Sir Goldsworthy Gurney, an eminent chemist, did for mechanical road propulsion what George Stephenson was doing for railway development. He boldly spent large sums on experimental vehicles, which took the form of six-wheeled coaches. The earliest of these were fitted with legs as well as driving-wheels, since he thought that in difficult country wheels alone would not have sufficient grip. (A similar fallacy was responsible for the cogged wheels on the first railways.) But in the later types legs were abandoned as unnecessary. His coaches easily climbed the steepest hills round London, including Highgate Hill, though a thoughtful mathematician had proved by calculations that a steam-carriage, so far from mounting a gradient, could not, without violating all natural laws, so much as move itself on the level!

Having satisfied himself of their power, Gurney took his coaches further afield. In 1829 was published the first account of a motor trip made by him and three companions through Reading, Devizes, and Melksham. The pace was, we read, at first only about six miles an hour, including stoppages. They drove very carefully to avoid injury to the persons or feelings of the country folk; but at Melksham, where a fair was in progress, they had to face a shower of stones, hurled by a crowd of roughs at the instigation of some coaching postilions, who feared losing their livelihood if the new method of locomotion became general. Two of the tourists were severely hurt, and Gurney was obliged to take shelter in a brewery, where constables guarded his coach. On the return journey the party timed their movements so as to pass through Melksham while the inhabitants were all safely in bed.

The coach ran most satisfactorily, improving every mile. "Our pace was so rapid," wrote one of the company, "that the horses of the mail-cart which accompanied us were hard put to it to keep up with us. At the foot of Devizes Hill we met a coach and another vehicle, which stopped to see us mount this hill, an extremely steep one. We ascended it at a rapid rate. The coach and passengers, delighted at this unexpected sight, honoured us with shouts of applause."

In 1830 Messrs. Ogle and Summers completely beat the road record on a vehicle fitted with a tubular boiler. This car, put through its trials before a Special Commission of the House of Commons, attained the astonishing speed of 35 miles an hour on the level, and mounted a hill near Southampton at 24½ miles an hour. It worked at a boiler pressure of 250 lbs. to the square inch, and though not hung on springs, ran 800 miles without a breakdown. This performance appears all the more extraordinary when we remember the roads of that day were not generally as good as they are now, and that in the previous year Stephenson's "Rocket," running on rails, had not reached a higher velocity.

The report of the Parliamentary Commission on horseless carriages was most favourable. It urged that the steam-driven car was swifter and lighter than the mail-coaches ; better able to climb and descend hills ; safer ; more economical ; and less injurious to the roads ; and, in conclusion, that the heavy charges levied at the toll-gates (often twenty times those on horse vehicles) were nothing short of iniquitous.

As a result of this report, motor services, inaugurated by Walter Hancock, Braithwayte, and others, commenced between Paddington and the Bank, London and Greenwich, London and Windsor, London and Stratford. Already, in 1829, Sir Charles Dance had a steam-coach running between Cheltenham and Gloucester. In four months it ran 3500 miles and carried 3000 passengers, traversing the nine miles in three-quarters of an hour ; although narrow-minded landowners placed ridges of stone eighteen inches deep on the road by way of protest.

The most ambitious service of all was that between London and Birmingham, established in 1833 by Dr. Church. The rolling-stock consisted of a single very much decorated coach.

The success of the road-steamer seemed now assured, when a cloud appeared on the horizon. It had already been too successful. The railway companies were up in arms. They saw plainly that if once the roads were covered with vehicles able to transport the public at low fares quickly from door to door on existing thoroughfares, the construction of expensive railroads would be seriously hindered, if not altogether stopped. So, taking advantage of two motor accidents, the companies appealed to Parliament—full of horse-loving squires and manufacturers, who scented profit in the railways—and though scientific opinion ran strongly in favour of the steam-coach, a law was passed in 1836 which rendered the steamers harmless by robbing them of their speed. The fiat went forth that in future *every road locomotive should be preceded at a distance of a hundred yards by a man on foot carrying a red flag to warn passengers of its approach.* This law marks the end of the first period of automobilism as far as England is concerned. At one blow it crippled a great industry, deprived the community of a very valuable means of transport, and crushed the energies of many clever inventors who would soon, if we may judge by the rapid advances already made in construction, have brought the steam-carriage to a high pitch of perfection. In the very year in which they were suppressed the steam services had proved their efficiency and safety. Hancock's London service alone traversed 4200 miles without serious accident, and was so popular that the coaches were generally crowded. It is therefore hard to believe that these vehicles did not supply a public want, or that they were regarded by those who used them as in any way inferior to horse-drawn coaches. Yet ignorant prejudice drove them off the road for sixty years; and to-day it surprises many Englishmen to learn that what is generally considered a novel method of travelling was already fairly well developed in the time of their grandfathers.

Second Period (1870 onwards).—To follow the further development of the automobile we must cross the Channel once again. French invention had not been idle while Gurney and Hancock were building their coaches. In 1835 M. Dietz established a service between Versailles and Paris, and the same year M. D'Asda carried out some successful trials of his steam "diligence" under the eyes of Royalty. But we find that for the next thirty-five years the steam-carriage was not much improved, owing to want of capital among its French admirers. No Gurney appeared, ready to spend his thousands in experimenting; also, though the law left road locomotion unrestricted, the railways offered a determined opposition to a possibly dangerous rival. So that, on the whole, road transport by steam fared badly till after the terrible Franco-Prussian war, when inventors again took courage. M. Bollée, of Mans, built in 1873 a car, "l'Obéissante," which ran from Mans to Paris; and became the subject of allusions in popular songs and plays, while its name was held up as an example to the Paris ladies. Three years later he constructed a steam omnibus to carry fifty persons, and in 1878 exhibited a car that journeyed at the rate of eighteen miles an hour from Paris to Vienna, where it aroused great admiration.

After the year 1880 French engineers divided their attention between the heavy motor omnibus and light vehicles for pleasure parties. In 1884 MM. Bouton and Trépardoux, working conjointly with the Comte de Dion, produced a steam-driven tricycle, and in 1887 M. Serpollet followed suit with another, fitted with the peculiar form of steam generator that bears his name. Then came in 1890 a very important innovation, which has made automobilism what it now is. Gottlieb Daimler, a German engineer, introduced the *petrol gas-motor*. Its comparative lightness and simplicity at once stamped it as the thing for which makers were waiting. Petrol-driven vehicles were soon abroad in considerable numbers and varieties, but they did not attract public attention to any great extent until, in 1894, M. Pierre Giffard, an editor of the *Petit Journal*, organised a motor race from Paris to Rouen. The proprietors of the paper offered handsome prizes to the successful competitors. There were ten starters, some on steam, others on petrol cars. The race showed that, so far as stability went, Daimler's engine was the equal of the steam cylinder. The next year another race of a more ambitious character was held, the course being from Paris to Bordeaux and back. Subscriptions for prizes flowed in freely. Serpollet, de Dion, and Bollée prepared steam cars that should win back for steam its lost supremacy, while the petrol faction secretly built motors of a strength to relegate steam once and for all to a back place. Electricity, too, made a bid unsuccessfully for the prize in the Jeantaud car, a special train being engaged in advance to distribute charged accumulators over the route. The steamers broke down soon after the start, so that the petrol cars "walked over" and won a most decisive victory.

The interest roused in the race led the Comte de Dion to found the Automobile Club of France, which drew together all the enthusiastic admirers of the new locomotion. Automobilism now became a sport, a craze. The French, with their fine straight roads, and a not too deeply ingrained love of horse-flesh, gladly welcomed the flying car, despite its noisy and malodorous properties.

Orders flowed in so freely that the motor makers could not keep pace with the demand, or promise delivery within eighteen months. Rich men were therefore obliged to pay double prices if they could find any one willing to sell—a state of things that remains unto this day with certain makes of French cars. Poorer folks contented themselves with De Dion motor tricycles, which showed up so well in the 1896 Paris-Marseilles race; or with the neat little three-wheeled cars of M. Bollée. Motor racing became the topic of the hour. Journals were started for the sole purpose of recording the doings of motorists; and few newspapers of any popularity omitted a special column of motor news. Successive contests on the highroads at increasing speeds attracted increased interest. The black-goggled, fur-clad *chauffeur* who carried off the prizes found himself a hero.

In short, the hold which automobilism has over our neighbours may be gauged from the fact that in 1901 it was estimated that nearly a thousand motor cars assembled to see the sport on the Longchamps Course (the scene of that ultra-"horsey" event, the Grand Prix), and the real interest of the meet did not centre round horses of flesh and blood.

The French have not a monopoly of devotion to automobilism. The speedy motor car is too much in accord with the bustling spirit of the age; its delights too easily appreciated to be confined to one country. Allowing France the first place, America, Germany, and Belgium are not far behind in their addiction to the "sport," and even in Britain, partially freed since 1896 from the red-flag tyranny, thanks to the efforts of Sir David Salomons, there are most visible signs that the era of the horse is beginning its end.

Types of Car.

Automobiles may be classified according to the purpose they serve, according to their size and weight, or according to their motive power. We will first review them under the latter head.

A. Petrol.—The petrol motor, suitable alike for

large cars of 40 to 60 horse-power and for the small bicycle weighing 70 lbs. or so, at present undoubtedly occupies the first place in popular estimation on account of its comparative simplicity, which more than compensates certain defects that affect persons off the vehicle more than those on it—smell and noise.

The chief feature of the internal explosion motor is that at one operation it converts fuel directly into energy, by exploding it inside a cylinder. It is herein more economical than steam, which loses power while passing from the boiler to the driving-gear.

Petrol cycles and small cars have usually only one cylinder, but large vehicles carry two, three, and sometimes four cylinders. Four and more avoid that bugbear of rotary motion, "dead points," during which the momentum of the machinery alone is doing work; and for that reason the engines of racing cars are often quadrupled.

For the sake of simplicity we will describe the working of a single cylinder, leaving the reader to imagine it acting alone or in concert with others as he pleases.

In the first place the fuel, petrol, is a very inflammable distillation of petroleum: so ready to ignite that it must be most rigorously guarded from naked lights; so quick to evaporate that the receptacles containing it, if not quite airtight, will soon render it "stale" and unprofitable for motor driving.

The engine, to mention its most important parts, consists of a single-action cylinder (giving a thrust one way only); a heavy flywheel revolving in an airtight circular case, and connected to the piston by a hinged rod which converts the reciprocating movement of the piston into a rotary movement of the crank-shaft built in with the wheel; inlet and outlet valves; a carburettor for generating petrol gas, and a device to ignite the gas-and-air mixture in the cylinder.

The action of the engine is as follows: as the piston moves outwards in its first stroke it sucks through the inlet valve a quantity of mixed air and gas, the proportions of which are regulated by special taps. The stroke ended, the piston returns, compressing the mixture and rendering it more combustible. Just as the piston commences its second outward stroke an electric spark passed through the mixture mechanically ignites it, and creates an explosion, which drives the piston violently forwards. The second return forces the burnt gas through the exhaust-valve, which is lifted by cog-gear once in every two revolutions of the crank, into the "silencer." The cycle of operations is then repeated.

We see that during three-quarters of the "cycle"—the suction, compression, and expulsion—the work is performed entirely by the flywheel. It follows that a single-cylinder motor, to work at all, must rotate the wheel at a high rate. Once stopped, it can be restarted only by the action of the handle or pedals; a task often so unpleasant and laborious that the driver of a car, when he comes to rest for a short time only, disconnects his motor from the driving-gear and lets it throb away idly beneath him.

The means of igniting the gas in the cylinders may be either a Bunsen burner or an electric spark. Tube ignition is generally considered inferior to electrical because it does not permit "timing" of the explosion. Large cars are often fitted with both systems, so as to have one in reserve should the other break down.

Electrical ignition is most commonly produced by the aid of an intensity coil, which consists of an inner core of coarse insulated wire, called the primary coil; and an outer, or secondary coil, of very fine wire. A current passes at intervals, timed by a cam on the exhaust-valve gear working a make-and-break contact blade, from an accumulator through the primary coil, exciting by induction a current of much greater intensity in the secondary. The secondary is connected to a "sparking plug," which screws into the end of the cylinder, and carries two platinum points about $\frac{1}{32}$ of an inch apart. The secondary current leaps this little gap in the circuit, and the spark, being intensely hot, fires the compressed gas. Instead of accumulators a small dynamo, driven by the motor, is sometimes used to produce the primary current.

By moving a small lever, known as the "advancing

lever," the driver can control the time of explosion relatively to the compression of the gas, and raise or lower the speed of the motor.

The strokes of the petrol-driven cylinder are very rapid, varying from 1000 to 3000 a minute. The heat of very frequent explosions would soon make the cylinder too hot to work were not measures adopted to keep it cool. Small cylinders, such as are carried on motor cycles, are sufficiently cooled by a number of radiating ribs cast in a piece with the cylinder itself; but for large machines a water jacket or tank surrounding the cylinder is a necessity. Water is circulated through the jacket by means of a small centrifugal pump working off the driving gear, and through a coil of pipes fixed in the front of the car to catch the draught of progression. So long as the jacket and tubes are full of water the temperature of the cylinder cannot rise above boiling point.

Motion is transmitted from the motor to the driving-wheels by intermediate gear, which in cycles may be only a leather band or couple of cogs, but in cars is more or less complicated. Under the body of the car, running usually across it, is the countershaft, fitted at each end with a small cog which drives a chain passing also over much larger cogs fixed to the driving-wheels. The countershaft engages with the cylinder mechanism by a "friction-clutch," a couple of circular faces which can be pressed against one another by a lever. To start his car the driver allows the motor to obtain a considerable momentum, and then, using the friction lever, brings more and more stress on to the countershaft until the friction-clutch overcomes the inertia of the car and produces movement.

Gearing suitable for level stretches would not be sufficiently powerful for hills: the motor would slow and probably stop from want of momentum. A car is therefore fitted with changing gears, which give two or three speeds, the lower for ascents, the higher for the level: and on declines the friction-clutch can be released, allowing the car to "coast."

B. Steam Cars.—Though the petrol car has come to the front of late years it still has a powerful rival in the steam car. Inventors have made strenuous efforts to provide steam-engines light enough to be suitable for small pleasure cars. At present the Locomobile (American) and Serpollet (French) systems are increasing their popularity. The Locomobile, the cost of which (about £120) contrasts favourably with that of even the cheaper petrol cars, has a small multitubular boiler wound on the outside with two or three layers of piano wire, to render it safe at high pressures. As the boiler is placed under the seat it is only fit and proper that it should have a large margin of safety. The fuel, petrol, is passed through a specially designed burner, pierced with hundreds of fine holes arranged in circles round air inlets. The feed-supply to the burner is governed by a spring valve, which cuts off the petrol automatically as soon as the steam in the boiler reaches a certain pressure. The locomobile runs very evenly and smoothly, and with very little noise, a welcome change after the very audible explosion motor.

The Serpollet system is a peculiar method of generating steam. The boiler is merely a long coil of tubing, into which a small jet of water is squirted by a pump at every stroke of the cylinders. The steam is generated and used in a moment, and the speed of the machine is regulated by the amount of water thrown by the pumps. By an ingenious device the fuel supply is controlled in combination with the water supply, so that there may not be any undue waste in the burner.

C. *Electricity.*—Of electric cars there are many patterns, but at present they are not commercially so practical as the other two types. The great drawbacks to electrically-driven cars are the weight of the accumulators (which often scale nearly as much as all the rest of the vehicle), and the difficulty of getting them recharged when exhausted. We might add to these the rapidity with which the accumulators become worn out, and the consequent expense of renewal. T. A. Edison is reported at work on an accumulator which will surpass all hitherto constructed, having a much longer life, and weighing very much less, power for power. The longest continuous run ever made with electricity, 187 miles at Chicago, compares badly with the feat of a petrol car which on November 23, 1900, travelled a thousand miles on the Crystal Palace track in 48 hours 24 minutes, without a single stop. Successful attempts have been made by MM. Pieper and Jenatsky to combine the petrol and electric systems, by an arrangement which instead of wasting power in the cylinders when less speed is required, throws into action electric dynamos to store up energy, convertible, when needed, into motive power by reversing the dynamo into a motor. But the simple electric car will not be a universal favourite until either accumulators are so light that a very large store of electricity can be carried without inconvenient addition of weight, or until charging stations are erected all over the country at distances of fifty miles or so apart.

Whether steam will eventually get the upper hand of the petrol engine is at present uncertain. The steam car has the advantage over the gas-engine car in ease of starting, the delicate regulation of power, facility of reversing, absence of vibration, noise and smell, and freedom from complicated gears. On the other hand the petrol car has no boiler to get out of order or burst, no troublesome gauges requiring constant attention, and there is small difficulty about a supply of fuel. Petrol sufficient to give motive power for hundreds of miles can be carried if need be ; and as long as there is petrol on board the car is ready for work at a moment's notice. Judging by the number of the various types of vehicles actually

By kind permission of] [*The Liquid Air Co.*

at work we should say that while steam is best for heavy traction, the gas-engine is most often employed on pleasure cars.

D. Liquid Air will also have to be reckoned with as a motive power. At present it is only on its probation; but the writer has good authority for stating that before these words appear in print there will be on the roads a car driven by liquid air, and able to turn off eighty miles in the hour.

Manufacture.—As the English were the pioneers of the steam car, so are the Germans and French the chief manufacturers of the petrol car. While the hands of English manufacturers were tied by short-sighted legislation, continental nations were inventing and controlling valuable patents, so that even now our manufacturers are greatly handicapped. Large numbers of petrol cars are imported annually from France, Germany, and Belgium. Steam cars come chiefly from America and France. The former country sent us nearly 2000 vehicles in 1901. There are signs, however, that English engineers mean to make a determined effort to recover lost ground; and it is satisfactory to learn that in heavy steam vehicles, such as are turned out by Thorneycroft and Co., this country holds the lead. We will hope that in a few years we shall be exporters in turn.

Having glanced at the history and nature of the various types of car, it will be interesting to turn to a consideration of their travelling capacities. As we have seen, a steam omnibus attained, in 1830, a speed of no less than thirty-five miles an hour on what we should call bad roads. It is therefore to be expected that on good modern roads the latest types of car would be able to eclipse the records of seventy years ago. That such has indeed been the case is evident when we examine the performances of cars in races organised as tests of speed. France, with its straight, beautifully-kept, military roads, is the country *par excellence* for the *chauffeur*. One has only to glance at the map to see how the main highways conform to Euclid's dictum that a straight line is the shortest distance between any two points, *e.g.* between Rouen and Dieppe, where a park of artillery, well posted, could rake the road either way for miles.

The growth of speed in the French races is remarkable. In 1894 the winning car ran at a mean velocity of thirteen miles an hour; in 1895, of fifteen. The year 1898 witnessed a great advance to twenty-three miles, and the next year to thirty miles. But all these speeds paled before that of the Paris to Bordeaux race of 1901, in which the winner, M. Fournier, traversed the distance of 327½ miles at a rate of 53¾ miles per hour! The famous Sud express, running between the same cities, and considered the fastest long-distance express in the world, was beaten by a full hour. It is interesting to note that in the same races a motor bicycle, a Werner, weighing 80 lbs. or less, successfully accomplished the course at an average rate of nearly thirty miles an hour. The motor-car, after waiting seventy years, had had its revenge on the railways.

This was not the only occasion on which an express service showed up badly against its nimble rival of the roads. In June, 1901, the French and German authorities forgot old animosities in a common enthusiasm for the automobile, and organised a race between Paris and Berlin. It was to be a big affair, in which the cars of all nations should fight for the speed championship. Every possible precaution was taken to insure the safety of the competitors and the spectators. Flags of various colours and placards marked out the course, which lay through Rheims, Luxembourg, Coblentz, Frankfurt, Eisenach, Leipsic, and Potsdam to the German capital. About fifty towns and large villages were "neutralised"—that is to say, the competitors had to consume a certain time in traversing them. At the entrance to each neutralised zone a "control" was established. As soon as a competitor arrived, he must slow down, and a card on which was written the time of his arrival was handed to a "pilot," who cycled in front of the car to the other "control" at the farther end of the zone, from which, when the proper time had elapsed, the car was dismissed. Among other rules were: that no car should be pushed or pulled during the race by any one else than the passengers; that at the end of the day only a certain time should be allowed for cleaning and repairs; and that a limited number of persons, varying with the size of the car, should be permitted to handle it during that period.

A small army of automobile club representatives, besides thousands of police and soldiers, were distributed along the course to restrain the crowds of spectators. It was absolutely imperative that for vehicles propelled at a rate of from 50 to 60 miles an hour a clear path should be kept.

At dawn, on July 27th, 109 racing machines assembled at the Fort de Champigny, outside Paris, in readiness to start for Berlin. Just before half-past three, the first competitor received the signal; two minutes later the second; and then at short intervals for three hours the remaining 107, among whom was one lady, Mme. de Gast. At least 20,000 persons were present, even at that early hour, to give the racers a hearty farewell, and demonstrate the interest attaching in France to all things connected with automobilism.

Great excitement prevailed in Paris during the three days of the race. Every few minutes telegrams arrived from posts on the route telling how the competitors fared. The news showed that during the first stage at least a hard fight for the leading place was in progress. The French cracks, Fournier, Charron, De Knyff, Farman, and Girardot pressed hard on Hourgières, No. 2 at the starting-point. Fournier soon secured the lead, and those who remembered his remarkable driving in the Paris-Bordeaux race at once selected him as the winner.

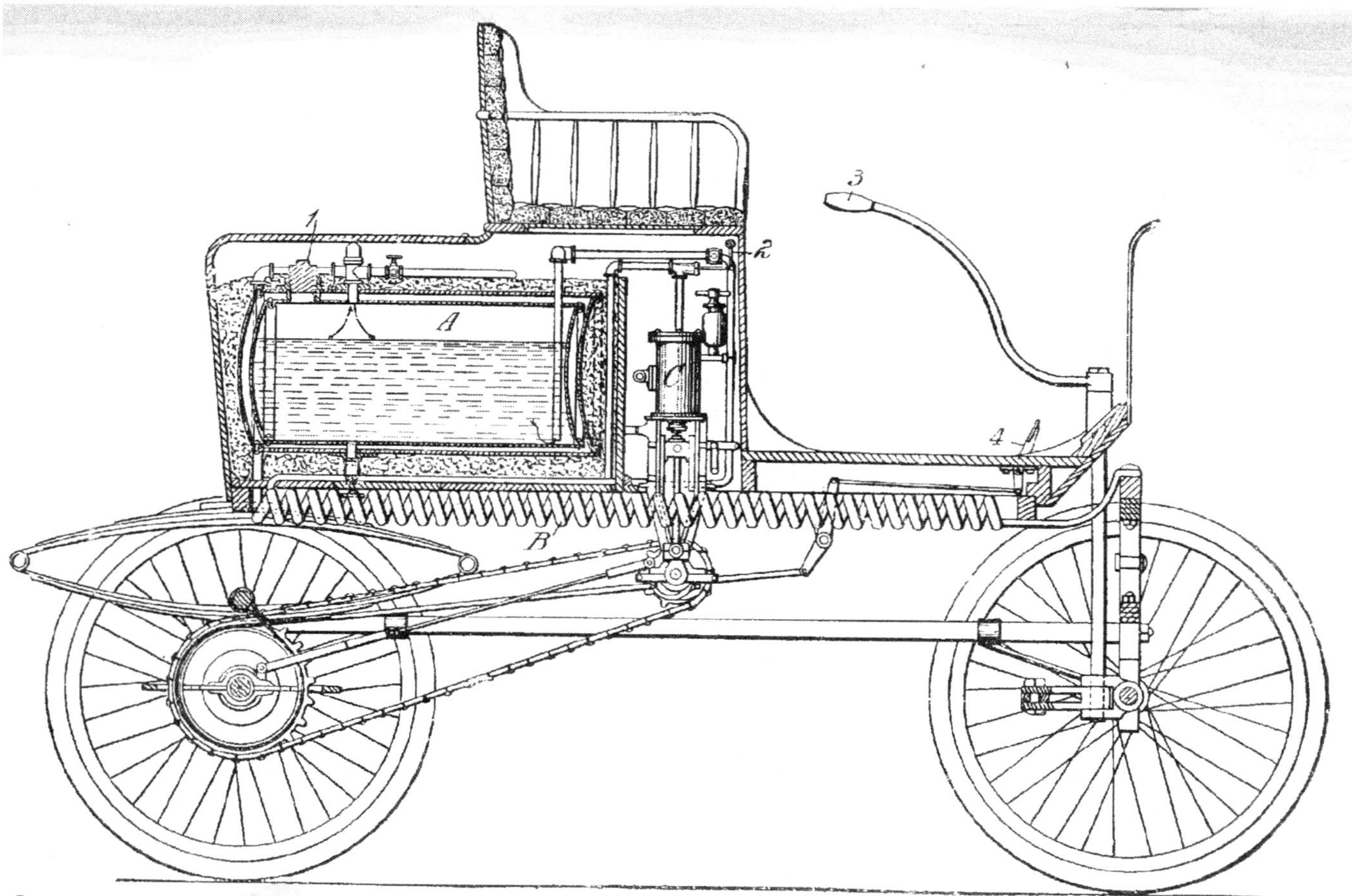

By kind permission of] [The Liquid Air Co.

Aix-la-Chapelle, 283 miles from Paris and the end of the first stage, was reached in 6 hours 28 minutes. Fournier first, De Knyff second by six minutes.

On the 28th the racing became furious. Several accidents occurred. Edge, driving the only English car, wrecked his machine on a culvert, the sharp curve of which flung the car into the air and broke its springs. Another ruined his chances by running over and killing a boy. But Fournier, Antony, De Knyff, and Girardot managed to avoid mishaps for that day, and covered the ground at a tremendous pace. At Dusseldorf Girardot won the lead from Fournier, to lose it again shortly. Antony, driving at a reckless speed, gained ground all day, and arrived a close second at Hanover, the halting-place, after a run averaging, in spite of bad roads and dangerous corners, no less than 54 miles an hour!

The *chauffeur* in such a race must indeed be a man of iron nerves. Through the great black goggles which shelter his face from the dust-laden hurricane set up by the speed he travels at he must keep a perpetual, piercingly keen watch. Though travelling at express speed, there are no signals to help him; he must be his own signalman as well as driver. He must mark every loose stone on the road, every inequality, every sudden rise or depression; he must calculate the curves at the corners and judge whether his mechanician, hanging out on the inward side, will enable a car to round a turn without slackening speed. His calculations and decisions must be made in the fraction of a second, for a moment's hesitation might be disaster. His driving must be furious and not reckless; the timid *chauffeur* will never win, the careless one will probably lose. His head must be cool although the car leaps beneath him like a wild thing, and the wind lashes his face. At least one well-tried driver found the mere mental strain too great to bear, and retired from the contest; and we may be sure that few of the competitors slept much during the nights of the race.

At four o'clock on the 29th Fournier started on the third stage, which witnessed another bout of fast travelling. It was now a struggle between him and Antony for first place. The pace rose at times to eighty miles an hour, a speed at which our fastest expresses seldom travel. Such a speed means huge risks, for stopping, even with the powerful brakes fitted to the large cars, would be a matter of a hundred yards or more. Not far from Hanover Antony met with an accident—Girardot now held second place; and Fournier finished an easy first. All along the route crowds had cheered him, and hurled bouquets into the car, and wished him good speed; but in Berlin the assembled populace went nearly frantic at his appearance. Fournier was overwhelmed with flowers, laurel wreaths, and other offerings; dukes, duchesses, and the great people of the land pressed for presentations; he was the hero of the hour.

Thus ended what may be termed a peaceful invasion of Germany by the French. Among other things it had shown that over an immense stretch of country, over roads in places bad as only German roads can be, the automobile was able to maintain an average speed superior to that of the express trains running between Paris and Berlin; also that, in spite of the large number of cars employed in the race, the accidents to the public were a negligible quantity. It should be mentioned that the actual time occupied by Fournier was 16 hours 5 minutes; that out of the 109 starters 47 reached Berlin; and that Osmont on a motor cycle finished only 3 hours and 10 minutes behind the winner.

In England such racing would be undesirable and impossible, owing to the crookedness of our roads. It would certainly not be permissible so long as the 12 miles an hour limit is observed. At the present time an agitation is on foot against this restriction, which, though reasonable enough among traffic and in towns, appears unjustifiable in open country. To help to convince the magisterial mind of the ease with which a car can be stopped, and therefore of its safety even at comparatively high speeds, trials were held on January 2, 1902, in Welbeck Park. The results showed that a car travelling at 13 miles an hour could be stopped dead in 4 yards; at 18 miles in 7 yards; at 20 miles in 13 yards; or in less than half the distance required to pull up a horse-vehicle driven at similar speeds.

Uses.—Ninety-five per cent of motors, at least in

England, are attached to pleasure vehicles, cycles, voiturettes, and large cars. On account of the costliness of cars motorists are far less numerous than cyclists ; but those people whose means enable them to indulge in automobilism find it extremely fascinating. Caricaturists have presented to us in plenty the gloomier incidents of motoring—the broken chain, the burst tyre, the "something gone wrong." It requires personal experience to understand how lightly these mishaps weigh against the exhilaration of movement, the rapid change of scene, the sensation of control over power which can whirl one along tirelessly at a pace altogether beyond the capacities of horseflesh. If proof were wanted of the motor car's popularity it will be seen in the unconventional dress of the *chauffeur*. The breeze set up by his rapid rush is such as would penetrate ordinary clothing ; he dons cumbrous fur cloaks. The dust is all-pervading at times ; he swathes himself in dust-proof overalls, and mounts large goggles edged with velvet, while a cap of semi-nautical cut tightly drawn down over neck and ears serves to protect those portions of his anatomy. The general effect is peculiarly unpicturesque ; but even the most artistically-minded driver is ready to sacrifice appearances to comfort and the proper enjoyment of his car.

In England the great grievance of motorists arises from the speed limit imposed by law. To restrict a powerful car to twelve miles an hour is like confining a thoroughbred to the paces of a broken-down cab horse. Careless drivińg is unpardonable, but its occasional existence scarcely justifies the intolerant attitude of the law towards motorists in general. It must, however, be granted in justice to the police that the *chauffeur*, from constant transgression of the law, becomes a bad judge of speed, and often travels at a far greater velocity than he is willing to admit.

The convenience of the motor car for many purposes is immense, especially for cross-country journeys, which may be made from door to door without the monotony or indirectness of railway travel. It bears the doctor swiftly on his rounds. It carries the business man from his country house to his office. It delivers goods for the merchant ; parcels for the post office.

In the warfare of the future, too, it will play its part, whether to drag heavy ordnance and stores, or to move commanding officers from point to point, or perform errands of mercy among the wounded. By the courtesy of the Locomobile Company we are permitted to append the testimony of Captain R. S. Walker, R.E., to the usefulness of a car during the great Boer War.

" Several months ago I noticed a locomobile car at Cape Town, and being struck with its simplicity and neatness, bought it and took it up country with me, with a view to making some tests with it over bad roads, &c. Its first trip was over a rough course round Pretoria, especially chosen to find out defects before taking it into regular use. Naturally, as the machine was not designed for this class of work, there were several. In about a month these had all been found out and remedied, and the car was in constant use, taking stores, &c., round the towns and forts. It also performed some very useful work in visiting out-stations, where searchlights were either installed or wanted, and in this way visited nearly all the bigger towns in the Transvaal. It was possible to go round all the likely positions for a searchlight in one day at every station, which frequently meant considerably over fifty miles of most indifferent roads—more than a single horse could have been expected to do—and the car generally carried two persons on these occasions. The car was also used as a tender to a searchlight plant, on a gun-carriage and limber, being utilised to fetch gasolene, carbons, water, &c. &c., and also to run the dynamo for charging the accumulators used for sparking, thus saving running the gasolene motor for this purpose. To do this the trail of the carriage, on which was the dynamo, was lowered on to the ground, the back of the car was pulled up, one wheel being supported on the dynamo pulley and the other clear of the ground, and two bolts were passed through the balance-gear to join it. On one occasion the car ran a 30 c.m. searchlight for an hour, driving a dynamo in this way. In consequence of this a trailer has been made to carry a dynamo and projector for searchlighting in the field, but so far this has not been so used. The trailer hooks into an eye, passing just behind the balance-gear. A Maxim, Colt, or small ammunition cart, &c., could be attached to this same eye.

"Undoubtedly the best piece of work done by the car so far was its trial trip with the trailer, when it blew up the mines at Klein Nek. These mines were laid some eight months previously, and had never been looked to in the interval. There had been several bad storms, the Boers and cattle had been frequently through the Nek, it had been on fire, and finally it was shelled with lyddite. The mines, eighteen in number, were found to be intact except two, which presumably had been fired off by the heat of the veldt fire. All the insulation was burnt off the wires, and the battery was useless. It had been anticipated that a dynamo exploder would be inadequate to fire these mines, so a 250 volt two h.p. motor, which happened to be in Pretoria, weighing about three or four hundredweight, was placed on the trailer ; a quarter of a mile of insulated cable, some testing gear, the kits of three men and their rations for three days, with a case of gasolene for the car, were also carried on the car and trailer, and the whole left Pretoria one morning and trekked to Rietfontein. Two of us were mounted, the third drove the car. At Rietfontein we halted for the night, and started next morning with an escort through Commando Nek, round the north of the Magaliesburg, to near Klein Nek, where the road had to be left, and the car taken across country through bush veldt. At the bottom the going was pretty easy; only a few bushes had to be charged down, and the grass, &c., rather wound itself around the wheels and chain. As the rise became steeper the stones became very large, and the car had to be taken along very gingerly to prevent breaking the wheels. A halt was made about a quarter of a mile from the top of the Nek, where the mines were. These were reconnoitered, and the wire, &c., was picked up; that portion which was useless was placed on top of the charges, and the remainder taken to the car. The dynamo was slid off the trailer, the car backed against it; one wheel was raised slightly and placed against the dynamo pulley, which was held up to it by a man using his rifle as a lever; the other wheel was on the ground with a stone under it. The balance gear being free, the dynamo was excited without the other wheel moving, and the load being on for a very short time (that is, from the time of touching lead on dynamo terminal to firing of the mine) no harm could come to the car. When all the leads had been joined to the dynamo the car was started, and after a short time, when it was judged to have excited, the second terminal was touched, a bang and clouds of dust resulted, and the Klein Nek Minefield had ceased to exist. The day was extremely hot, and the work had not been light, so the tea, made with water drawn direct from the boiler, which we were able to serve round to the main body of our escort was much appreciated, and washed down the surplus rations we dispensed with to accommodate the battery and wire, which we could not leave behind for the enemy.

"On the return journey we found this extra load too much for the car, and had great difficulty getting up to Commando Nek, frequently having to stop to get up steam, so these materials were left at the first blockhouse, and the journey home continued in comfort.

"A second night at Rietfontein gave us a rest after our labour, and the third afternoon saw us on our way back to Pretoria. As luck would have it, a sandstorm overtook the car, which had a lively time of it. The storm began by blowing the sole occupant's hat off, so, the two mounted men being a long way behind, he shut off steam and chased his hat. In the meantime the wind increased, and the car sailed off 'on its own,' and was only just caught in time to save a smash. Luckily the gale was in the right direction, for the fire was blown out, and it was impossible to light a match in the open. The car sailed into a poort on the outskirts of Pretoria, got a tow from a friendly cart through it, and then steamed home after the fire had been relit.

"The load carried on this occasion (without the battery, &c.) must have been at least five hundredweight besides the driver, which, considering the car is designed to carry two on ordinary roads, and that these roads were by no means ordinary, was no mean feat. The car, as ordinarily equipped for trekking, carries the following: Blankets, waterproof sheets, &c., for two men; four planks for crossing ditches, bogs, stones, &c.; all necessary tools and spare parts, a day's supply of gasolene, a couple of telephones, and one mile of wire. In addition, on the trailer, if used for searchlighting: One 30 c.m. projector, one automatic lamp for projector, one dynamo (100 volts 20 ampères), two short lengths of wire, two pairs of carbons, tools, &c. This trailer would normally be carried with the baggage, and only picked up by the car when wanted as a light; that is, as a rule, after arriving in camp, when a good many other things could be left behind."

Perhaps the most useful work in store for the motor is to help relieve the congestion of our large towns and to restore to the country some of its lost prosperity. There is no stronger inducement to make people live in the country than rapid and safe means of locomotion, whether public or private. At present the slow and congested suburban train services on some sides of London consume as much time as would suffice a motor car to cover twice or three times the distance. We must welcome any form of travel which will tend to restore the balance between country and town by enabling the worker to live far from his work. The gain to the health of the nation arising from more even distribution of population would be inestimable.

A world's tour is among the latest projects in automobilism. On April 29, 1902, Dr. Lehwess and nine friends started from Hyde Park Corner for a nine months' tour on three vehicles, the largest of them a luxuriously appointed 24 horse-power caravan, built to accommodate four persons. Their route lies through France, Germany, Russia, Siberia, China, Japan, and the United States.

HIGH-SPEED RAILWAYS

A CENTURY ago a long journey was considered an exploit, and an exploit to be carried through as quickly as possible on account of the dangers of the road and the generally uncomfortable conditions of travel. To-day, though our express speed is many times greater than that of the lumbering coaches, our carriages comparatively luxurious, the risk practically nil, the same wish lurks in the breast of ninety-nine out of a hundred railway passengers—to spend the shortest time in the train that the time-table permits of. Time differences that to our grandfathers would have appeared trifling are now matters of sufficient importance to make rival railway companies anxious to clip a few minutes off a 100-mile "run" simply because their passengers appreciate a few minutes' less confinement to the cars.

During the last fifty years the highest express speeds have not materially altered. The Great Western Company in its early days ran trains from Paddington to Slough, 18 miles, in 15½ minutes, or at an average pace of 69½ miles an hour.

On turning to the present regular express services

of the world we find America heading the list with a 50-mile run between Atlantic City and Camden, covered at the average speed of 68 miles an hour; Britain second with a 33-mile run between Forfar and Perth at 59 miles; and France a good third with an hourly average of rather more than 58 miles between Les Aubrais and S. Pierre des Corps. These runs are longer than that on the Great Western Railway referred to above (which now occupies twenty-four minutes), but their average velocity is less. What is the cause of this decrease of speed? Not want of power in modern engines; at times our trains attain a rate of 80 miles an hour, and in America a mile has been turned off in the astonishing time of thirty-two seconds. We should rather seek it in the need for economy and in the physical limitations imposed by the present system of plate-laying and railroad engineering. An average speed of ninety miles an hour would, as things now stand, be too wasteful of coal and too injurious to the rolling-stock to yield profit to the proprietors of a line; and, except in certain districts, would prove perilous for the passengers. Before our services can be much improved the steam locomotive must be supplanted by some other application of motive power, and the metals be laid in a manner which will make special provision for extreme speed.

Since rapid transit is as much a matter of commercial importance as of mere personal convenience it must not be supposed that an average of 50 miles an hour will continue to meet the needs of travellers. Already practical experiments have been made with two systems that promise us an ordinary speed of 100 miles an hour and an express speed considerably higher.

One of these, the monorail or single-rail system, will be employed on a railroad projected between Manchester and Liverpool. At present passengers between these two cities—the first to be connected by a railroad of any kind—enjoy the choice of three rival services covering 34½ miles in three-quarters of an hour. An eminent engineer, Mr. F. B. Behr, now wishes to add a fourth of unprecedented swiftness. Parliamentary powers have been secured for a line starting from Deansgate, Manchester, and terminating behind the pro-Cathedral in Liverpool, on which single cars will run every ten minutes at a velocity of 110 miles an hour.

A monorail track presents a rather curious appearance. The ordinary parallel metals are replaced by a single rail carried on the summit of A-shaped trestles, the legs of which are firmly bolted to sleepers. A monorail car is divided lengthwise by a gap that allows it to hang half on either side of the trestles and clear them as it moves. The double flanged wheels to carry and drive the car are placed at the apex of the gap. As the "centre of gravity" is below the rail the car cannot turn over, even when travelling round a sharp curve.

The first railway built on this system was constructed by M. Charles Lartigue, a French engineer, in Algeria, a district where an ordinary two-rail track is often blocked by severe sand-storms. He derived the idea of balancing trucks over an elevated rail from caravans of camels laden on each flank with large bags. The camel, or rather its legs, was transformed by the engineer's eye into iron trestles, while its burden became a car. A line built as a result of this observation, and supplied with mules as tractive power, has for many years played an important part in the esparto-grass trade of Algeria.

In 1886 Mr. Behr decided that by applying steam to M. Lartigue's system he could make it successful as a means of transporting passengers and goods. He accordingly set up in Tothill Fields, Westminster, on the site of the new Roman Catholic Cathedral, a miniature railway which during nine months of use showed that the monorail would be practical for heavy traffic, safe, and more cheaply maintained than the ordinary double-metal railway. The train travelled easily round very sharp curves and climbed unusually steep gradients without slipping.

Mr. Behr was encouraged to construct a monorail in Kerry, between Listowel, a country town famous for its butter, and Ballybunion, a seaside resort of increasing popularity. The line, opened on the 28th of February 1888, has worked most satisfactorily ever since, without injury to a single employé or passenger.

On each side of the trestles, two feet below the apex, run two guide-rails, against which press small wheels attached to the carriages to prevent undue oscillation and "tipping" round curves. At the three stations there are, instead of points, turn-tables or switches on to which the train runs for transference to sidings.

Road traffic crosses the rail on drawbridges, which are very easily worked, and which automatically set signals against the train. The bridges are in two portions and act on the principle of the Tower Bridge, each half falling from a perpendicular position towards the centre, where the ends rest on the rail, specially strengthened at that spot to carry the extra weight. The locomotive is a twin affair; has two boilers, two funnels, two fireboxes; can draw 240 tons on the level at fifteen miles an hour, and when running light travels a mile in two minutes. The carriages, 18 feet long and carrying twelve passengers on each side, are divided longitudinally into two parts. Trucks too are used, mainly for the transport of sand—of which each carries three tons—from Ballybunion to Listowel: and in the centre of each train is a queer-looking vehicle serving as a bridge for any one who may wish to cross from one side of the rail to the other.

Several lines on the pattern of the Ballybunion-Listowel have been erected in different countries. Mr. Behr was not satisfied with his first success, however, and determined to develop the monorail in the direction of fast travelling, which he thought would be most easily attained on a trestle-track. In 1893 he startled engineers by proposing a Lightning-Express service, to transport passengers at a velocity of 120 miles an hour. But the project seemed too ideal to tempt money from the pockets of financiers, and Mr. Behr soon saw that if a high-speed railway after his own heart were constructed it must be at his own expense. He had sufficient faith in his scheme to spend £40,000 on an experimental track at the Brussels Exhibition of 1897. The exhibition was in two parts, connected by an electric railway, the one at the capital, the other at Tervueren, seven miles away. Mr. Behr built his line at Tervueren.

The greatest difficulty he encountered in its construction arose from the opposition of landowners, mostly small peasant proprietors, who were anxious to make advantageous terms before they would hear of the rail passing through their lands. Until he had concluded two hundred separate contracts, by most of which the peasants benefited, his platelayers could not get to work. Apart from this opposition the conditions were not favourable. He was obliged to bridge no less than ten roads; and the contour of the country necessitated steep gradients, sharp curves, long cuttings and embankments, the last of which, owing to a wet summer, could not be trusted to stand quite firm. The track was doubled for three miles, passing at each end round a curve of 1600 feet radius.

The rail ran about four feet above the track on trestles bolted down to steel sleepers resting on ordinary ballast. The carriage—Mr. Behr used but one on this line—weighed 68 tons, was 59 feet long and 11 feet wide, and could accommodate one hundred persons. It was handsomely fitted up, and had specially-shaped seats which neutralised the effect of rounding curves, and ended fore and aft in a point, to overcome the wind-resistance in front and the air-suction behind. Sixteen pairs of wheels on the under side of the carriage engaged with the two pairs of guide rails flanking the trestles, and eight large double-flanged wheels, 4½ feet in diameter, carried the weight of the vehicle. The inner four of these wheels were driven by as many powerful electric motors contained, along with the guiding mechanism, in the lower part of the car. The motors picked up current from the centre rail and from another steel rail laid along the sleepers on porcelain insulators.

The top speed attained was about ninety miles an hour. On the close of the Exhibition special experiments were made at the request of the Belgian, French, and Russian Governments, with results that proved that the Behr system deserved a trial on a much larger scale.

The engineer accordingly approached the British Government with a Bill for the construction of a high-speed line between Liverpool and Manchester. A Committee of the House of Commons rejected the Bill on representations of the Salford Corporation. The Committee had to admit, nevertheless, that the evidence called was mainly in favour of the system; and, the plans of the rail having been altered to meet certain objections, Parliamentary consent was obtained to commence operations when the necessary capital had been subscribed. In a few years the great seaport and the great cotton town will probably be within a few minutes' run of each other.

A question that naturally arises in the mind of the reader is this: could the cars, when travelling at 110 miles an hour, be arrested quickly enough to avoid an accident if anything got on the line?

The Westinghouse air-brake has a retarding force of three miles a second. It would therefore arrest a train travelling at 110 miles per hour in 37 seconds, or 995 yards. Mr. Behr proposes to reinforce the Westinghouse with an electric brake, composed of magnets 18 inches long, exerting on the guide rails by means of current generated by the reversed motors an attractive force of 200 lbs. per square inch. One great advantage of this brake is that its efficiency is greatest when the speed of the train is highest and when it is most needed. The united brakes are expected to stop the car in half the distance of the Westinghouse alone; but they would not both be applied except in emergencies. Under ordinary conditions the slowing of a car would take place only at the termini, where the line ascends gradients into the stations. There would, however, be small chance of collisions, the railway being securely fenced off throughout its entire length, and free from level crossings, drawbridges and points. Furthermore, each train would be its own signalman. Suppose the total 34½ miles divided into "block" lengths of 7 miles. On leaving a terminus the train sets a danger signal behind it; at 7 miles it sets another, and at 14 miles releases the first signal. So that the driver of a car would have at least 7 miles to slow down in after seeing the signals against him. In case of fog he would consult a miniature signal in his cabin working electrically in unison with the large semaphores.

The Manchester-Liverpool rail will be reserved for express traffic only. Mr. Behr does not believe in mixing speeds, and considers it one of the advantages of his system that slow cars and waggons of the ordinary two-rail type cannot be run on the monorail; because if they could managers might be tempted to place them there.

A train will consist of a single vehicle for forty, fifty, or seventy passengers, as the occasion requires. It is calculated that an average of twelve passengers at one penny per mile would pay all the expenses of running a car.

Mr. Behr maintains that monorails can be constructed far more cheaply than the two-rail, because they permit sharper curves, and thereby save a lot of cutting and embankment; and also because the monorail itself, when trestles and rail are specially strengthened, can serve as its own bridge across roads, valleys and rivers.

Though the single-rail has come to the front of late, it must not be supposed that the two-rail track is for ever doomed to moderate speeds only. German engineers have built an electric two-rail military line between Berlin and Zossen, seventeen miles long, over which cars have been run at a hundred miles an hour. The line has very gradual curves, and in this respect is inferior to the more sinuous monorail. Its chief virtue is the method of applying motive power—a method common to both systems.

The steam locomotive creates its own motive force, and as long as it has fuel and water can act independently. The electric locomotive, on the other hand, receives its power through metallic conductors from some central station. Should the current fail all the traffic on the line is suspended. So far the advantage rests with the steamer. But as regards economy the superiority of the current is obvious. In the electric systems under consideration—the monorail and Berlin-Zossen—there is less weight per passenger to be shifted, since a comparatively light motor supersedes the heavy locomotive. The cars running singly, bridges and track are subjected to less strain, and cost less to keep in repair. But the greatest saving of all is made in fuel. A steam locomotive uses coal wastefully, sending a lot of latent power up the funnel in the shape of half-expanded steam. Want of space prevents the designer from fitting to a moving engine the more economical machinery to be found in the central power-station of an electric railway, which may be so situated—by the water-side or near a pit's mouth—that fuel can be brought to it at a trifling cost. Not only is the expense of distributing coal over the system avoided, but the coal itself, by the help of triple and quadruple expansion engines should yield two or three times as much energy per ton as is developed in a locomotive furnace.

Many schemes are afoot for the construction of high-speed railways. The South-Eastern plans a monorail between Cannon Street and Charing Cross to avoid the delay that at present occurs in passing from one station to the other. We hear also of a projected railway from London to Brighton, which will reduce the journey to half-an-hour; and of another to connect Dover and London. It has even been suggested to establish monorails on existing tracks for fast passenger traffic, the expresses passing overhead, the slow and goods trains plodding along the double metals below.

But the most ambitious programme of all comes from the land of the Czar. M. Hippolyte Romanoff, a Russian engineer, proposes to unite St. Petersburg and Moscow by a line that shall cover the intervening 600 miles in three hours—an improvement of ten hours on the present time-tables. He will use T-shaped supports to carry two rails, one on each arm, from which the cars are to hang. The line being thus double will permit the cars—some four hundred in number—to run to and fro continuously, urged on their way by current picked up from overhead wires. Each car is to have twelve wheels, four drivers arranged vertically and eight horizontally, to prevent derailment by gripping the rail on either side. The stoppage or breakdown of any car will automatically stop those following by cutting off the current.

In the early days of railway history lines were projected in all directions, regardless of the fact whether they would be of any use or not. Many of these lines began, where they ended, on paper. And now that the high-speed question has cropped up, we must not believe that every projected electric railway will be built, though of the ultimate prevalence of far higher speeds than we now enjoy there can be no doubt.

The following is a time-table drawn up on the two-mile-per-minute basis.

A man leaving London at 10 A.M. would reach—

Brighton . . .	50 miles away, at			10.25 A.M.
Portsmouth . .	60	,,	,,	10.30 A.M.
Birmingham . .	113	,,	,,	10.57 A.M.
Leeds	188	,,	,,	11.34 A.M.
Liverpool . .	202	,,	,,	11.41 A.M.
Holyhead . .	262	,,	,,	12.11 P.M.
Edinburgh . .	400	,,	,,	1.20 P.M.
Aberdeen . .	540	,,	,,	2.30 P.M.

What would become of the records established in the "Race to the North" and by American "fliers"?

And what about continental travel?

Assuming that the Channel Tunnel is built—perhaps a rather large assumption—Paris will be at our very doors. A commercial traveller will step into the lightning express at London, sleep for two hours and twenty-four minutes and wake, refreshed, to find the blue-smocked Paris porters bawling in his ear. Or even if we prefer to keep the "little silver streak" free from subterranean burrows, he will be able to catch the swift turbine steamers—of which more anon—at Dover, slip across to Calais in half-an-hour, and be at the French capital within four hours of quitting London. And if M. Romanoff's standard be reached, the latest thing in hats despatched from

Paris at noon may be worn in Regent Street before two o'clock.

Such speeds would indeed produce a revolution in travelling comparable to the substitution of the steam locomotive for the stage coach. As has been pithily said, the effect of steam was to make the bulk of population travel, whereas they had never travelled before, but the effect of the electric railway will be to make those who travel travel much further and much oftener.

SEA EXPRESSES.

In the year 1836 the *Sirius*, a paddle-wheel vessel, crossed the Atlantic from Cork Harbour to New York in nineteen days. Contrast with the first steam-passage from the Old World to the New a return journey of the *Deutschland*, a North German liner, which in 1900 averaged over twenty-seven miles an hour between Sandy Hook and Plymouth, accomplishing the whole distance in the record time of five days seven hours thirty-eight minutes.

This growth of speed is even more remarkable than might appear from the mere comparison of figures. A body moving through water is so retarded by the inertia and friction of the fluid that to quicken its pace a force quite out of proportion to the increase of velocity must be exerted. The proportion cannot be reduced to an exact formula, but under certain conditions the speed and the power required advance in the ratio of their cubes; that is, to double a given rate of progress eight times the driving-power is needed; to treble it, twenty-seven times.

The mechanism of our fast modern vessels is in every way as superior to that which moved the

Sirius, as the beautifully-adjusted safety cycle is to the clumsy "boneshaker" which passed for a wonder among our grandfathers. A great improvement has also taken place in the art of building ships on lines calculated to offer least resistance to the water, and at the same time afford a good carrying capacity. The big liner, with its knife-edged bow and tapering hull, is by its shape alone eloquent of the high speed which has earned it the title of Ocean Greyhound; and as for the fastest craft of all, torpedo-destroyers, their designers seem to have kept in mind Euclid's definition of a line-length without breadth. But whatever its shape, boat or ship may not shake itself free of Nature's laws. Her restraining hand lies heavy upon it. A single man paddles his weight-carrying dinghy along easily at four miles an hour; eight men in the pink of condition, after arduous training, cannot urge their light, slender, racing shell more than twelve miles in the same time.

To understand how mail boats and "destroyers" attain, despite the enormous resistance of water, velocities that would shame many a train-service, we have only to visit the stokeholds and engine-rooms of our sea expresses and note the many devices of marine engineers by which fuel is converted into speed.

We enter the stokehold through air-locks, closing one door before we can open the other, and find ourselves among sweating, grimy men, stripped to the waist. As though life itself depended upon it they shovel coal into the rapacious maws of furnaces glowing with a dazzling glare under the "forced-draught" sent down into the hold by the fans whirling overhead. The ignited furnace gases on their way to the outer air surrender a portion of their heat to the water from which they are separated by a skin of steel. Two kinds of marine boiler are used—the fire-tube and the water-tube. In fire-tube boilers the fire passes inside the tubes and the water outside; in water-tube boilers the reverse is the case, the crown and sides of the furnace being composed of sheaves of small parallel pipes through which water circulates. The latter type, as generating steam very quickly, and being able to bear very high pressures, is most often found in war vessels of all kinds. The quality sought in boiler construction is that the heating surface should be very large in proportion to the quantity of water to be heated. Special coal, anthracite or Welsh, is used in the navy on account of its great heating power and freedom from smoke; experiments have also been made with crude petroleum, or liquid fuel, which can be more quickly put on board than coal, requires the services of fewer stokers, and may be stored in odd corners unavailable as coal bunkers.

From the boiler the steam passes to the engine-room, whither we will follow it. We are now in a bewildering maze of clanking, whirling machinery;

our noses offended by the reek of oil, our ears deafened by the uproar of the moving metal, our eyes wearied by the efforts to follow the motions of the cranks and rods.

On either side of us is ranged a series of three or perhaps even four cylinders, of increasing size. The smallest, known as the high-pressure cylinder, receives steam direct from the boiler. It takes in through a slide-valve a supply for a stroke ; its piston is driven from end to end ; the piston-rod flies through the cylinder-end and transmits a rotary motion to a crank by means of a connecting-rod. The half-expanded steam is then ejected, not into the air as would happen on a locomotive, but into the next cylinder, which has a larger piston to compensate the reduction of pressure. Number two served, the steam does duty a third time in number three, and perhaps yet a fourth time before it reaches the condensers, where its sudden conversion into water by cold produces a vacuum suction in the last cylinder of the series. The secret of a marine engine's strength and economy lies then in its treatment of the steam, which, like clothes in a numerous family, is not thought to have served its purpose till it has been used over and over again.

Reciprocating (*i.e.* cylinder) engines, though brought to a high pitch of efficiency, have grave disadvantages, the greatest among which is the annoyance caused by their intense vibration to all persons in the vessel. A revolving body that is not exactly balanced runs unequally, and transmits a tremor to anything with which it may be in contact. Turn a cycle upside down and revolve the driving-wheel rapidly by means of the pedal. The whole machine soon begins to tremble violently, and dance up and down on the saddle springs, because one part of the wheel is heavier than the rest, the mere weight of the air-valve being sufficient to disturb the balance. Now consider what happens in the engine-room of high-powered vessels. On destroyers the screws make 400 revolutions a minute. That is to say, all the momentum of the pistons, cranks, rods, and valves (weighing tons), has to be arrested thirteen or fourteen times every second. However well the moving parts may be balanced, the vibration is felt from stem to stern of the vessel. Even on luxuriously-appointed liners, with engines running at a far slower speed, the throbbing of the screw (*i.e.* engines) is only too noticeable and productive of discomfort.

We shall be told, perhaps, that vibration is a necessary consequence of speed. This is true enough of all vehicles, such as railway trains, motor-cars, cycles, which are shaken by the irregularities of the unyielding surface over which they run, but does not apply universally to ships and boats. A sail or oar-propelled craft may be entirely free from vibration, whatever its speed, as the motions arising from water are usually slow and deliberate. In fact, water in its calmer moods is an ideal medium to travel on, and the trouble begins only with the introduction of steam as motive force.

But even steam may be robbed of its power to annoy us. The steam-turbine has arrived. It works a screw propeller as smoothly as a dynamo, and at a speed that no cylinder engine could maintain for a minute without shaking itself to pieces.

The steam-turbine is most closely connected with the name of the Hon. Charles Parsons, son of Lord Rosse, the famous astronomer. He was the first to show, in his speedy little *Turbinia,* the possibilities of the turbine when applied to steam navigation. The results have been such as to attract the attention of the whole shipbuilding world.

The principle of the turbine is seen in the ordinary windmill. To an axle revolving in a stationary bearing are attached vanes which oppose a current of air, water, or steam, at an angle to its course, and by it are moved sideways through a circular path. Mr. Parsons' turbine has of course been specially adapted for the action of steam. It consists of a cylindrical, air-tight chest, inside which rotates a drum, fitted round its circumference with rows of curved vanes. The chest itself has fixed immovably to its inner side a corresponding number of vane rings, alternating with those on the drum, and so arranged as to deflect the steam on to the latter at the most efficient angle. The diameter of the chest and drum is not constant, but increases towards the exhaust end, in order to give the expanding and weakening steam a larger leverage as it proceeds.

The steam entering the chest from the boiler at a pressure of some hundreds of pounds to the square inch strikes the first set of vanes on the drum, passes them and meets the first set of chest-vanes, is turned from its course on to the second set of drum-vanes, and so on to the other end of the chest. Its power arises entirely from its expansive velocity, which, rather than turn a number of sharp corners, will, if possible, compel the obstruction to move out of its way. If that obstruction be from any cause difficult to stir, the steam must pass round it until its pressure overcomes the inertia. Consequently the turbine differs from the cylinder engine in this respect, that steam *can* pass through and be wasted without doing any work at all, whereas, unless the gear of a cylinder moves, and power is exerted, all steam ways are closed, and there is no waste. In practice, therefore, it is found that a turbine is most effective when running at high speed.

The first steam-turbines were used to drive dynamos. In 1884 Mr. Parsons made a turbine in which fifteen wheels of increasing size moved at the astonishing rate of 300 revolutions per second, and developed 10 horse-power. In 1888 followed a 120 horse-power turbine, and in 1892 one of 2000

horse-power, provided with a condenser to produce suction. So successful were these steam fans for electrical work, pumping water and ventilating mines, that Mr. Parsons determined to test them as a means of propelling ships. A small vessel 100 feet long and 9 feet in beam was fitted with three turbines—high, medium, and low pressure, of a total 2000 horse-power—a proportion of motive force to tonnage hitherto not approached. Yet when tried over the test course the *Turbinia*, as the boat was fitly named, ran in a most disappointing fashion. The screws revolved *too fast*, producing what is known as *cavitation*, or the scooping out of the water by the screws, so that they moved in a partial vacuum and utilised only a fraction of their force, from lack of anything to "bite" on. This defect was remedied by employing screws of coarser pitch and larger blade area, three of which were attached to each of the three propeller shafts. On a second trial the *Turbinia* attained $32\frac{3}{4}$ knots over the "measured mile," and later the astonishing speed of forty miles an hour, or double that of the fast Channel packets. At the Spithead Review in 1897 one of the most interesting sights was the little nimble *Turbinia* rushing up and down the rows of majestic warships at the rate of an express train.

After this success Mr. Parsons erected works at Wallsend-on-Tyne for the special manufacture of turbines. The Admiralty soon placed with him an order for a torpedo-destroyer—the *Viper*—of 350 tons; which on its trial trip exceeded forty-one miles an hour at an estimated horse-power (11,000) equalling that of our largest battleships. A sister vessel, the *Cobra*, of like size, proved as speedy. Misfortune, however, overtook both destroyers. The *Viper* was wrecked August 3, 1901, on the coast of Alderney during the autumn naval manœuvres, and the *Cobra* foundered in a severe storm on September 12 of the same year in the North Sea. This double disaster casts no reflections on the turbine engines; being attributed to fog in the one case and to structural weakness in the other. The Admiralty has since ordered another turbine destroyer, and before many years are past we shall probably see all the great naval powers providing themselves with like craft to act as the "eyes of the fleet," and travel at even higher speeds than those of the *Viper* and *Cobra*.

The turbine has been applied to mercantile as well as warlike purposes. There is at the present time a turbine-propelled steamer, the *King Edward*, running in the Clyde on the Fairlie-Campbelltown route. This vessel, 250 feet long, 30 broad, 18 deep, contains three turbines. In each the steam is expanded fivefold, so that by the time it passes into the condensers it occupies 125 times its boiler volume. (On the *Viper* the steam entered the turbine through an inlet eight inches in diameter, and left them by an outlet four feet square.) In cylinder engines thirty-fold expansion is considered a high ratio; hence the turbine extracts a great deal more power in proportion from its steam. As a turbine cannot be reversed, special turbines are attached to the two outside of the three propeller shafts to drive the vessel astern. The steamer attained 20½ knots over the "Skelmorlie mile" in fair and calm weather, with 3500 horse-power produced at the turbines. The *King Edward* is thus the fastest by two or three knots of all the Clyde steamers, as she is the most comfortable. We are assured that as far as the turbines are concerned it is impossible by placing the hand upon the steam-chest to tell whether the drum inside is revolving or not!

Every marine engine is judged by its economy in the consumption of coal. Except in times of national peril extra speed produced by an extravagant use of fuel would be severely avoided by all owners and captains of ships. At low speeds the turbine develops less power than cylinders from the same amount of steam, but when working at high velocity it gives at least equal results. A careful record kept by the managers of the Caledonian Steamship Company compares the *King Edward* with the *Duchess of Hamilton*, a paddle steamer of equal tonnage used on the same route and built by the same firm. The record shows that though the paddle-boat ran a fraction of a mile further for every ton of coal burnt in the furnaces, the *King Edward* averaged two knots an hour faster, a superiority of speed quite out of proportion to the slight excess of fuel. Were the *Duchess* driven at 18½ knots instead of 16½ her coal bill would far exceed that of the turbine.

As an outcome of these first trials the Caledonian Company are launching a second turbine vessel. Three high-speed turbine yachts are also on the stocks; one of 700 tons, another of 1500 tons, and a third of 170 tons. The last, the property of Colonel M'Calmont, is designed for a speed of twenty-four knots.

Mr. Parsons claims for his system the following advantages: Greatly increased speed; increased carrying power of coal; economy in coal consumption; increased facilities for navigating shallow waters; greater stability of vessels; reduced weight of machinery (the turbines of the *King Edward* weigh but one-half of cylinders required to give the same power); cheapness of attending the machinery; absence of vibration, lessening wear and tear of the ship's hull and assisting the accurate training of guns; lowered centre of gravity in the vessel, and consequent greater safety during times of war.

The inventor has suggested a cruiser of 2800 tons, engined up to 80,000 horse-power, to yield a speed of forty-four knots (about fifty miles) an hour. Figures such as these suggest that we may be on the eve of a revolution of ocean travel comparable to that made by the substitution of steam for wind power. Whether the steam-turbine will make for increased speed all round, or for greater economy, remains to be seen; but we may be assured of a higher degree of comfort. We can easily believe that improvements will follow in this as in other mechanical contrivances, and that the turbine's efficiency has not yet reached a maximum; and even if our ocean expresses, naval and mercantile, do not attain the one-mile-a-minute standard, which is still regarded as creditable to the fastest methods of land locomotion, we look forward to a time in the near future when much higher speeds will prevail, and the tedium of long voyages be greatly shortened. Already there is talk of a service which shall reduce the trans-Atlantic journey to three-and-a-half days. The means are at hand to make it a fact.

Note.—In the recently-launched turbine destroyer *Velox* a novel feature is the introduction of ordinary reciprocating engines fitted in conjunction with the steam turbines. These engines are of triple-compound type, and are coupled direct to the main turbines. They take steam from the boilers direct and exhaust into the high-pressure turbine. These reciprocating engines are for use at cruising speeds. When higher power is needed the steam will be admitted to the turbines direct from the boilers, and the cylinders be thrown out of gear.

MECHANICAL FLIGHT.

FEW, if any, problems have so strongly influenced the imagination and exercised the ingenuity of mankind as that of aërial navigation. There is something in our nature that rebels against being condemned to the condition of "featherless bipeds" when birds, bats, and even minute insects have the whole realm of air and the wide heavens open to them. Who has not, like Solomon, pondered upon "the way of a bird in the air" with feelings of envy and regret that he is chained to earth by his gross body; contrasting our laboured movements from point to point of the earth's surface with the easy gliding of the feathered traveller? The unrealised wish has found expression in legends of Dædalus, Pegasus, in the "flying carpet" of the fairy tale, and in the pages of Jules Verne, in which last the adventurous Robur on his "Clipper of the Clouds" anticipates the future in a most startling fashion.

Aeromobilism—to use its most modern title—is regarded by the crowd as the mechanical counterpart of the Philosopher's Stone or the Elixir of Life; a highly desirable but unattainable thing. At times this incredulity is transformed by highly-coloured press reports into an equally unreasonable readiness to believe that the conquest of the air is completed, followed by a feeling of irritation that facts are not as they were represented in print.

The proper attitude is of course half-way between these extremes. Reflection will show us that money, time, and life itself would not have been freely and ungrudgingly given or risked by many men—hard-headed, practical men among them—in pursuit of a Will-o'-the-Wisp, especially in a century when scientific calculation tends always to calm down any too imaginative scheme. The existing state of the aërial problem may be compared to that of a railway truck which an insufficient number of men are trying to move. Ten men may make no impression on it, though they are putting out all their strength. Yet the arrival of an eleventh may enable them to overcome the truck's inertia and move it at an increasing pace.

Every new discovery of the scientific application of power brings us nearer to the day when the truck will move. We have metals of wonderful strength in proportion to their weight; pigmy motors containing the force of giants; a huge fund of mechanical experience to draw upon; in fact, to paraphrase the Jingo song, "We've got the things, we've got the men, we've got the money too"—but we haven't as yet got the machine that can mock the bird like the flying express mocks the strength and speed of horses.

The reason of this is not far to seek. The difficulties attending the creation of a successful flying-machine are immense, some unique, not being found in aquatic and terrestrial locomotion.

In the first place, the airship, flying-machine, aerostat, or whatever we please to call it, must not merely move, but also lift itself. Neither a ship nor a locomotive is called upon to do this. Its ability to lift itself must depend upon either the employment of large balloons or upon sheer power. In the first case the balloon will, by reason of its size, be unmanageable in a high wind; in the second case, a breakdown in the machinery would probably prove fatal.

Even supposing that our aerostat can lift itself successfully, we encounter the difficulties connected with steering in a medium traversed by ever-shifting currents of air, which demands of the helmsman a caution and capacity seldom required on land or water. Add to these the difficulties of leaving the ground and alighting safely upon it; and, what is more serious than all, the fact that though success can be attained only by experiment, experiment is in this case extremely expensive and risky, any failure often resulting in total ruin of the machine, and sometimes in loss of life. The list of those who have perished in the search for the power of flight is a very long one.

Yet in spite of these obstacles determined attempts have been and are being made to conquer the air. Men in a position to judge are confident that the day of conquest is not very far distant, and that the next generation may be as familiar with aerostats as we with motor-cars. Speculation as to the future is, however, here less profitable than a consideration of what has been already done in the direction of collecting forces for the final victory.

To begin at the beginning, we see that experimenters must be divided into two great classes: those who pin their faith to airships lighter than air, *e.g.* Santos Dumont, Zeppelin, Roze; and those who have small respect for balloons, and see the ideal air-craft in a *machine* lifted entirely by means of power and surfaces pressing the air after the manner of a kite. Sir Hiram Maxim and Professor S. P. Langley, Mr. Lawrence Hargrave, and Mr. Sydney Hollands are eminent members of the latter cult.

As soon as we get on the topic of steerable balloons the name of Mr. Santos Dumont looms large. But before dealing with his exploits we may notice the airship of Count Zeppelin, an ingenious and costly structure that was tested over Lake Constance in 1900.

The balloon was built in a large wooden shed,

450 by 78 by 66 feet, that floated on the lake on ninety pontoons. The shed alone cost over £10,000.

The balloon itself was nearly 400 feet long, with a cylindrical diameter of 39 feet, except at its ends, which were conical, to offer as little resistance as possible to the air. Externally it afforded the appearance of a single-compartment bag, but in reality it was divided into seventeen parts, each gas-tight, so that an accident to one part of the fabric should not imperil the whole.

A framework of aluminium rods and rings gave the bag a partial rigidity.

Its capacity was 12,000 cubic yards of hydrogen gas, which, as our readers doubtless know, is much lighter though more expensive than ordinary coal-gas; each inflation costing several hundreds of pounds.

Under the balloon hung two cars of aluminium, the motors and the screws; and also a great sliding weight of 600 lbs. for altering the "tip" of the airship; and rudders to steer its course.

On June 30 a great number of scientific men and experts assembled to witness the behaviour of a balloon which had cost £20,000. For two days wind prevented a start, but on July 2, at 7.30 P.M., the balloon emerged from its shed, and at eight o'clock commenced its first journey, with and against a light easterly wind for a distance of three and a half miles. A mishap to the steering-gear occurred early

The air-ship of M. Santos Dumont rounding the Eiffel Tower during its successful run for the Henri Deutsch Prize.

[*To face p.* 288.

in the trip, and prevented the airship appearing to advantage, but a landing was effected easily and safely. In the following October the Count made a second attempt, returning against a wind blowing at three yards a second, or rather more than six miles an hour.

Owing to lack of funds the fate of the "Great Eastern" has overtaken the Zeppelin airship—to be broken up, and the parts sold.

The aged Count had demonstrated that a petroleum motor could be used in the neighbourhood of gas without danger. It was, however, reserved for a younger man to give a more decided proof of the steerableness of a balloon.

In 1900 M. Henri Deutsch, a member of the French Aero Club, founded a prize of £4000, to win which a competitor must start from the Aero Club Park, near the Seine in Paris, sail to and round the Eiffel Tower, and be back at the starting-point within a time-limit of half-an-hour.

M. Santos Dumont, a wealthy and plucky young Brazilian, had, previously to this offer, made several successful journeys in motor balloons in the neighbourhood of the Eiffel Tower. He therefore determined to make a bid for the prize with a specially constructed balloon "Santos Dumont V." The third unsuccessful attempt ended in disaster to the airship, which fell on to the houses, but fortunately without injuring its occupant.

Another balloon—"Santos Dumont VI."—was then built. On Saturday, October 19th, M. Dumont reached the Tower in nine minutes and recrossed the starting line in 20½ more minutes, thus complying with the conditions of the prize with half-a-minute to spare. A dispute, however, arose as to whether the prize had been actually won, some of the committee contending that the balloon should have come to earth within the half-hour, instead of merely passing overhead; but finally the well-merited prize was awarded to the determined young aeronaut.

The successful airship was of moderate proportions as compared with that of Count Zeppelin. The cigar-shaped bag was 112 feet long and 20 feet in diameter, holding 715 cubic yards of gas. M. Dumont showed originality in furnishing it with a smaller balloon inside, which could be pumped full of air so as to counteract any leakage in the external bag and keep it taut. The motor, on which everything depended, was a four-cylinder petrol-driven engine, furnished with "water-jackets" to prevent over-heating. The motor turned a large screw—made of silk and stretched over light frames—200 times a minute, giving a driving force of 175 lbs. Behind, a rudder directed the airship, and in front hung down a long rope suspended by one end that could be drawn towards the centre of the frame to alter the trim of the ship. The aeronaut stood in a large wicker basket flanked on either side by bags of sand ballast. The fact that the motor, once stopped, could only be restarted by coming to earth again added an element of great uncertainty to all his trips ; and on one occasion the mis-firing of one of the cylinders almost brought about a collision with the Eiffel Tower.

From Paris M. Dumont went to Monaco at the invitation of the prince of that principality, and cruised about over the bay in his balloon. His fresh scheme was to cross to Corsica, but it was brought to an abrupt conclusion by a leakage of gas, which precipitated balloon and balloonist into the sea. Dumont was rescued, and at once set about new projects, including a visit to the Crystal Palace, where he would have made a series of ascents this summer (1902) but for damage done to the silk of the gas-bag by its immersion in salt water and the other vicissitudes it had passed through. Dumont's most important achievement has been, like that of Count Zeppelin, the application of the gasolene motor to aeromobilism. In proportion to its size this form of motor develops a large amount of energy, and its mechanism is comparatively simple—a matter of great moment to the aeronaut. He has also shown that under favourable conditions a balloon may be steered against a head-wind, though not with the certainty that is desirable before air travel can be pronounced an even moderately simple undertaking.

The fact that many inventors, such as Dr. Barton, M. Roze, Henri Deutsch, are fitting motors to balloons in the hopes of solving the aërial problem shows that the airship has still a strong hold on the minds of men. But on reviewing the successes of such combinations of lifting and driving power it must be confessed, with all due respect to M. Dumont, that they are somewhat meagre, and do not show any great advance.

The question is whether these men are not working on wrong lines, and whether their utmost endeavours and those of their successors will ever produce anything more than a very semi-successful craft. Their efforts appear foredoomed to failure. As Sir Hiram Maxim has observed, a balloon by its very nature is light and fragile, it is a mere bubble. If it were possible to construct a motor to develop 100 horse-power for every pound of its weight, it would still be impossible to navigate a balloon against a wind of more than a certain strength. The mere energy of the motor would crush the gas-bag against the pressure of the wind, deform it, and render it unmanageable. Balloons therefore must be at the mercy of the wind, and obliged to submit to it under conditions not always in accordance with the wish of the aeronaut.

Sir Hiram in condemning the airship was ready with a substitute. On looking round on the patterns of Nature, he concluded that, inasmuch as all things that fly are heavier than air, the problem of aërial navigation must be solved by a machine whose natural tendency is to fall to the ground, and which can be sustained only by the exertion of great force. Its very weight would enable it to withstand, at least to a far greater extent than the airship, the varying currents of the air.

The lifting principle must be analogous to that by which a kite is suspended. A kite is prevented from rising beyond a certain height by a string, and the pressure of the wind working against it at an angle tends to lift it, like a soft wedge continuously driven under it. In practice it makes no difference whether the kite be stationary in a wind or towed rapidly through a dead calm; the wedge-like action of the air remains the same.

Maxim decided upon constructing what was practically a huge compound kite driven by very powerful motors.

But before setting to work on the machine itself he made some useful experiments to determine the necessary size of his kites or aeroplanes, and the force requisite to move them.

He accordingly built a "whirling-table," consisting of a long arm mounted on a strong pivot at one end, and driven by a 10 horse-power engine. To the free end, which described a circle of 200 feet in circumference, he attached small aeroplanes, and by means of delicate balances discovered that at

40 miles an hour the aeroplane would lift 133 lbs. per horse-power, and at 60 miles per hour every square foot of surface sustained 8 lbs. weight. He, in common with other experimenters on the same lines, became aware of the fact that if it took a certain strain to suspend a stationary weight in the air, *to advance it rapidly as well as to suspend it took a smaller strain.* Now, as on sea and land, increased speed means a very rapid increase in the force required, this is a point in favour of the flying-machine. Professor Langley found that a brass plate weighing a pound, when whirled at great speed, was supported in the air by a pulling pressure of less than one ounce. And, of course, as the speed increased the plate became more nearly horizontal, offering less resistance to the air.

It is on this behaviour of the aeroplane that the hopes of Maxim and others have been based. The swiftly moving aeroplane, coming constantly on to fresh air, the inertia of which had not been disturbed, would resemble the skater who can at high speed traverse ice that would not bear him at rest.

Maxim next turned his attention to the construction of the aeroplanes and engines. He made a special machine for testing fabrics, to decide which would be most suitable for stretching over strong frames to form the planes. The fabric must be light, very strong, and offer small frictional resistance to the air. The testing-machine was fitted with a nozzle, through which air was forced at a known pace on to the substance under trial, which met the air current at a certain angle and by means of indicators showed the strength of its "lift" or tendency to rise, and that of its "drift" or tendency to move horizontally in the direction of the air-current. A piece of tin, mounted at an angle of one in ten to the air-current, showed a "lift" of ten times its "drift." This proportion was made the standard. Experiments conducted on velvet, plush, silk, cotton and woollen goods proved that the drift of crape was several times that of its lift, but that fine linen had a lift equal to nine times its drift; while a sample of Spencer's balloon fabric was as good as tin.

Accordingly he selected this balloon fabric to stretch over light but strong frames. The stretching of the material was no easy matter, as uneven tension distorted it; but eventually the aeroplanes were completed, tight as drumheads.

The large or central plane was 50 feet wide and 40 long; on either side were auxiliary planes, five pairs; giving a total area of 5400 square feet.

The steam-engine built to give the motive power was perhaps the most interesting feature of the whole construction. Maxim employed steam in preference to any other power as being one with which he was most familiar, and yielding most force in proportion to the weight of the apparatus. He designed and constructed a pair of high-pressure compound engines, the high-pressure cylinders 5 inches in diameter, the low-pressure 8 inches, and both 1 foot stroke. Steam was supplied to the high-pressure cylinders at 320 lbs. per square inch from a tubular boiler heated by a gasolene burner so powerful in its action as to raise the pressure from 100 to 200 lbs. in a minute. The total weight of the boiler, burner, and engines developing 350 horse-power was 2000 lbs., or about 6 lbs. per horse-power.

The two screw-propellers driven by the engine measured 17 feet 11 inches in diameter.

The completed flying-machine, weighing 7500 lbs., was mounted on a railway-truck of 9-foot gauge, in Baldwyn's Park, Kent, not far from the gun-factories for which Sir Hiram is famous. Outside and parallel to the 9-foot track was a second track, 35 feet across, with a reversed rail, so that as soon as the machine should rise from the inner track long spars furnished with flanged wheels at their extremities should press against the under side of the outer track and prevent the machine from rising too far. Dynamometers, or instruments for measuring strains, were fitted to decide the driving and lifting power of the screws. Experiments proved that with the engines working at full power the screw-thrust against the air was 2200 lbs., and the lifting force of the aeroplanes 10,000 lbs., or 1500 in excess of the machine's weight.

Everything being ready the machine was fastened to a dynamometer and steam run up until it strained at its tether with maximum power; when the moorings were suddenly released and it bounded forward at a terrific pace, so suddenly that some of the crew were flung violently down on to the platform. When a speed of 42 miles was reached the inner wheels left their track, and the outer wheels came into play. Unfortunately, the long 35-foot axletrees were too weak to bear the strain, and one of them broke. The upper track gave way, and for the first time in the history of the world a flying-machine actually left the ground fully equipped with engines, boiler, fuel, and a crew. The journey, however, was a short one, for part of the broken track fouled the screws, snapped a propeller blade and necessitated the shutting off of the steam, which done, the machine settled to earth, the wheels sinking into the sward and showing by the absence of any marks that it had come directly downwards and not run along the surface.

The inventor was prevented by other business, and by the want of a sufficiently large open space, from continuing his experiments, which had demonstrated that a large machine heavier than air could be made to lift itself and move at high speed. Misfortune alone prevented its true capacities being shown.

Another experimenter on similar lines, but on a less heroic scale than Sir Hiram Maxim, is Professor S. P. Langley, the secretary of the Smithsonian Institution, Washington. For sixteen years he has devoted himself to a persevering course of study of the flying-machine, and after oft-repeated failures has scored a decided success in his Aerodrome, which, though only a model, has made considerable flights. His researches have proved beyond doubt that the amount of energy required for flight is but one-fiftieth of what was formerly regarded as a minimum. A French mathematician had proved by figures that a swallow must develop the power of a horse to maintain its rapid flight! Professor Langley's aerodrome has told a very different tale, affording another instance of the truth of the saying that an ounce of practice is worth a pound of theory.

A bird is nearly one thousand times heavier than the air it displaces. As a motor it develops huge power for its weight, and consumes a very large amount of fuel in doing so. An observant naturalist has calculated that the homely robin devours per diem, in proportion to its size, what would be to a man a sausage two hundred feet long and three inches thick! Any one who has watched birds pulling worms out of the garden lawn and swallowing them wholesale can readily credit this.

Professor Langley therefore concentrated himself on the production of an extremely light and at the same time powerful machine. Like Maxim, he turned to steam for motive-power, and by rigid economy of weight constructed an engine with boilers weighing 5 lbs., cylinders of 26 ozs., and an energy of 1 to 1½ horse-power! Surely a masterpiece of mechanical workmanship! This he enclosed in a boat-shaped cover which hung from two pairs of aeroplanes 12½ feet from tip to tip. The whole apparatus weighed nearly 30 lbs., of which one quarter represented the machinery. Experiments with smaller aerodromes warned the Professor that rigidity and balance were the two most difficult things to attain; also that the starting of the machine on its aerial course was far from an easy matter.

A soaring bird does not rise straight from the ground, but opens its wings and runs along the ground until the pressure of the air raises it sufficiently to give a full stroke of its pinions. Also it rises *against* the wind to get the full benefit of its lifting force. Professor Langley hired a houseboat on the Potomac River, and on the top of it built an apparatus from which the aerodrome could be launched into space at high velocity.

On May 6, 1896, after a long wait for propitious weather, the aerodrome was despatched on a trial trip. It rose in the face of the wind and travelled for over half a mile at the rate of twenty-five miles an hour. The water and fuel being then exhausted it settled lightly on the water and was again launched. Its flight on both occasions was steady, and limited only by the rapid consumption of its power-producing elements. The Professor believes that larger machines would remain in the air for a long period and travel at speeds hitherto unknown to us.

In both the machines that we have considered the propulsive power was a screw. No counterpart of it is seen in Nature. This is not a valid argument against its employment, since no animal is furnished with driving-wheels, nor does any fish carry a revolving propeller in its tail. But some inventors are strongly in favour of copying Nature as regards the employment of wings. Mr. Sydney H. Hollands, an enthusiastic aeromobilist, has devised an ingenious cylinder-motor so arranged as to flap a pair of long wings, giving them a much stronger impulse on the down than on the up stroke. The pectoral muscles of a bird are reproduced by two strong springs which are extended by the upward motion of the wings and store up energy for the down-stroke. Close attention is also being paid to the actual shape of a bird's wing, which is not flat but hollow on its under side, and at the front has a slightly downward dip. "Aerocurves" are therefore likely to supersede the "aeroplane," for Nature would not have

built bird's wings as they are without an object. The theory of the aerocurve's action is this: that the front of the wing, on striking the air, gives it a downwards motion, and if the wing were quite flat its rear portion would strike air already in motion, and therefore less buoyant. The curvature of a floating bird's wings, which becomes more and more pronounced towards the rear, counteracts this yielding of the air by pressing harder upon it as it passes towards their hinder edge.

The aerocurve has been used by a very interesting group of experimenters, those who, putting motors entirely aside, have floated on wings, and learnt some of the secrets of balancing in the air. For a man to propel himself by flapping wings moved by legs or arms is impossible. Sir Hiram Maxim, in addressing the Aeronautical Society, once said that for a man to successfully imitate a bird his lungs must weigh 40 lbs., to consume sufficient oxygen, his breast muscles 75 lbs., and his breast bone be extended in front 21 inches. And unless his total weight were increased his legs must dwindle to the size of broomsticks, his head to that of an apple! So that for the present we shall be content to remain as we are!

Dr. Lilienthal, a German, was the first to try scientific wing-sailing. He became a regular air gymnast, running down the sides of an artificial mound until the wings lifted him up and enabled him to float a considerable distance before reaching earth again. His wings had an area of 160 square feet, or about a foot to every pound weight. He was killed by the wings collapsing in mid-air. A similar fate also overtook Mr. Percy Pilcher, who abandoned the initial run down a sloping surface in favour of being towed on a rope attached to a fast-moving vehicle. At present Mr. Octave Chanute, of Chicago, is the most distinguished member of the "gliding" school. He employs, instead of wings, a species of kite made up of a number of small aerocurves placed one on the top of another a small distance apart. These box kites are said to give a great lifting force for their weight.

These and many other experimenters have had the same object in view—to learn the laws of equilibrium in the air. Until these are fully understood the construction of large flying-machines must be regarded as somewhat premature. Man must walk before he can run, and balance himself before he can fly.

There is no falling off in the number of aërial machines and schemes brought from time to time into public notice. We may assure ourselves that if patient work and experiment can do it the problem of "how to fly" is not very far from solution at the present moment.

As a sign of the times, the War Office, not usually

very ready to take up a new idea, has interested itself in the airship, and commissioned Dr. F. A. Barton to construct a dirigible balloon which combines the two systems of aerostation. Propulsion is effected by six sets of triple propellers, three on each side. Ascent is brought about partly by a balloon 180 feet long, containing 156,000 cubic feet of hydrogen, partly by nine aeroplanes having a total superficial area of nearly 2000 square feet. The utilisation of these aeroplanes obviates the necessity to throw out ballast to rise, or to let out gas for a descent. The airship, being just heavier than air, is raised by the 135 horse-power motors pressing the aeroplanes against the air at the proper angle. In descent they act as parachutes.

The most original feature of this war balloon is the automatic water-balance. At each end of the "deck" is a tank holding forty gallons of water. Two pumps circulate water through these tanks, the amount sent into a tank being regulated by a heavy pendulum which turns on the cock leading to the end which may be highest in proportion as it turns off that leading to the lower end. The idea is very ingenious, and should work successfully when the time of trial comes.

Valuable money prizes will be competed for by aeronauts at the coming World's Fair at St. Louis in 1903. Sir Hiram Maxim has expressed an intention of spending £20,000 in further experiments and prizes. In this country, too, certain journals have offered large rewards to any aeronaut who shall make prescribed journeys in a given time. It has also been suggested that aeronautical research should be endowed by the state, since England has nothing to fear more than the flying machine and the submarine boat, each of which tends to rob her of the advantages of being an island by exposing her to unexpected and unseen attacks.

Tennyson, in a fine passage in "Locksley Hall," turns a poetical eye towards the future. This is what he sees—

> "For I dipt into the future, far as human eye could see,
> Saw the vision of the world and all the wonder that would be,
> Saw the heavens fill with commerce, argosies of magic sail,
> Pilots of the purple twilight dropping down with costly bales,
> Heard the heavens fill with shouting, then there rained a ghostly dew,
> From the nations' airy navies, grappling in the central blue."

Expressed in more prosaic language, the flying-machine will primarily be used for military purposes. A country cannot spread a metal umbrella over itself to protect its towns from explosives dropped from the clouds.

Mail services will be revolutionised. The pleasure aerodrome will take the place of the yacht and motor-car, affording grand opportunities for the mountaineer and explorer (if the latter could find anything new to explore). Then there will also be a direct route to the North Pole over the top of those terrible icefields that have cost civilisation so many gallant lives. And possibly the ease of transit will bring the nations closer together, and produce good-fellowship and concord among them. It is pleasanter to regard the flying-machine of the future as a bringer of peace than as a novel means of spreading death and destruction.

TYPE-SETTING BY MACHINERY.

To the Assyrian brickmakers who, thousands of years ago, used blocks wherewith to impress on their unbaked bricks hieroglyphics and symbolical characters, must be attributed the first hesitating step towards that most marvellous and revolutionary of human discoveries—the art of printing. Not, however, till the early part of the fifteenth century did Gutenberg and Coster conceive the brilliant but simple idea of printing from separate types, which could be set in different orders and combinations to represent different ideas. For Englishmen, 1474 deserves to rank with 1815, as in that year a very Waterloo was won on English soil against the forces of ignorance and oppression, though the effects of the victory were not at once evident. Considering the stir made at the time by the appearance of Caxton's first book at Westminster, it seems strange that an invention of such importance as the printing-press should have been frowned upon by those in power, and so discouraged that for nearly two centuries printing remained an ill-used and unprogressive art, a giant half strangled in his cradle. Yet as soon as prejudice gave it an open field, improved methods followed close on one another's heels. To-day we have in the place of Caxton's rude hand-made press great cylinder machines capable of absorbing paper by the mile, and grinding out 20,000 impressions an hour as easily as a child can unwind a reel of cotton.

Side by side with the problem how to produce the greatest possible number of copies in a given time from one machine, has arisen another :—how to set up type with a proportionate rapidity. A press without type is as useless as a chaff-cutter without hay or straw. The type once assembled, as many casts or stereotypes can be made from it as there are machines to be worked. But to arrange a large body of type in a short time brings the printer face to face with the need of employing the expensive services of a small army of compositors—unless he can attain his end by some equally efficient and less costly means. For the last century a struggle has been in progress between the machine compositor and the human compositor, mechanical ingenuity against eye and brains. In the last five years the battle has turned most decidedly in favour of the machine. To-day there are in existence two wonderful contrivances which enable a man to set up type six times as fast as he could by hand from a box of type, with an ease that reminds one of the mythical machine for the conversion of live pigs into strings of sausages by an uninterrupted series of movements.

These machines are called respectively the Linotype and Monotype. Roughly described, they are to the compositor what a typewriter is to a clerk—forming words in obedience to the depression of keys on a keyboard. But whereas the typewriter merely imprints a single character on paper, the linotype and monotype cast, deliver, and set up type from which an indefinite number of impressions can be taken. They meet the compositor more than half-way, and simplify his labour while hugely increasing his productiveness.

As far back as 1842 periodicals were mechanically composed by a machine which is now practically forgotten. Since that time hundreds of other inventions have been patented, and some scores of different machines tried, though with small success in most cases; as it was found that quality of composition was sacrificed to quantity, and that what at first appeared a short cut to the printing-press was after all the longest way round, when corrections had all been attended to. A really economical type-setter must be accurate as well as prolific. Slipshod work will not pay in the long run.

Such a machine was perfected a few years ago by Ottmar Mergenthaler of Baltimore, who devised the plan of casting a whole *line of type*. The Linotype Composing Machine, to give it its full title, produces type all ready for the presses in "slugs" or lines—hence the name, Lin' o' type. It deserves at least a short description.

The Linotype occupies about six square feet of floor space, weighs one ton, and is entirely operated by one man. Its most prominent features are a slop-

By kind permission of] [*The Linotype Co.*

The Linotype Machine. By pressing keys on the key-board the operator causes lines of type to be set up, cast, and arranged on the "galley" ready for the printers.

[*To face p.* 308.

ing magazine at the top to hold the brass matrices, or dies from which the type is cast, a keyboard controlling the machinery to drop and collect the dies, and a long lever which restores the dies to the magazine when done with.

The operator sits facing the keyboard, in which are ninety keys, variously coloured to distinguish the different kinds of letters. His hands twinkle over the keys, and the brass dies fly into place. When a key is depressed a die shoots from the magazine on to a travelling belt and is whirled off to the assembling-box. Each die is a flat, oblong brass plate, of a thickness varying with the letter, having a large V-shaped notch in the top, and the letter cut half-way down on one of the longer sides. A corresponding letter is stamped on the side nearest to the operator so that he may see what he is doing and make needful corrections.

As soon as a word is complete, he touches the "spacing" lever at the side of the keyboard. The action causes a "space" to be placed against the last die to separate it from the following word. The operations are repeated until the tinkle of a bell warns him that, though there may be room for one or two more letters, the line will not admit another whole syllable. The line must therefore be "justified," that is, the spaces between the words increased till the vacant room is filled in. In hand composition this takes a considerable time, and is irksome; but at the linotype the operator merely twists a handle and the wedge-shaped "spaces," placed thin end upwards, are driven up simultaneously, giving the lateral expansion required to make the line of the right measure.

A word about the "spaces," or space-bands. Were each a single wedge the pressure would be on the bottom only of the dies, and their tops, being able to move slightly, would admit lead between them. To obviate this a small second wedge, thin end *downwards*, is arranged to slide on the larger wedge, so that in all positions parallelism is secured. This smaller wedge is of the same shape as the dies and remains stationary in line with them, the larger one only moving.

The line of dies being now complete, it is automatically borne off and pressed into contact with the casting wheel. This wheel, revolving on its centre, has a slit in it corresponding in length and width to the size of line required. At first the slit is horizontal, and the dies fit against it so that the row of sunk letters on the faces are in the exact position to receive the molten lead, which is squirted through the slit from behind by an automatic pump, supplied from a metal-pot. The pot is kept at a proper heat of 550° Fahrenheit by the flames of a Bunsen burner.

The lead solidifies in an instant, and the "slug" of type is ready for removal, after its back has been carefully trimmed by a knife. The wheel revolves for a quarter-turn, bringing the slit into a vertical position; a punch drives out the "slug," which is slid into the galley to join its predecessors. The wheel then resumes its former horizontal position in readiness for another cast.

The assembled dies have for the time done their work and must be returned to the magazine. The mechanism used to effect this is peculiarly ingenious.

An arm carrying a ribbed bar descends. The dies are pushed up, leaving the "spaces" behind to be restored to their proper compartment, till on a level with the ribbed bar, on to which they are slid by a lateral movement, the notches of the V-shaped opening in the top side of each die engaging with the ribs on the bar. The bar then ascends till it is in line with a longer bar of like section passing over the open top of the entire magazine. A set of horizontal screw-bars, rotating at high speed, transfer the dies from the short to the long bar, along which they move till, as a die comes above its proper division of the magazine, the arrangement of the teeth allows it to drop. While all this has been going on, the operator has composed another line of moulds, which will in turn be transferred to the casting wheel, and then back to the magazine. So that the three operations of composing, casting, and sorting moulds are in progress simultaneously in different parts of the machine; with the result that as many as 20,000 letters can be formed by an expert in the space of an hour, against the 1500 letters of a skilled hand compositor.

How about corrections? Even a comma too few or too many needs the whole line cast over again. It is a convincing proof of the difference in speed between the two methods that a column of type can be corrected much faster by the machine, handicapped as it is by its solid "slugs," than by hand. No wonder then that more than 1000 linotypes are to be found in the printing offices of Great Britain.

The Monotype, like the Linotype, aims at speed in composition, but in its mechanism it differs essentially from the linotype. In the first place, the apparatus is constructed in two quite separate parts. There is a keyboard, which may be on the third floor of the printing offices, and the casting machine, which ceaselessly casts and sets type in the basement. Yet they are but one whole. The connecting link is the long strip of paper punched by the keyboard mechanism, and then transferred to the casting machine to bring about the formation of type. The keyboard is the servant of man; the casting machine is the slave of the keyboard.

Secondly, the Monotype casts type, not in blocks or a whole line, but in separate letters. It is thus a complete type-foundry. Order it to cast G's and it will turn them out by the thousand till another letter is required.

Thirdly, by means of the punched paper roll, the same type can be set up time after time without a second recourse to the keyboard, just as a tune is ground repeatedly out of a barrel organ.

The keyboard has a formidable appearance. It contains 225 keys, providing as many characters; also thirty keys to regulate the spacing of the words. At the back of the machine a roll of paper runs over

By kind permission of] [*The Monotype Co.*

The Monotype Casting Machine. A punched paper roll fed through the top of the machine automatically casts and set, up type in separate letters.

[*To face p.* 312.

rollers and above a row of thirty little punches worked by the keys. A key being depressed, an opened valve admits air into two cylinders, each driving a punch. The punches fly up and cut two neat little holes in the paper. The roll then moves forward for the next letter. At the end of the word a special lever is used to register a space, and so on to the end of the line. The operator then consults an automatic indicator which tells him exactly how much space is left, and how much too long or too short the line would be if the spaces were of the normal size. Supposing, for instance, that there are ten spaces, and that there is one-tenth of an inch to spare. It is obvious that by extending each space one-hundredth of an inch the vacant room will be exactly filled. Similarly, if the ten normal spaces would make the line one-tenth of an inch too *long*, by *decreasing* the spaces each one-hundredth inch the line will also be "justified."

But the operator need not trouble his head about calculations of this kind. His indicator, a vertical cylinder covered with tiny squares, in each of which are printed two figures, tell him exactly what he has to do. On pressing a certain key the cylinder revolves and comes to rest with the tip of a pointer over a square. The operator at once presses down the keys bearing the numbers printed on that square, confident that the line will be of the proper length.

As soon as the roll is finished, it is detached from the keyboard and introduced to the casting machine.

Hitherto passive, it now becomes active. Having been placed in position on the rollers it is slowly unwound by the machinery. The paper passes over a hollow bar in which there are as many holes as there were punches in the keyboard, and in precisely the same position. When a hole in the paper comes over a hole in the hollow bar air rushes in, and passing through a tube actuates the type-setting machinery in a certain manner, so as to bring the desired die into contact with molten lead. The dies are, in the monotype, all carried in a magazine about three inches square, which moves backwards or forwards, to right or left, in obedience to orders from the perforated roll. The dies are arranged in exactly the same way as the keys on the keyboard. So that, supposing A to have been stamped on the roll, one of the perforations causes the magazine to slide one way, while the other shoves it another, until the combined motions bring the matrix engraved with the A underneath the small hole through which molten lead is forced. The letter is ejected and moves sideways through a narrow channel, pushing preceding letters before it, and the magazine is free for other movements.

At the end of each word a "space" or blank lead is cast, its size exactly determined by the "justifying" hole belonging to that line. Word follows word till the line is complete; then a knife-like lever rises, and the type is propelled into the "galley." Though a slave the casting machine will not tolerate injustice

Should the compositor have made a mistake, so that the line is too long or too short, automatic machinery at once comes into play, and slips the driving belt from the fixed to the loose pulley, thus stopping the machine till some one can attend to it. But if the punching has been correctly done, the machine will work away unattended till, a whole column of type having been set up, it comes to a standstill.

The advantages of the Monotype are easily seen. In order to save money a man need not possess the complete apparatus. If he has the keyboard only he becomes to a certain extent his own compositor, able to set up the type, as it were by proxy, at any convenient time. He can give his undivided attention to the keyboard, stop work whenever he likes without keeping a casting-machine idle, and as soon as his roll is complete forward it to a central establishment where type is set. There a single man can superintend the completion of half-a-dozen men's labours at the keyboard. That means a great reduction of expense.

In due time he receives back his copy in the shape of set-up type, all ready to be corrected and transferred to the printing machines. The type done with, he can melt it down without fear of future regret, for he knows that the paper roll locked up in his cupboard will do its work a second time as well as it did the first. Should he need the same matter re-setting, he has only to send the roll through the post to the central establishment.

Thanks to Mr. Lanston's invention we may hope for the day when every parish will be able to do its own printing, or at least set up its own magazine. The only thing needful will be a monotype keyboard supplied by an enlightened Parish Council—as soon as the expense appears justifiable—and kept in the Post Office or Village Institute. The payment of a small fee will entitle the Squire to punch out his speech on behalf of the Conservative Candidate, the Schoolmaster to compose special information for his pupils, the Rector to reduce to print pamphlets and appeals to charity. And if those of humbler degree think they can strike eloquence from the keys, they too will of course be allowed to turn out their ideas literally by the yard.

PHOTOGRAPHY IN COLOURS.

WHILE photography was still in its infancy many people believed that, a means having been found of impressing the representation of an object on a sensitised surface, a short time only would have to elapse before the discovery of some method of registering the colours as well as the forms of nature.

Photography has during the last forty years passed through some startling developments, especially as regards speed. Experts, such as M. Marey, have proved the superiority of the camera over the human eye in its power to grasp the various phases of animal motion. Even rifle bullets have been arrested in their lightning flight by the sensitised plate. But while the camera is a valuable aid to the eye in the matter of form, the eye still has the advantage so far as colour is concerned. It is still impossible for a photographer by a simple process similar to that of making an ordinary black-and-white negative, to affect a plate in such a manner that from it prints may be made by a single operation showing objects in their natural colours. Nor, for the matter of that, does colour photography direct from nature seem any nearer attainment now than it was in the time of Daguerre.

There are, however, extant several methods of making colour photographs in an indirect or roundabout way. These various "dodges" are, apart from their beautiful results, so extremely ingenious and interesting that we propose to here examine three of the best known.

The reader must be careful to banish from his mind those *coloured* photographs so often to be seen in railway carriages and shop windows, which are purely the result of hand-work and mechanical printing, and therefore not *colour* photographs at all.

Before embarking on an explanation of these three methods it will be necessary to examine briefly the nature of those phenomena on which all are based—light and colour. The two are really identical, light is colour and colour is light.

Scientists now agree that the sensation of light arises from the wave-like movements of that mysterious fluid, the omnipresent ether. In a beam of white light several rates of wave vibrations exist side by side. Pass the beam through a prism and the various rapidities are sorted out into violet, indigo, blue, green, yellow, orange and red, which are called the pure colours, since if any of them be passed again through a prism the result is still that colour. Crimson, brown, &c., the composite colours, would, if subjected to the prism, at once split up into their component pure colours.

There are several points to be noticed about the relationship of the seven pure colours. In the first place, though they are all allies in the task of making white light, there is hostility among them, each being jealous of the others, and only waiting a chance to show it. Thus, suppose that we have on a strip of paper squares of the seven colours, and look at the strip through a piece of red glass we see only one square—the red—in its natural colour, since that square is in harmony only with red rays. (Compare the sympathy of a piano with a note struck on another instrument; if C is struck, say on a violin, the piano strings producing the corresponding note will sound, but the other strings will be silent.) The orange square suggests orange, but the green and blue and violet appear black. Red glass has arrested their ether vibrations and said "no way here." Green and violet would serve just the same trick on red or on each other. It is from this readiness to absorb or stop dissimilar rays that we have the different colours in a landscape flooded by a common white sunlight. The trees and grass absorb all but the green rays, which they reflect. The dandelions and buttercups capture and hold fast all but the yellow rays. The poppies in the corn send us back red only, and the cornflowers only blue; but the daisy is more generous and gives up all the seven. Colour therefore is not a thing that can be touched, any more than sound, but merely the capacity to affect the retina of the eye with a certain number of ether vibrations per second, and it makes no difference whether light is reflected from a substance or refracted through a substance; a red brick and a piece of red glass have similar effects on the eye.

This then is the first thing to be clearly grasped, that whenever a colour has a chance to make prisoners of other colours it will do so.

The second point is rather more intricate, viz. that this imprisonment is going on even when friendly concord appears to be the order of the day. Let us endeavour to present this clearly to the reader. Of the pure colours, violet, green and red—the extremes and the centre—are sufficient to produce white, because each contains an element of its neighbours. Violet has a certain amount of indigo, green some yellow, red some orange; in fact every colour of the spectrum contains a greater or less degree of several of the others, but not enough to destroy its own identity. Now, suppose that we have three lanterns projecting their rays on to the same portion of a white sheet, and that in front of the first is placed a violet glass, in front of the second a green glass, in front of the third a red glass. What is the result? A white light. Why? Because they meet *on equal terms*, and as no one of them is in a point of advantage no prisoners can be made and they must work in harmony. Next, turn down the violet lantern, and green and red produce a yellow, half-way between them; turn down red and turn up violet, indigo-blue results. All the way through a compromise is effected.

But supposing that the red and green glasses are put in front of the *same* lantern and the white light sent through them—where has the yellow gone to? only a brownish-black light reaches the screen. The same thing happens with red and violet or green and violet.

Prisoners have been taken, because one colour has had to *demand passage* from the other. Red says to green, "You want your rays to pass through me, but they shall not." Green retorts, "Very well; but I myself have already cut off all but green rays, and if they don't pass you, nothing shall." And the consequence of the quarrel is practical darkness.

The same phenomenon may be illustrated with blue and yellow. Lights of these two colours projected simultaneously on to a sheet yield white; but white light sent through blue and yellow glass *in succession* produces a green light. Also, blue paint mixed with yellow gives green. In neither case is there darkness or entire cutting-off of colour, as in the case of Red + Violet or Green + Red.

The reason is easy to see.

Blue light is a compromise of violet and green;

yellow of green and red. Hence the two coloured lights falling on the screen make a combination which can be expressed as an addition sum.

$$\begin{aligned} \text{Blue} &= \text{green} + \text{violet.} \\ \text{Yellow} &= \underline{\text{green} + \text{red.}\qquad\qquad} \\ & \text{green} + \text{violet} + \text{red} = \text{white.} \end{aligned}$$

But when light is passed *through* two coloured glasses in succession, or reflected from two layers of coloured paints, there are prisoners to be made.

Blue passes green and violet only.

Yellow passes green and red only.

So violet is captured by yellow, and red by blue, green being free to pass on its way.

There is, then, a great difference between the *mixing* of colours, which evokes any tendency to antagonism, and the *adding* of colours under such conditions that they meet on equal terms. The first process happens, as we have seen, when a ray of light is passed through colours *in succession;* the second, when lights stream simultaneously on to an object. A white screen, being capable of reflecting any colour that falls on to it, will with equal readiness show green, red, violet, or a combination; but a substance that is in white light red, or green, or violet will capture any other colour. So that if for the white screen we substituted a red one, violet or green falling simultaneously, would yield blackness, because red takes *both* prisoners; if it were violet, green would be captured, and so on.

From this follows another phenomenon: that whereas projection of two or more lights may yield white, white cannot result from any mixture of pigments. A person with a whole boxful of paints could not get white were he to mix them in an infinitude of different ways; but with the aid of his lanterns and as many differently coloured glasses the feat is easy enough.

Any two colours which meet on equal terms to make white are called *complementary* colours.

Thus yellow (=red+green lights) is complementary of violet.

Thus pink (=red+violet lights) is complementary of green.

Thus blue (=violet+green lights) is complementary of red.

This does not of course apply to mixture of paints, for complementary colours must act together, not in antagonism.

If the reader has mastered these preliminary considerations he will have no difficulty in following out the following processes.

(*a*) *The Joly Process*, invented by Professor Joly of Dublin. A glass plate is ruled across with fine parallel lines—350 to the inch, we believe. These lines are filled in alternately with violet, green, and red matter, every third being violet, green or red as the case may be. The colour-screen is placed in the camera in front of the sensitised plate. Upon an exposure being made, all light reflected from a red object (to select a colour) is allowed to pass through the red lines, but blocked by all the green and violet lines. So that on development that part of the negative corresponding to the position of the red object will be covered with dark lines separated by transparent belts of twice the breadth. From the negative a positive is printed, which of course shows transparent lines separated by opaque belts of twice their breadth. Now, suppose that we take the colour-screen and place it again in front of the plate in the position it occupied when the negative was taken, the red lines being opposite the transparent parts of the positive will be visible, but the green and violet being blocked by the black deposit behind them will not be noticeable. So that the object is represented by a number of red lines, which at a small distance appear to blend into a continuous whole.

The violet and green affect the plate in a corresponding manner; and composite colours will affect two sets of lines in varying degrees, the lights from the two sets blending in the eye. Thus yellow will obtain passage from both green and red, and when the screen is held up against the positive, the light streaming through the green and red lines will blend into yellow in the same manner as they would make yellow if projected by lanterns on to a screen. The same applies to all the colours.

The advantage of the Joly process is that in it only one negative has to be made.

(*b*) *The Ives Process.*—Mr. Frederic Eugene Ives, of Philadelphia, arrives at the same result as Professor Joly, but by an entirely different means. He takes three negatives of the same object, one through a violet-blue, another through a green, and a third through a red screen placed in front of the lens. The red negative is affected by red rays only; the green by green rays only, and the violet-blue by violet-blue rays only, in the proper gradations. That is to say, each negative will have opaque patches wherever the rays of a certain kind strike it; and the positive printed off will be by consequence transparent at the same places. By holding the positive made from the red-screen negative against a piece of red glass, we should see light only in those parts of the positive which were transparent. Similarly with the green and violet positives if viewed through glasses of proper colour. The most ingenious part of Mr. Ives' method is the apparatus for presenting all three positives (lighted through their coloured glasses) to the eye simultaneously. When properly adjusted, so that their various parts exactly coincide, the eye blends the three together, seeing green, red, or violet separately, or blended in correct proportions. The Kromoscope, as the viewing apparatus is termed, contains three mirrors, projecting the reflections from the positives in a single line. As the three slides are taken stereoscopically the result gives the impression of solidity as well as of colour, and is most realistic.

(*c*) *The Sanger Shepherd Process.*—This is employed mostly for lantern transparencies. As in the Ives process, three negatives and three transparent positives are made. But instead of coloured glasses being used to give effect to the positives the positives themselves are dyed, and placed one on the top of another in close contact, so that the light from the lantern passes through them in succession. We have therefore now quitted the realms of harmony for that of discord, in which prisoners are made; and Mr. Shepherd has had to so arrange matters that in every case the capture of prisoners does not interfere with the final result, but conduces to it.

In the first place, three negatives are secured through violet, green, and red screens. Positives are printed by the carbon process on thin celluloid films. The carbon film contains gelatine and bichromate of potassium. The light acts on the bichromate in such a way as to render the gelatine insoluble. The result is that, though in the positives there is at first no colour, patches of gelatine are left which will absorb dyes of various colours. The dyeing process requires a large amount of care and patience.

Now, it would be a mistake to suppose that each positive is dyed in the colour of the screen through which its negative was taken. A moment's consideration will show us why.

Let us assume that we are photographing a red object, a flower-pot for instance. The red negative represents the pot by a dark deposit. The positive printed off will consequently show clear glass at that spot, the unaffected gelatine being soluble. So that to dye the plate would be to make all red *except* the very part which we require red; and on holding it up to the light the flower-pot would appear as a white transparent patch.

How then is the problem to be solved?

Mr. Shepherd's process is based upon an ordered system of prisoner-taking. Thus, as red in this particular case is wanted it will be attained by the *other two* positives (which are placed in contact with the red positive, so that all three coincide exactly), robbing white light of all *but* its red rays.

Now if the other positives were dyed green and violet, what would happen? They would not produce red, but by robbing white light between them of red, green, and violet, would produce blackness, and we should be as far as ever from our object.

The positives are therefore dyed, not in the same colours as the screens used when the negatives were made, but in their *complementary* colours, *i.e.* as explained above, those colours which added to the colour of the screen would make white.

The red screen negative is therefore dyed (violet + green) = blue. The green negative (red + violet) = pink. The violet negative (red + green) = yellow.

To return to our flower-pot. The red-screen positive (dyed blue) is, as we saw, quite transparent where the pot should be. But behind the transparent gap are the pink and yellow positives.

White light (= violet + green + red) passes through pink (= violet + red), and has to surrender all its green rays. The violet and red pass on and encounter yellow (= green + red), and violet falls a victim to green, leaving red unmolested.

If the flower-pot had been white all three positives would have contained clear patches unaffected by the three dyes, and the white light would have been unobstructed. The gradations and mixtures of colours are obtained by two of the screens being influenced by the colour of the object. Thus, if it were crimson, both violet and red-screen negatives would be affected by the rays reflected by it, and the green screen negative not at all. Hence the pink positive would be pink, the yellow clear, and the blue clear.

White light passing through is robbed by pink of green, leaving red + violet = crimson.

Colour Printing.

Printing in ink colours is done in a manner very similar to the Sanger Shepherd lantern slide process. Three blocks are made, by the help of photography, through violet, green and red screens, and etched away with acid, like ordinary half-tone black-and-white blocks. The three blocks have applied to them ink of a complementary colour to the screen they represent, just as in the Sanger Shepherd process the positives were dyed. The three inks are laid over one another on the paper by the blocks, the relieved parts of which (corresponding to the undissolved gelatine of the Shepherd positives) only take the ink. White light being reflected through layers of coloured inks is treated in just the same way as it would be were it transmitted through coloured glasses, yielding all the colours in approximately correct gradations.

LIGHTING.

THE production of fire by artificial means has been reasonably regarded as the greatest invention in the history of the human race. Prior to the day when a man was first able to call heat from the substances about him the condition of our ancestors must have been wretched indeed. Raw food was their portion; metals mingled with other matter mocked their efforts to separate them; the cold of winter drove them to the recesses of gloomy caverns, where night reigned perpetual.

The production of fire also, of course, entailed the creation of light, which in its developments has been of an importance second only to the improved methods of heating. So accustomed are we to our candles, our lamps, our gas-jets, our electric lights, that it is hard for us to imagine what an immense effect their sudden and complete removal would have on our existence. At times, when floods, explosions, or other accidents cause a temporary stoppage of the gas or current supply, a town may for a time be plunged into darkness; but this only for a short period, the distress of which can be alleviated by recourse to paraffin lamps, or the more homely candle.

The earliest method of illumination was the rough-and-ready one of kindling a pile of brushwood or logs. The light produced was very uncertain and feeble, but possibly sufficient for the needs of the cave-dweller. With the advance of civilisation arose an increasing necessity for a more steady illuminant, discovered in vegetable oils, burned in lamps of various designs. Lamps have been found in old Egyptian and Etruscan tombs constructed thousands of years ago. These lamps do not differ essentially from those in use to-day, being reservoirs fitted with a channel to carry a wick.

But probably from the difficulty of procuring oil, lamps fell into comparative disuse, or rather were almost unknown, in many countries of Europe as late as the fifteenth century; when the cottage and baronial hall were alike lit by the blazing torch fixed into an iron sconce or bracket on the wall.

The rushlight, consisting of a peeled rush, coated by repeated dipping into a vessel of melted fat, made a feeble effort to dispel the gloom of long winter evenings. This was succeeded by the tallow and more scientifically made wax candle, which last still maintains a certain popularity.

How our grandmothers managed to "keep their eyes" as they worked at stitching by the light of a couple of candles, whose advent was the event of the evening, is now a mystery. To-day we feel aggrieved if our lamps are not of many candle-power, and protest that our sight will be ruined by what one hundred and fifty years ago would have seemed a marvel of illumination. In the case of lighting necessity has been the mother of invention. The tendency of modern life is to turn night into day. We go to bed late and we get up late; this is perhaps foolish, but still we do it. And, what is more, we make increasing use of places, such as basements, underground tunnels, and "tubes," to which the light of heaven cannot penetrate during any of the daily twenty-four hours.

The nineteenth century saw a wonderful advance in the science of illumination. As early as 1804 the famous scientist, Sir Humphrey Davy, discovered the electric arc, presently to be put to such universal use. About the same time gas was first manufactured and led about in pipes. But before electricity for lighting purposes had been rendered sufficiently cheap the discovery of the huge oil deposits in Pennsylvania flooded the world with an inexpensive illuminant. As early as the thirteenth century Marco Polo, the explorer, wrote of a natural petroleum spring at Baku, on the Caspian Sea: "There is a fountain of great abundance, inasmuch as a thousand shiploads might be taken from it at one time. This oil is not good to use with food, but it is *good to burn;* and is also used to anoint camels that have the mange. People come from vast distances to fetch it, for in all other countries there is no oil." His last words have been confuted by the American oil-fields, yielding many thousands of barrels a day—often in such quantities that the oil runs to waste for lack of a buyer.

The rivals for pre-eminence in lighting to-day are electricity, coal gas, petroleum, and acetylene gas. The two former have the advantage of being easily turned on at will, like water; the third is more generally available.

The invention of the dynamo by Gramme in 1870 marks the beginning of an epoch in the history of illumination. With its aid current of such intensity as to constantly bridge an air-gap between carbon points could be generated for a fraction of the cost entailed by other previous methods. Paul Jablochkoff devised in 1876 his "electric candle"—a couple of parallel carbon rods separated by an insulating medium that wasted away under the influence of heat at the same rate as the rods. The "candles" were used with rapidly-alternating currents, as the positive "pole" wasted twice as quickly as the negative. During the Paris Exhibition of 1878 visitors to Paris were delighted by the new method of illumination installed in some of the principal streets and theatres.

The arc-lamp of to-day, such as we see in our streets, factories, and railway stations, is a modification of M. Jablochkoff's principle. Carbon rods are used, but they are pointed towards each other, the distance between their extremities being kept constant by ingenious mechanical contrivances. Arc-lamps of all types labour under the disadvantage of being, by necessity, very powerful; and were they only available the employment of electric lighting would be greatly restricted. As it is, we have, thanks to the genius of Mr. Edison, a means of utilising current in but small quantities to yield a gentler light. The glow-lamp, as it is called, is so familiar to us that we ought to know something of its antecedents.

In the arc-lamp the electric circuit is *broken* at the point where light is required. In glow or incandescent lamps the current is only *hindered* by the interposition of a bad conductor of electricity, which must also be incombustible. Just as a current of water flows in less volume as the bore of a pipe is reduced, and requires that greater pressure shall be exerted to force a constant amount through the pipe, so is an electric current *choked* by its conductor being reduced in size or altered in nature. Edison in 1878 employed as the current-choker a very fine platinum wire, which, having a melting temperature of 3450 degrees Fahrenheit, allowed a very white heat to be generated in it. The wire was enclosed in a glass bulb almost entirely exhausted of air by a mercury-pump before being sealed. But it was found that even platinum could not always withstand the heating effect of a strong current; and accordingly Edison looked about for some less combustible material. Mr. J. W. Swan of Newcastle-on-Tyne had already experimented with carbon filaments made from cotton threads steeped in sulphuric acid. Edison and Swan joined hands to produce the present well-known lamp, "The Ediswan," the filament of which is a bamboo fibre, carbonised during the exhaustion of air in the bulb to one-millionth of an atmosphere pressure by passing the electric current through it. These bamboo filaments are very elastic and capable of standing almost any heat.

Glow-lamps are made in all sizes—from tiny globes small enough to top a tie-pin to powerful lamps of 1000 candle-power. Their independence of atmospheric air renders them most convenient in places where other forms of illumination would be dangerous or impossible; *e.g.* in coal mines, and under water during diving operations. By their aid great improvements have been effected in the lighting of theatres, which require a quick switching on and off of light. They have also been used in connection with minute cameras to explore the recesses of the human body. In libraries they illuminate without injuring the books. In living rooms they do not foul the air or blacken the ceiling like oil or gas burners. The advantages of the "Edison lamp" are, in short, multitudinous.

Cheapness of current to work them is, of course, a very important condition of their economy. In some small country villages the cottages are lit by electricity even in England, but these are generally within easy reach of water power. Mountainous districts, such as Norway and Switzerland, with their rushing streams and high water-falls, are peculiarly suited for electric lighting: the cost of which is mainly represented by the expense of the generating apparatus and the motive power.

One of the greatest engineering undertakings in the world is connected with the manufacture of electric current. Niagara, the "Thunder of the Waters" as the Indians called it, has been harnessed to produce electrical energy, convertible at will into motion, heat, or light. The falls pass all the water overflowing from nearly 100,000 square miles of lakes, which in turn drain a far larger area of territory. Upwards of 10,000 cubic yards of water leap over the falls every second, and are hurled downwards for more than 200 feet, with an energy of eight or nine million horse-power! In 1886 a company determined to turn some of this huge force to account. They bought up land on the American bank, and cut a tunnel 6700 yards long, beginning a mile and a half above the falls, and terminating below them. Water drawn from the river thunders into the tunnel through a number of wheel pits, at the bottom of each of which is a water-turbine developing 5000 horse-power. The united force of the turbines is said to approximate 100,000 horse-power; and as if this were but a small thing, the same Company has obtained concessions to erect plant on the Canadian bank to double or treble the total power.

So cheaply is current thus produced that the Company is in a position to supply it at rates which appear small compared with those that prevail in this country. A farthing will there purchase what would here cost from ninepence to a shilling. Under such conditions the electric lamp need fear no competitor.

But in less favoured districts gas and petroleum are again holding up their heads.

Both coal and oil-gas develop a great amount of heat in proportion to the light they yield. The hydrogen they contain in large quantities burns, when pure, with an almost invisible flame, but more hotly than any other known gas. The particles of carbon also present in the flame are heated to whiteness by the hydrogen, but they are not sufficient in number to convert more than a fraction of the heat into light.

A German, Auer von Welsbach, conceived the idea of suspending round the flame a circular "mantle" of woven cotton steeped in a solution of certain rare earths (*e.g.* lanthanum, yttrium, zirconium), to arrest the heat and compel it to produce bright incandescence in the arresting substance.

With the same gas consumption a Welsbach burner yields seven or more times the light of an ordinary batswing burner. The light itself is also of a more pleasant description, being well supplied with the blue rays of the spectrum.

The mantle is used with other systems than the ordinary gas-jet. Recently two methods of illumination have been introduced in which the source of illumination is supplied under pressure.

The high-pressure incandescent gas installations of Mr. William Sugg supply gas to burners at five or six times the ordinary pressure of the mains. The effect is to pulverise the gas as it issues from the nozzle of the burners, and, by rendering it more inflammable, to increase its heating power until the surrounding mantle glows with a very brilliant and white light of great penetration. Gas is forced through the pipes connected with the lamps by hydraulic rams working gas-pumps, which alternately suck in and expel the gas under a pressure of twelve inches (*i.e.* a pressure sufficient to maintain a column of water twelve inches high). The gas under this pressure passes into a cylinder of a capacity considerably greater than the capacity of the pumps. This cylinder neutralises the shock of the rams, when the stroke changes from up- to downstroke, and *vice versâ*. On the top of the cylinder is fixed a governor consisting of a strong leathern gas-holder, which has a stroke of about three inches, and actuates a lever which opens and closes the valve through which the supply of water to the rams flows, and reduces the flow of the water when it exceeds ten or twelve inches pressure, according to circumstances. The gas-holder of the governor is lifted by the pressure of the gas in the cylinder, which passes through a small opening from the cylinder to the governor so as not to cause any sudden rise or fall of the gas-holder. By this means a nearly constant pressure is maintained; and from the outlet of the cylinder the gas passes to another governor sufficient to supply the number of lights the apparatus is designed for, and to maintain the pressure without variation whether all or a few lamps are in action. For very large installations steam is used.

Each burner develops 300 candle-power. A double-cylinder steam-engine working a double pump supplies 300 of these burners, giving a total lighting-power of 90,000 candles. As compared with the cost of low-pressure incandescent lighting the high-pressure system is very economical, being but half as expensive for the same amount of light.

It is largely used in factories and railway stations. It may be seen on the Tower Bridge, Blackfriars Bridge, Euston Station, and in the terminus of the Great Central Railway, St. John's Wood.

Perhaps the most formidable rival to the electric arc-lamp for the lighting of large spaces and buildings is the Kitson Oil Lamp, now so largely used in America and this country.

The lamp is usually placed on the top of an iron post similar to an ordinary gas-light standard. At the bottom of the post is a chamber containing a steel reservoir capable of holding from five to forty gallons of petroleum. Above the oil is an air-space into which air has been forced at a pressure of fifty lbs. to the square inch, to act as an elastic cushion to press the oil into the burners. The oil passes upwards through an extremely fine tube scarcely thicker than electric incandescent wires to a pair of cross tubes above the burners. The top one of these acts as a filter to arrest any foreign matter that finds its way into the oil; the lower one, in diameter about the size of a lead-pencil and eight inches long, is immediately above the mantles, the heat from which vaporises the small quantity of oil in the tube. The oil-gas then passes through a tiny hole no larger than a needle-point into an open mixing-tube where sufficient air is drawn in for supporting combustion. The mixture then travels down to the mantle, inside which it burns.

An ingenious device has lately been added to the system for facilitating the lighting of the lamp. At the base of the lamp-post a small hermetically-closed can containing petroleum ether is placed, and connected by very fine copper-tubing with a burner under the vaporising tube. When the lamp is to be lit a small rubber bulb is squeezed, forcing a quantity of the ether vapour into the burner, where it is ignited by a platinum wire rendered incandescent by a current passing from a small accumulator also placed in the lamp-post. The burner rapidly heats the vaporising tube, and in a few moments oil-gas is passing into the mantles, where it is ignited by the burner.

So economical is the system that a light of 1000 candle-power is produced by the combustion of about half-a-pint of petroleum per hour! Comparisons are proverbially odious, but in many cases very instructive. Professor V. B. Lewes thus tabulates the results of experiments with various illuminants:—

Cost of 1000 *candles per hour.*

		s.	*d.*
Electricity	Per unit, 3½d.		
"	Incandescent,	1	2
"	Arc,	0	3¾
Coal-gas	Flat flame,	1	6
"	Incandescent,	0	2¼
"	" high pressure,	0	1¾
Oil	Lamp (oil at 8d. per gall.),	0	7¼
"	Incandescent lamp,	0	2¼
"	Kitson lamp,	0	1

Petroleum, therefore, at present comes in a very good first in England.

The system that we have noticed at some length has been adapted for lighthouse use, as it gives a light peculiarly fog-piercing. It is said to approximate most closely to ordinary sunlight, and on that account has been found very useful for the taking of photographs at night-time. The portability of the apparatus makes it popular with contractors; and the fact that its installation requires no tearing up of the streets is a great recommendation with the long-suffering public of some of our large towns.

Another very powerful light is produced by burning the gas given off by carbide of calcium when immersed in water. *Acetylene* gas, as it is called, is now widely used in cycle and motor lamps, which emit a shaft of light sometimes painfully dazzling to those who have to face it. In Germany the gas is largely employed in village streets; and in this country it is gaining ground as an illuminant of country houses, being easy to manufacture—in small gasometers of a few cubic yards capacity—and economical to burn.

Well supplied as we are with lights, we find, nevertheless, that savants are constantly in pursuit of an *ideal* illuminant.

From the sun are borne to us through the ether light waves, heat waves, magnetic waves, and other waves of which we have as yet but a dim perception. The waves are commingled, and we are unable to separate them absolutely. And as soon as we try to copy the sun's effects as a source of heat or light we find the same difficulty. The fire that cooks our food gives off a quantity of useless light-waves; the oil-lamp that brightens one's rooms gives off a quantity of useless, often obnoxious, heat.

The ideal illuminant and the ideal heating agent must be one in which the required waves are in a great majority. Unfortunately, even with our most perfected methods, the production of light is accompanied by the exertion of a disproportionate amount of wasted energy. In the ordinary incandescent lamp, to take an instance, only 5 or 6 per cent. of the energy put into it as electricity results in light. The rest is dispelled in overcoming the resistance of the filament and agitating the few air-molecules in the bulb. To this we must add the fact that the current itself represents but a fraction of the power exerted to produce it. The following words of Professor Lodge are to the point on this subject:—

"Look at the furnaces and boilers of a steam-engine driving a group of dynamos, and estimate the energy expended; and then look at the incandescent filaments of the lamps excited by them, and estimate how much of their radiated energy is of real service to the eye. It will be as the energy of a pitch-pipe to an entire orchestra.

"It is not too much to say that a boy turning a handle could, if his energy were properly directed, produce quite as much real light as is produced by all this mass of mechanism and consumption of material." [1]

The most perfect light in nature is probably that of the glow-worm and firefly—a phosphorescent or "cold" light, illuminating without combustion owing to the absence of all waves but those of the requisite

[1] Professor Oliver Lodge, in a lecture to the Ashmolean Society, 3rd June 1889.

frequency. The task before mankind is to imitate the glow-worm in the production of isolated light-waves.

The nearest approach to its achievement has occurred in the laboratories of Mr. Nikola Tesla, the famous electrician. By means of a special oscillator, invented by himself, he has succeeded in throwing the ether particles into such an intense state of vibration that they become luminous. In other words, he has created vibrations of the enormous rapidity of light, and this without the creation of heat waves to any appreciable extent.

An incandescent lamp, mounted on a powerful coil, is lit *without* contact by ether waves transmitted from a cable running round the laboratory, or bulbs and tubes containing highly rarefied gases are placed between two large plate-terminals arranged on the end walls. As soon as the bulbs are held in the path of the currents passing through the ether from plate to plate they become incandescent, shining with a light which, though weak, is sufficiently strong to take photographs by with a long exposure. Tesla has also invented what he calls a "sanitary" light, as he claims for it the germ-killing properties of sunshine. The lamps are glass tubes several feet long, bent into spirals or other convolutions, and filled before sealing with a certain gas. The ends of the glass tube are coated with metal and provided with hooks to connect the lamp with an electric current. The gas becomes *luminous* under the influence of current, but not strictly incandescent, as there is very little heat engendered. This means economy in use. The lamps are said to be cheaply manufactured, but as yet they are not "on the market." We shall hear more of them in the near future, which will probably witness no more interesting development than that of lighting.

Before closing this chapter a few words may be said about new heating methods. Gas stoves are becoming increasingly popular by reason of the ease with which they can be put in action and made to maintain an even temperature. But the most up-to-date heating apparatus is undoubtedly electrical. Utensils of all sorts are fitted with very thin heating strips (formed by the deposition of precious metals, such as gold, platinum, &c., on exceedingly thin mica sheets), through which are passed powerful currents from the mains. The resistance of the strip converts the electromotive energy of the current into heat, which is either radiated into the air or into water for cookery, &c.

In all parts of the house the electric current may be made to do work besides that of lighting. It warms the passages by means of special radiators—replacing the clumsy coal and "stuffy" gas stove; in the kitchen it boils, stews, and fries, heats the flat-irons and ovens; in the breakfast room boils the kettle, keeps the dishes, teapots, and coffee-pots warm; in the bathroom heats the water; in the smoking-room replaces matches; in the bedroom electrifies footwarmers, and—last wonder of all—even makes possible an artificially warm bed-quilt to heat the chilled limbs of invalids !

The great advantage of electric heating is the freedom from all smell and smoke that accompanies it. But until current can be provided at cheaper rates than prevail at present, its employment will be chiefly restricted to the houses of the wealthy or to large establishments, such as hotels, where it can be used on a sufficient scale to be comparatively economical.

THE END

Printed by BALLANTYNE, HANSON & Co.
Edinburgh & London

CPSIA information can be obtained
at www.ICGtesting.com
Printed in the USA
BVOW04s1628161017
497788BV00017B/681/P

9 781247 666099